300 BEST SELLING HOME PLANS

No. 10587
Curved Stairway Highlights Plan

■ This plan features:
— Three bedrooms
— Two and one half baths

■ A Family Room with vaulted ceilings and a wood-burning fireplace

■ A sunken Living Room with a fireplace and an open view of the Dining Room

■ A Laundry room surrounded by the bedrooms for convenience

FIRST FLOOR — 2,036 SQ. FT.
SECOND FLOOR — 1,554 SQ. FT.
GARAGE — 533 SQ. FT.

TOTAL LIVING AREA:
3,590 SQ. FT.

No. 10587

No. 10785
Farmhouse Flavor

■ This plan features:

— Three bedrooms

— Two and one half baths

■ A inviting wrap-around porch with old fashioned charm

■ Two-story foyer

■ A wood stove in Living Room that warms the entire house

■ A Modern Kitchen flowing easily into bayed Dining Room

■ A first floor Master Bedroom with private Master Bath

■ Two additional bedrooms with walk-in closets and cozy gable sitting nooks

FIRST FLOOR — 1,269 SQ. FT.
SECOND FLOOR — 638 SQ. FT.
BASEMENT — 1,269 SQ. FT.

TOTAL LIVING AREA:
1,907 SQ. FT.

Slab/Crawl Space Option

First Floor

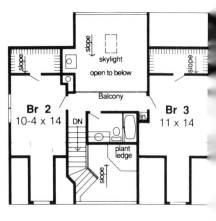

No. 10785

A Karl Kreeger Design

No. 20165
Classic Drama

- ■ This plan features:
- — Three bedrooms
- — Two and one half baths

■ A central Foyer, crowned by a balcony sloping upward to meet the high ceiling of a fireplaced Living Room

■ A sky lit Dining Room with three-sided view of the adjoining Deck

■ A gourmet Kitchen with built-in desk and an abundance of cabinet space

■ Master Bedroom offering a sloping ceiling, walk-in closet and luxurious bath

■ Generous closet and storage space throughout the home

FIRST FLOOR — 901 SQ. FT.
SECOND FLOOR — 864 SQ. FT.
BASEMENT — 901 SQ. FT.
GARAGE — 594 SQ. FT.

TOTAL LIVING AREA: 1,765 SQ. FT.

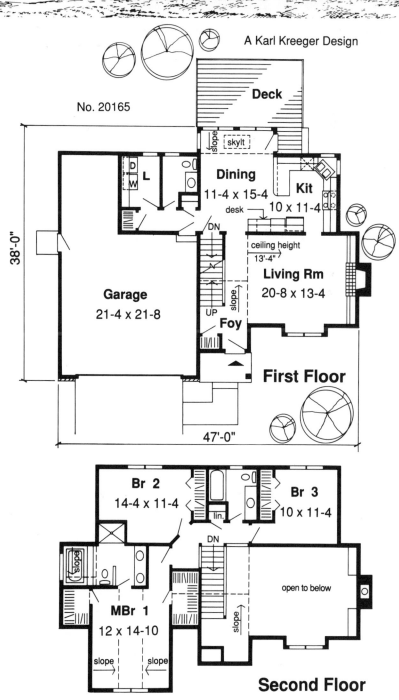

A Karl Kreeger Design

No. 20165

38'-0"

47'-0"

Deck

skylt

Dining
11-4 x 15-4

Kit
10 x 11-4

desk

DN

ceiling height
13'-4"

Garage
21-4 x 21-8

Living Rm
20-8 x 13-4

slope

UP

Foy

First Floor

Br 2
14-4 x 11-4

Br 3
10 x 11-4

lin.

DN

open to below

MBr 1
12 x 14-10

slope   slope

slope

Second Floor

No. 24400
National Treasure

■ This plan features:

— Three bedrooms

— Two and one half baths

■ A wrap-around covered porch

■ Decorative vaulted ceilings in the fireplaced Living room

■ A large Kitchen with central island/breakfast bar

■ A sun-lit sitting area

FIRST FLOOR — 1,034 SQ. FT.
SECOND FLOOR — 944 SQ. FT.
BASEMENT — 944 SQ. FT.
GARAGE & STORAGE — 684 SQ. FT.

TOTAL LIVING AREA:
1,978 SQ. FT.

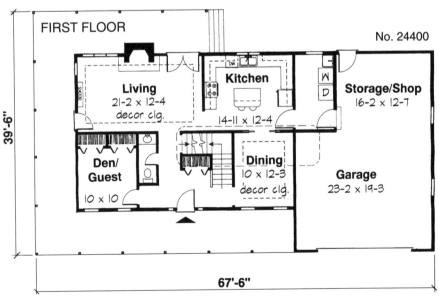

An Upright Design

No. 20176
Gabled Grace

■ This plan features:

— Four bedrooms

— Three full and one half bath

■ An angular Kitchen with built-in pantry, double sinks, peninsula counter that opens to the sunny Breakfast bay and the Hearth Room

■ A cozy fireplace that warms the Hearth Room, Breakfast bay and Kitchen

■ A sloped ceiling with skylights in the Living Room

■ A Master Suite with private Master Bath and a walk-in closet

■ Three additional bedrooms, two with walk-in closets, one with private bath

FIRST FLOOR — 1,625 SQ. FT.
SECOND FLOOR — 916 SQ. FT.
BASEMENT — 1,618 SQ. FT.
GARAGE — 521 SQ. FT.

TOTAL LIVING AREA:
2,541 SQ. FT.

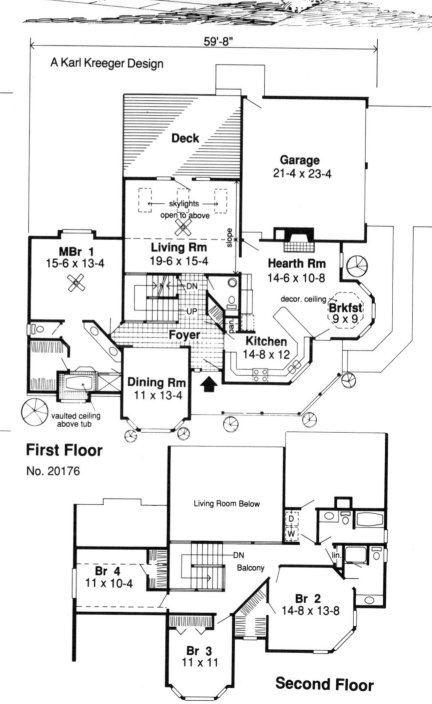

A Karl Kreeger Design

59'-8"

55'-8"

Deck

skylights →
open to above

Garage
21-4 x 23-4

MBr 1
15-6 x 13-4

Living Rm
19-6 x 15-4

slope

Hearth Rm
14-6 x 10-8

decor. ceiling

DN
UP

Brkfst
9 x 9

pan.

Foyer

Kitchen
14-8 x 12

vaulted ceiling
above tub

Dining Rm
11 x 13-4

First Floor

No. 20176

Living Room Below

D
W

Br 4
11 x 10-4

DN
Balcony

lin.

Br 2
14-8 x 13-8

Br 3
11 x 11

Second Floor

No. 10274

Fireplace Center of Circular Living Area

■ This plan features:

— Three bedrooms

— One and one half baths

■ A dramatically positioned fire-place as a focal point for the main living area

■ The Kitchen, Dining and Living Rooms forming a circle that allow work areas to flow into living areas

■ Sliding glass doors giving access to wood Deck

■ A convenient Laundry Room located off Kitchen

■ A double Garage providing excellent storage

FIRST FLOOR — 1,783 SQ. FT.
GARAGE — 576 SQ. FT.

TOTAL LIVING AREA: 1,783 SQ. FT.

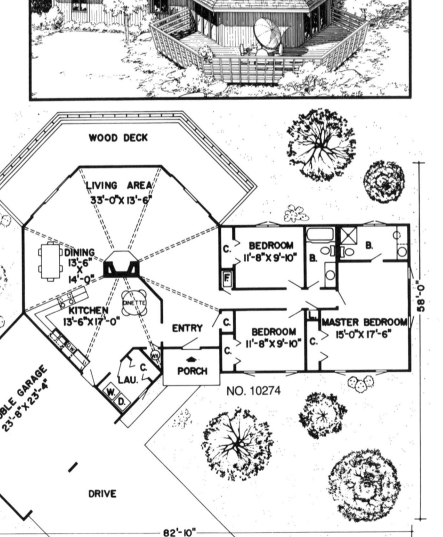

WOOD DECK

LIVING AREA
33'-0" X 13'-6"

DINING
13'-6"
X
14'-0"

KITCHEN
13'-6" X 17'-0"

DINETTE

ENTRY

BEDROOM
11'-8" X 9'-10"

BEDROOM
11'-8" X 9'-10"

MASTER BEDROOM
15'-0" X 17'-6"

C.

C.

C.

C.

B.

B.

F

LAU.

W. D.

PORCH

DOUBLE GARAGE
23'-8" X 23'-4"

S.

DRIVE

NO. 10274

58'-0"

82'-10"

No. 10220

Bedrooms Sliders Open Onto Wooden Deck

■ This plan features:

— Two bedrooms

— One full bath

■ A fifty foot deck setting the stage for a relaxing lifestyle encouraged by this home

■ A simple, yet complete floor plan centering around the large Family Area, warmed by a prefab fireplace with sliders to the deck

■ An efficient L-shaped Kitchen that includes a double sink with a window above, and direct access to the rear yard and the Laundry Room

■ Two bedrooms privately located, each outfitted with sliding doors to the deck and a large window for plenty of light

MAIN AREA — 888 SQ. FT.

TOTAL LIVING AREA:
888 SQ. FT.

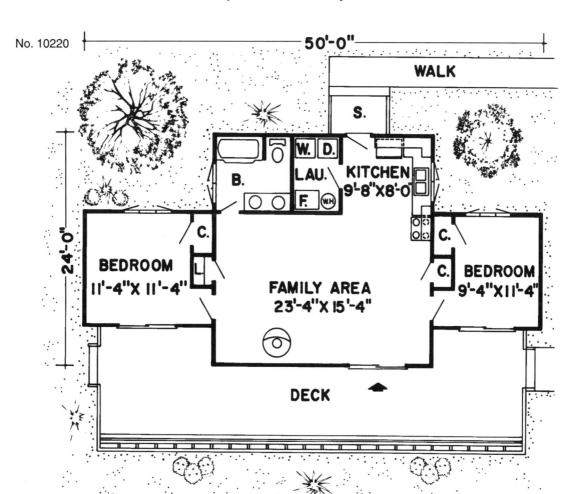

No. 10787
Compact Comfort

■ This plan features:

— Three bedrooms

— Two and one half baths

■ Soaring ceilings and a wall of stacked windows

■ A formal Dining Room perfect for entertaining

■ A Kitchen-Family Room combination with cozy fireplace

■ An efficient Kitchen layout

■ Three bedrooms upstairs and two full baths, including the luxury bath in the Master Bedroom

FIRST FLOOR — 1,064 SQ. FT.
SECOND FLOOR — 708 SQ. FT.
BASEMENT — 1,064 SQ. FT.
GARAGE — 576 SQ. FT.

TOTAL LIVING AREA:
1,772 SQ. FT.

Second Floor

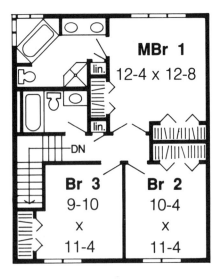

MBr 1
12-4 x 12-8

lin.

lin.

DN

Br 3
9-10
x
11-4

Br 2
10-4
x
11-4

No. 10787

First Floor

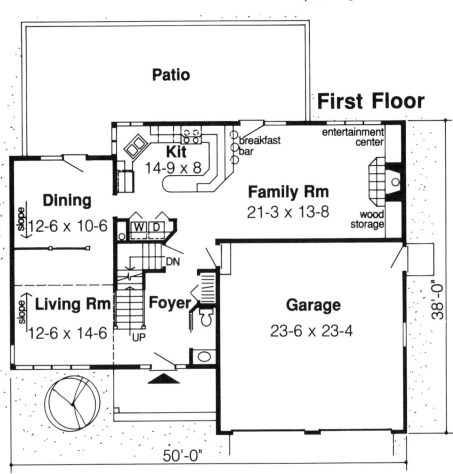

Patio

Kit
14-9 x 8

breakfast bar

entertainment center

Dining
12-6 x 10-6

Family Rm
21-3 x 13-8

wood storage

W D

DN

Living Rm
12-6 x 14-6

Foyer

UP

Garage
23-6 x 23-4

38'-0"

50'-0"

No. 20208
Desirable Family Plan

■ This plan features:

— Three bedrooms

— Three full baths

■ A sloped ceiling in the Living Room with a fantastic fireplace

■ A spacious U-shaped Kitchen and adjoining Dining Room with access to the deck

■ A Master Suite with large walk-in closet and a private Master Bath with a vaulted ceiling

■ Two additional bedroom sharing a full bath

FIRST FLOOR — 989 SQ. FT.
SECOND FLOOR — 932 SQ. FT.
BASEMENT — 950 SQ. FT.
GARAGE — 475 SQ. FT.

TOTAL LIVING AREA:
1,921 SQ. FT.

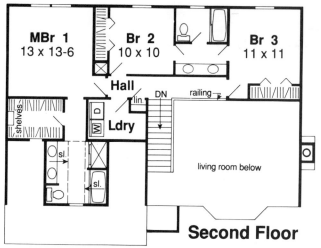

Second Floor

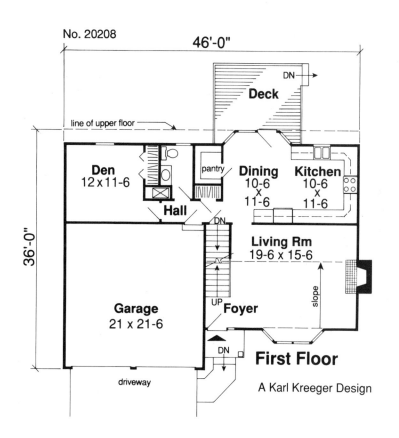

First Floor

A Karl Kreeger Design

No. 24302

Champagne Style on a Soda-Pop Budget

Donald L. Marshall Architect

■ This plan features:

— Three bedrooms

— Two full baths

■ Multiple gables, circle-top windows, and a unique exterior setting this delightful ranch apart in any neighborhood

■ Living and Dining Rooms flowing together to create a very roomy feeling

■ Sliding doors leading from the Dining Room to a covered patio

■ A Master Bedroom with a private bath

FIRST FLOOR — 988 SQ. FT.
BASEMENT — 988 SQ. FT.
GARAGE — 280 SQ. FT
OPTIONAL 2-CAR GARAGE — 384 SQ. FT.

TOTAL LIVING AREA:
988 SQ. FT.

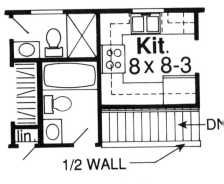

Kit.
8 x 8-3

DN

1/2 WALL

Basement Option

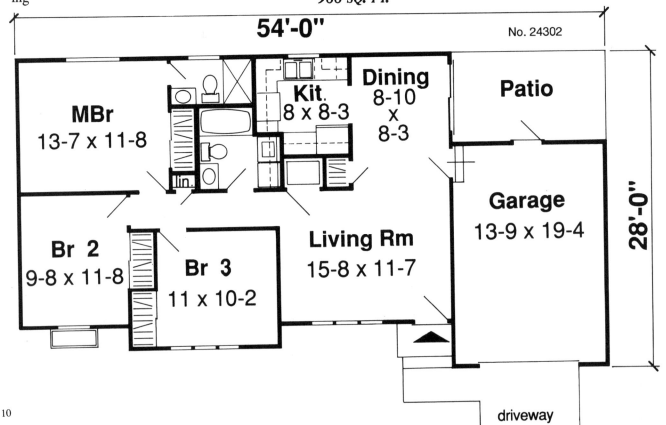

54'-0"

No. 24302

MBr
13-7 x 11-8

Kit.
8 x 8-3

Dining
8-10
x
8-3

Patio

Br 2
9-8 x 11-8

Br 3
11 x 10-2

Living Rm
15-8 x 11-7

Garage
13-9 x 19-4

28'-0"

driveway

An Energetic Enterprises Design

No. 24256

Beautiful Combination of Old and New

■ This plan features:

— Three bedrooms

— Two full baths

■ Vaulted ceilings in the family living areas; Living Room, Dining Room, Family Room and Eating Nook

■ An open layout between the Kitchen, Nook, and Family Room, making the rooms appear even more spacious

■ A corner fireplace in the Family Room, which also has access to the patio

■ A peninsula counter in the island Kitchen that doubles as an eating bar

■ A lavish Master Suite that is equipped with a private bath and walk-in closet

■ Two family bedrooms that share a full hall bath

MAIN LIVING AREA — 2,108 SQ. FT.

TOTAL LIVING AREA: 2,108 SQ. FT.

BATH

OPTIONAL CABINETS

DN

FOYER

2-CAR GARAGE

OPTIONAL DEN
9'-8"x12'-8"

PORCH

OPTIONAL DEN

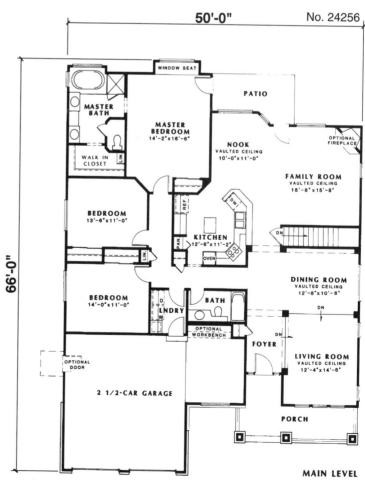

50'-0"   No. 24256

66'-0"

WINDOW SEAT

PATIO

MASTER BATH

MASTER BEDROOM
14'-2"x16'-6"

NOOK
VAULTED CEILING
10'-0"x11'-0"

OPTIONAL FIREPLACE

WALK IN CLOSET

FAMILY ROOM
VAULTED CEILING
18'-8"x15'-8"

BEDROOM
13'-8"x11'-0"

REF.

KITCHEN
12'-8"x11'-2"

PAN.

OVEN

DN

BEDROOM
14'-0"x11'-0"

LNDRY
D W

BATH

DINING ROOM
VAULTED CEILING
12'-8"x10'-8"

DN

OPTIONAL WORKBENCH

FOYER

DN

OPTIONAL DOOR

2 1/2-CAR GARAGE

LIVING ROOM
VAULTED CEILING
12'-4"x14'-6"

PORCH

MAIN LEVEL

BEDROOM

LNDRY

BATH

OPTIONAL WORKBENCH

DN

FOYER

OPTIONAL DOOR

OPTIONAL 3-CAR GARAGE

PORCH

OPTIONAL 3-CAR GARAGE

No. 34043

A Home for Today and Tomorrow

■ This plan features:

— Three bedrooms

— Two full baths

■ An intriguing Breakfast nook off the Kitchen

■ A wide open fireplaced Living Room with glass sliders to deck

■ A step-saving arrangement of the Kitchen between the Breakfast and formal Dining Room

■ A handsome Master Bedroom with sky-lit compartmentalized bath

MAIN LIVING AREA — 1,583 SQ. FT.
BASEMENT — 1,583 SQ. FT.
GARAGE — 484 SQ. FT.

TOTAL LIVING AREA:
1,583 SQ. FT.

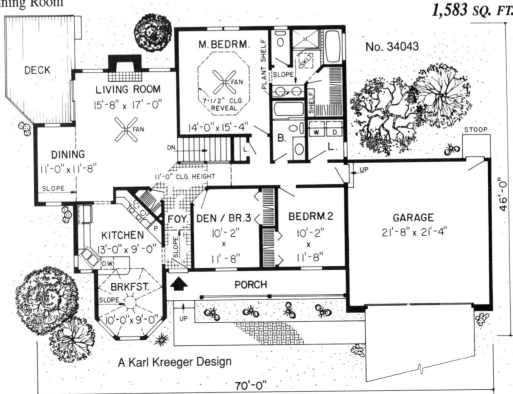

A Karl Kreeger Design

No. 10570

Ranch Design Utilizes Skylights

■ This plan features:

— Four bedrooms

— Two baths

■ A partial stone veneer front making this large ranch design very inviting

■ A large Library/Den next to the foyer sharing a two-way fireplace with the Living Room

■ A Living Room leading to a deck or screened porch

■ A very large hexagonal Kitchen with a connecting Dining Room

FIRST FLOOR — 2,450 SQ. FT.
BASEMENT — 2,450 SQ. FT.
GARAGE — 739 SQ. FT.

TOTAL LIVING AREA: 2,450 SQ. FT.

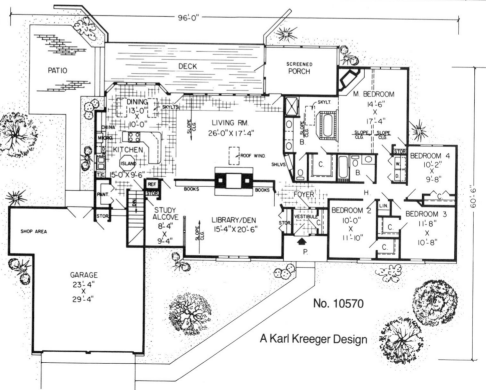

No. 10570

A Karl Kreeger Design

No. 10540

Stone and Stucco Gives this House Class

■ This plan features:

— Four bedrooms

— Two and one half baths

■ A large, majestic foyer flowing into the formal Dining Room

■ A Great Room accented by a wet bar, a stone fireplace, and access to a spacious deck

■ A spacious Kitchen highlighted by a writing area, work area, and a beamed Breakfast Room

■ A huge Master Bedroom with a dressing room and a separate whirlpool bath

■ A lower level featuring a recreation area and two additional bedrooms

First floor — 2,473 sq. ft.
Lower floor — 1,624 sq. ft.
Basement — 732 sq. ft.
Garage & storage — 686 sq. ft.

Total living area: 4,097 sq. ft.

A Karl Kreeger Design
No. 10540

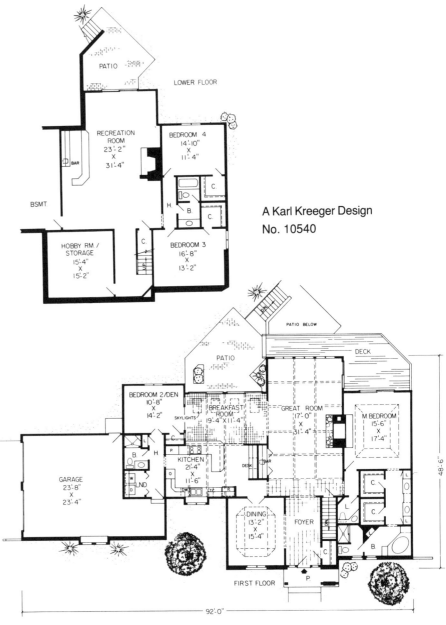

No. 34011

Windows Add Warmth To All Living Areas

■ This plan features:

— Three bedrooms

— Two full baths

■ A Master Suite with huge his and hers walk-in closets and private bath

■ Second and third bedroom with ample closet space

■ A Kitchen equipped with an island counter and flowing easily into the Dining and Family Rooms

■ A Laundry Room conveniently located near all three bedrooms

■ An optional garage

FIRST FLOOR — 1,672 SQ. FT.
OPTIONAL GARAGE — 566 SQ. FT.

TOTAL LIVING AREA: 1,672 SQ. FT.

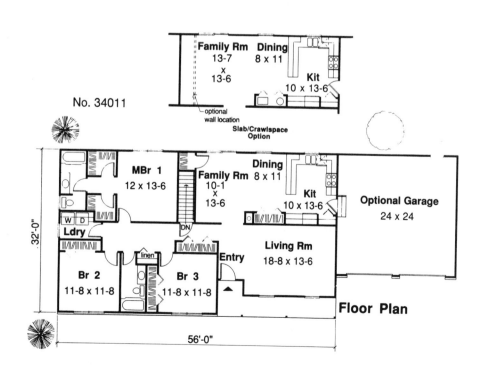

No. 34011

Family Rm
13-7
x
13-6

Dining
8 x 11

Kit
10 x 13-6

optional
wall location

Slab/Crawlspace
Option

MBr 1
12 x 13-6

Family Rm
10-1
x
13-6

Dining 8 x 11

Kit
10 x 13-6

Optional Garage
24 x 24

W D

Ldry

DN

Br 2
11-8 x 11-8

linen

Br 3
11-8 x 11-8

Entry

Living Rm
18-8 x 13-6

32'-0"

56'-0"

Floor Plan

No. 9269
Vaulted Ceilings Effect Impressive Entry

- This plan features:
- — Three bedrooms
- — Two full baths
- Vaulted ceilings and a wood-burning fireplace

- A Living Room adjoining an open Kitchen and Family Room, separated by a breakfast bar
- A Hobby Room which can be easily converted into a guest room
- A covered patio accessible through the Family Room

FIRST FLOOR — 1,285 SQ. FT.
SECOND FLOOR — 476 SQ. FT.
GARAGE — 473 SQ. FT.

TOTAL LIVING AREA: 1,761 SQ. FT.

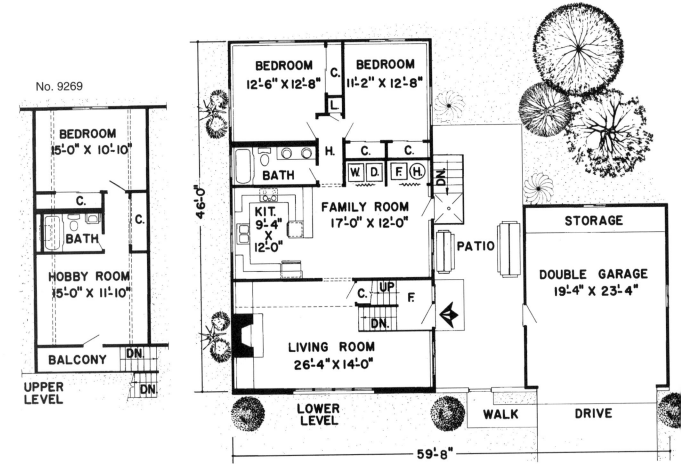

No. 10802

A Spacious Abode with Plenty of Growing Room

■ This plan features:

— Three bedrooms

— Two and one half baths

■ A central foyer creating a dazzling impression for entering guests

■ Formal Living and Dining Rooms overlooking the front yard for elegant entertaining

■ A Family Room with a fireplace, built in bar, and bookcases

■ An island Kitchen designed for the modern two-cook family

■ An adjoining rear deck as a great place for a barbecue

■ A Master Suite with a sunny well-appointed bath, walk-in closet, and sky-lit secret room over the three car Garage

FIRST FLOOR — 1,522 SQ. FT.
SECOND FLOOR — 1,545 SQ. FT.

TOTAL LIVING AREA: 3,067 SQ. FT.

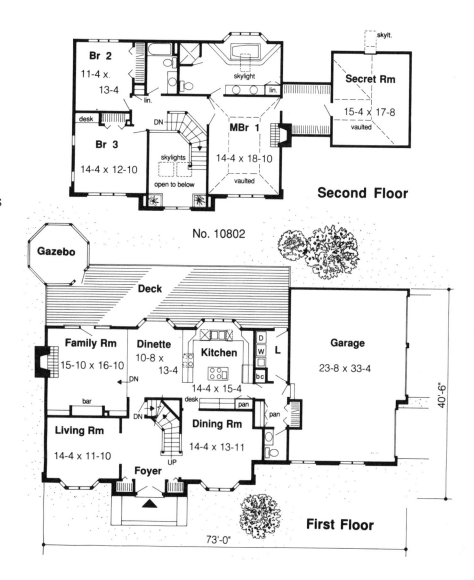

No. 20124

Romantic Porch Mirrors Dining Bay

■ This plan features:

— Four bedrooms

— Two and one half baths

■ Bay and bump-out windows, sliders and skylights adding space to every room

■ Formal Living and Dining Rooms flanking the attractive foyer

■ An island Kitchen serving all the active areas with ease

■ A first-floor Master Suite with a garden tub and step-in shower

■ A walk-in closet in every bedroom

FIRST FLOOR — 1,798 SQ. FT.
SECOND FLOOR — 879 SQ. FT.
BASEMENT — 1,789 SQ. FT.
GARAGE — 484 SQ. FT.

TOTAL LIVING AREA:
2,677 SQ. FT.

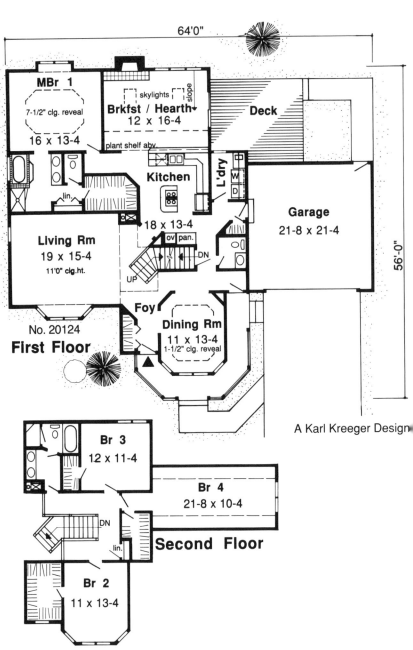

First Floor

64'0"

MBr 1
7-1/2" clg. reveal
16 x 13-4

Brkfst / Hearth
12 x 16-4
skylights
slope

Deck

plant shelf abv.

Kitchen

L'dry
W D

Garage
21-8 x 21-4

18 x 13-4

Living Rm
19 x 15-4
11'0" clg. ht.

ov pan.
DN
UP

56'-0"

No. 20124

Foy

Dining Rm
11 x 13-4
1-1/2" clg. reveal

A Karl Kreeger Design

Br 3
12 x 11-4

Br 4
21-8 x 10-4

DN

Second Floor

lin.

Br 2
11 x 13-4

No. 20144
Country Comforts

- ■ This plan features:
- — Four bedrooms
- — Three full and one half bath
- ■ A sprawling front porch
- ■ A two-way fireplace warming the Hearth Room and the Living Room
- ■ A formal, bayed Dining Room with decorative ceiling
- ■ An efficient, well-appointed Kitchen with peninsula counter and double sinks
- ■ A vaulted ceiling in the Master Suite which is equipped with a private Master Bath
- ■ Three additional bedrooms each with adjoining full baths

FIRST FLOOR — 1,737 SQ. FT.
SECOND FLOOR — 826 SQ. FT.
BASEMENT — 1,728 SQ. FT.

TOTAL LIVING AREA:
2,563 SQ. FT.

A Karl Kreeger Design

No. 20144

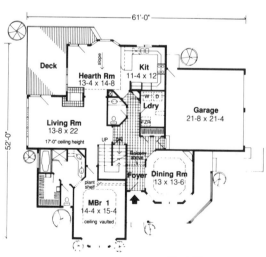

First Floor

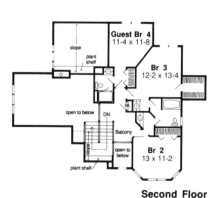

Second Floor

No. 24320
Step Saving One Floor Living

■ This plan features:

— Three bedrooms

— Two full baths

■ A covered entrance leads to the Foyer and opens into the Living, Breakfast and Kitchen areas

■ A fireplace and corner windows in the Living area

■ A galley Kitchen offers a breakfast bar, a built-in pantry and easy access to the covered Porch and Garage

■ The Master Bedroom features a double closet and a private bath

■ Two additional bedrooms sharing a full hall bath

MAIN LIVING AREA — 1,235 SQ. FT.
GARAGE — 425 SQ. FT.

TOTAL LIVING AREA: 1,235 SQ. FT.

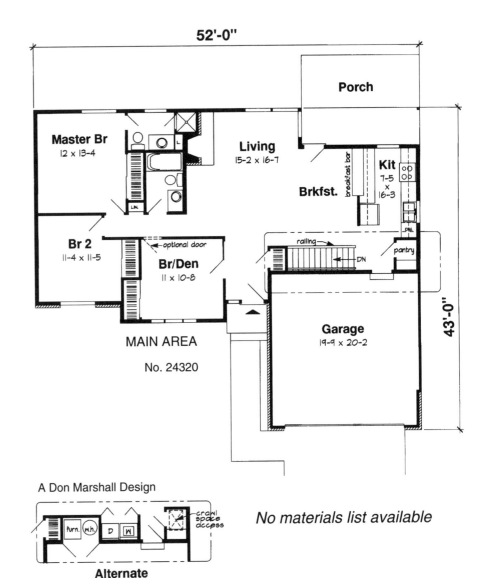

MAIN AREA

No. 24320

A Don Marshall Design

Alternate Foundation Plan

No materials list available

No. 10495

Sun Space Warmth

- ■ This plan features:
- — Four bedrooms
- — Three baths
- ■ Tile used to soak up solar heat in the sun space and also to add a tailored accent
- ■ Tile separating the activity area from the sleeping areas
- ■ Utilitarian areas of the home enhanced by direct access to the sun space
- ■ A large Master Bedroom with private bath and large walk in closet

FIRST FLOOR — 1,691 SQ. FT.
SECOND FLOOR — 512 SQ. FT.
SUN SPACE — 108 SQ. FT.
BASEMENT — 1,691 SQ. FT.
GARAGE — 484 SQ. FT.

TOTAL LIVING AREA:
2,203 SQ. FT.

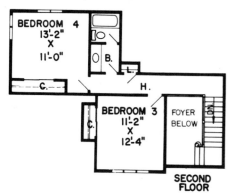

BEDROOM 4
13'-2"
X
11'-0"
B.
C.
H.
BEDROOM 3
11'-2"
X
12'-4"
FOYER BELOW

SECOND FLOOR

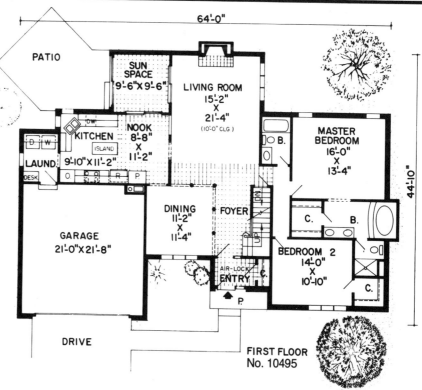

64'-0"

PATIO

SUN SPACE
9'-6" X 9'-6"

LIVING ROOM
15'-2"
X
21'-4"
(10'-0" CLG)

MASTER BEDROOM
16'-0"
X
13'-4"

KITCHEN
9'-10"X11'-2"

NOOK
8'-8"
X
11'-2"

LAUND.

DESK

DINING
11'-2"
X
11'-4"

FOYER

GARAGE
21'-0"X21'-8"

BEDROOM 2
14'-0"
X
10'-10"

AIR-LOCK
ENTRY

44'-10"

DRIVE

FIRST FLOOR
No. 10495

A Karl Kreeger Design

No. 10679
Dine On The Deck

■ This plan features:

— Three bedrooms

— Two and one half baths

■ A rear-facing Master Suite with his and hers walk-in closets and a luxurious bath overlooking the deck

■ A sunken Living Room with expansive stacked windows and sloping ceilings

■ A range-top island Kitchen open to the Dining area

■ A Sewing Room, Laundry Room and large Garage

FIRST FLOOR — 1,445 SQ. FT.
SECOND FLOOR — 739 SQ. FT.
BASEMENT — 1,229 SQ. FT.
GARAGE — 724 SQ. FT.

TOTAL LIVING AREA:
2,184 SQ. FT.

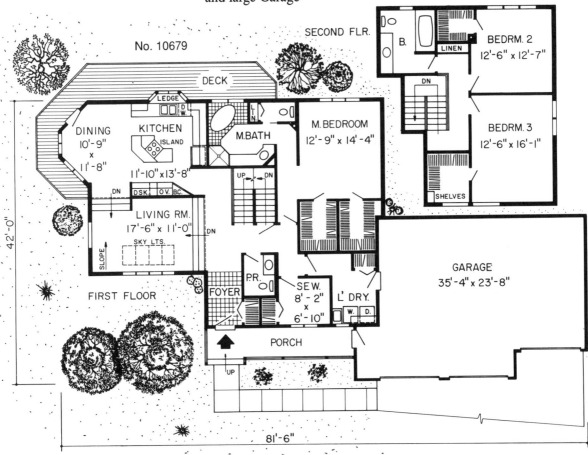

No. 10638

Traditional Warmth With a Modern Accent

■ This plan features

— Four bedrooms

— Two and one half baths

■ Recessed ceilings in the Living Room, Dining and Master Bedrooms

■ Rustic beams, a fireplace and built-in shelves located in the Family Room

■ A laundry room close by the Kitchen with it's cozy breakfast area

■ A Master Suite complete with private bath and bay window sitting nook

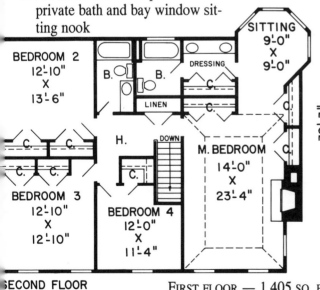

SITTING 9'-0" X 9'-0"

BEDROOM 2 12'-10" X 13'-6"

DRESSING

LINEN

M. BEDROOM 14'-0" X 23'-4"

DOWN

BEDROOM 3 12'-10" X 12'-10"

BEDROOM 4 12'-0" X 11'-4"

SECOND FLOOR

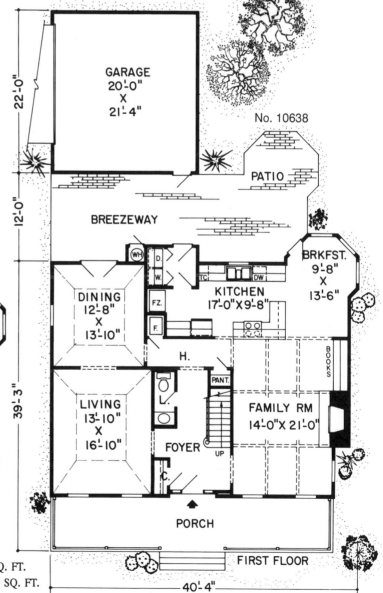

GARAGE 20'-0" X 21'-4"

No. 10638

PATIO

22'-0"

12'-0"

BREEZEWAY

WH

DINING 12'-8" X 13'-10"

KITCHEN 17'-0"X9'-8"

BRKFST. 9'-8" X 13'-6"

BOOKS

39'-3"

LIVING 13'-10" X 16'-10"

FAMILY RM 14'-0"X 21'-0"

PANT.

FOYER

UP

PORCH

FIRST FLOOR

40'-4"

FIRST FLOOR — 1,405 sq. ft.
SECOND FLOOR — 1,364 sq. ft.
GARAGE — 458 sq. ft.

TOTAL LIVING AREA:

2,769 sq. ft.

No. 24324

Focus on the Family

■ This plan features:

— Three bedrooms

— Two full and one half baths

■ Cozy front porch

■ A fireplaced Family Room only divided from the Kitchen by an eating bar

■ A U-shaped Kitchen with a pantry and ample cabinet space

■ A pan-vaulted ceiling in the formal Dining Room adds a decorative accent

■ A spacious Living Room, flowing easily into the Dining Room and viewing the front porch

■ A Master Suite enhanced with a walk-in closet, a double vanity, a whirlpool tub, a step-in shower and a compartmentalized toilet

■ Two additional bedrooms, one with a walk-in closet, share the second full bath

FIRST FLOOR — 916 SQ. FT.
SECOND FLOOR — 884 SQ. FT.
GARAGE — 480 SQ. FT.

TOTAL LIVING AREA:
1,800 SQ. FT.

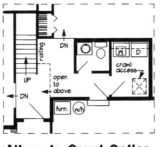

Alternate Crawl Option

A Don Marshall Design

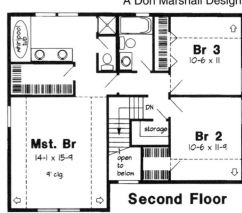

Second Floor

No. 24324

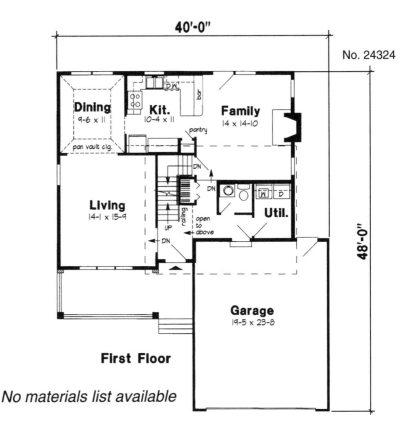

First Floor

No materials list available

No. 20138
Towering Tudor

■ This plan features:

— Four bedrooms

— Three baths

■ A bay window tower gracing the front of this impressive home

■ A two-story foyer flanked by a large formal Living Room and a private Master Suite with every amenity

■ A formal Dining Room with bump-out window overlooking the backyard

■ A gourmet Kitchen with a range - top island

■ A sky-lit Breakfast area adjoining the cozy Hearth Room which includes a fireplace

FIRST FLOOR — 2,136 SQ. FT.
SECOND FLOOR — 873 SQ. FT.
BASEMENT — 2,130 SQ. FT.
GARAGE — 720 SQ. FT.

TOTAL LIVING AREA:
3,009 SQ. FT.

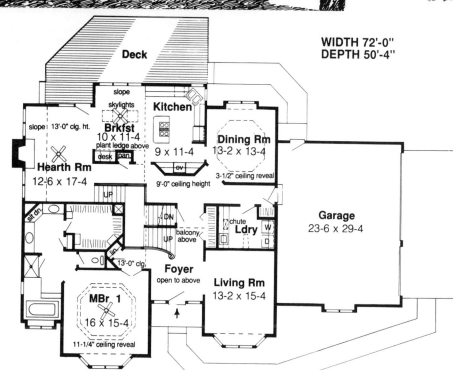

WIDTH 72'-0"
DEPTH 50'-4"

Deck

slope
skylights
Kitchen

Brkfst
10 x 11-4
plant ledge above
slope 13'-0" clg. ht.
9 x 11-4

Dining Rm
13-2 x 13-4

desk | pan.
slope
ov
9'-0" ceiling height
3-1/2" ceiling reveal

Hearth Rm
12-6 x 17-4

UP
sit dn
DN
chute
Ldry
W
D

UP
balcony above

Garage
23-6 x 29-4

lin.
13'-0" clg.

Foyer
open to above

Living Rm
13-2 x 15-4

MBr 1
16 x 15-4

11-1/4" ceiling reveal

First Floor

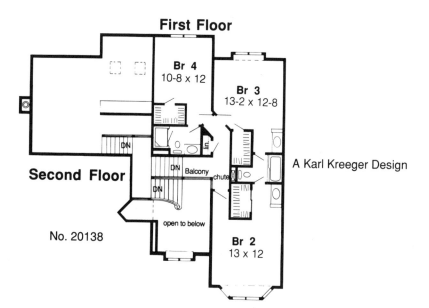

First Floor

Br 4
10-8 x 12

Br 3
13-2 x 12-8

DN

DN
Balcony
chute

Second Floor

DN

A Karl Kreeger Design

open to below

No. 20138

Br 2
13 x 12

No. 24550

Impressive Brick

■ This plan features:

— Four bedrooms

— Two full and one half bath

■ Decorative facade of brick and windows, and a covered entrance leading into a two-story, raised Foyer with a splendid, curved staircase

■ A Family Room with the unique fireplace and built-in entertainment center opens to the Breakfast/Kitchen area

■ An efficient, island Kitchen with an atrium sink, walk-in pantry, built-in desk expanding to bright Breakfast area and outdoors as well as Utility room and Garage

■ A Master Suite with a vaulted ceiling, over-sized walk-in closet, and a plush Bath with a corner window tub, two vanities and an oversized shower

■ Three additional bedrooms, on second floor, sharing a full bath

FIRST FLOOR — 1,433 SQ. FT.
SECOND FLOOR — 1,283 SQ. FT.
BASEMENT — 1.433 SQ. FT.
GARAGE — 923 SQ. FT.

TOTAL LIVING AREA:
2,716 SQ. FT.

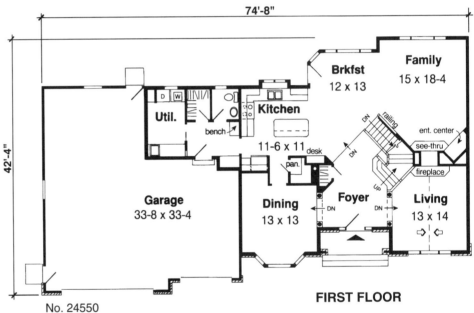

FIRST FLOOR

No. 24550

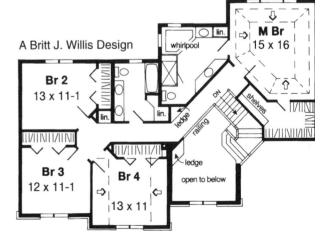

A Britt J. Willis Design

SECOND FLOOR

No. 24325

Homey Country Porch

■ This plan features:

— Three bedrooms

— Two full and one half baths

■ A covered front Porch wraps around to connect with Patio that extends around back of home

■ A spacious Living Room with a cozy fireplace, triple front window and atrium door to Patio

■ A Family Room flowing into the Dining Room and Kitchen creates a comfortable gathering space

■ An efficient Kitchen including a peninsula counter/snackbar, double sink, walk-in pantry and a broom closet

■ A Master Suite with a walk-in closet, private Bath and a built-in audio/video center

■ A Laundry Room ideally located near the bedrooms

■ Two additional bedrooms that share a full hall bath

FIRST FLOOR — 908 SQ. FT.
SECOND FLOOR — 908 SQ. FT.
GARAGE — 462 SQ. FT.

TOTAL LIVING AREA:
1,816 SQ. FT.

Alternate Crawl Option

A Don Marshall Design

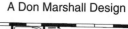

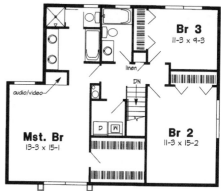

Second Floor

Br 3
11-3 x 9-3

linen

audio/video

Mst. Br
13-3 x 15-1

Br 2
11-3 x 15-2

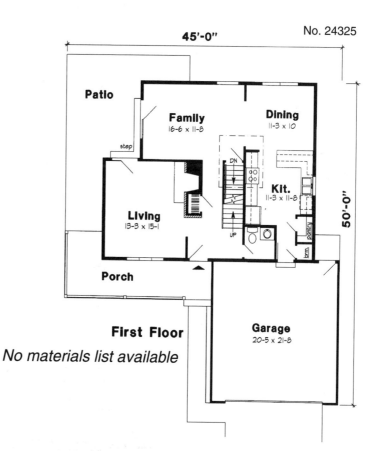

No. 24325

45'-0"

50'-0"

Patio

Family
16-6 x 11-8

Dining
11-3 x 10

step

Kit.
11-3 x 11-8

Living
13-3 x 15-1

Porch

First Floor

Garage
20-5 x 21-8

No materials list available

No. 20050
Perfect for Entertaining

This plan features:

— Three bedrooms

— Two full and one half baths

■ A beautiful front door surrounded by windows, leads into a tiled, vaulted Foyer and an expansive Living Room

■ A sloped ceiling, a wall of windows and a large fireplace enhance the Living Room that leads directly into the Dining Room

■ A formal Dining Room with a decorative ceiling conveniently adjacent to the Kitchen

■ A Kitchen equipped with a corner sink, a cooktop island/snack bar and a built-in pantry

■ A Master Suite featuring a double closet and a Bath with a raised garden tub and a double vanity

■ Two additional bedrooms on the second floor

FIRST FLOOR — 1,303 SQ. FT.
SECOND FLOOR — 596 SQ. FT.
BASEMENT — 1,303 SQ. FT.
GARAGE — 460 SQ. FT.

TOTAL LIVING AREA : 1,899 SQ. FT.

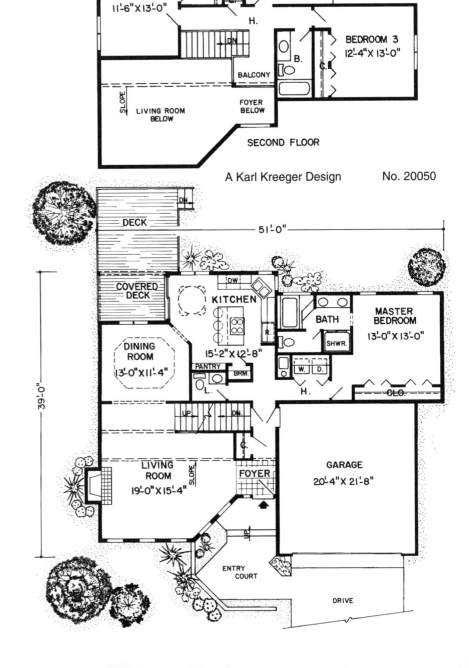

A Karl Kreeger Design   No. 20050

No. 10779

Fireplaces Add Warmth

■ This plan features:

— Three bedrooms

— Three full and one half bath

■ A balcony giving a sweeping view of the vaulted Great Room, the two-story foyer, and the bi-level Master Suite

■ A sunken formal Dining Room

■ A country Kitchen with a cook top island and a greenhouse window for growing herbs

■ A book-lined Study next to the Living Room

■ A Master Suite with ample closet space, double vanities, and a large fireplace

FIRST FLOOR — 2,962 SQ. FT.
SECOND FLOOR — 1,883 SQ. FT.
LOWER FLOOR(NOT SHOWN) — 1,888 SQ. FT.
BASEMENT — 1,074 SQ. FT.
GARAGE — 890 SQ. FT.

TOTAL LIVING AREA: 6,733 SQ. FT.

No. 10779

No. 10791

Super Starter

■ This plan features:

— Three bedrooms

— One full bath

■ An entry opening to a spacious Living Room brightened by a triple window arrangement

■ An open Kitchen and Dining Room combination including sliding glass doors to the back-yard

■ A handy side entry

■ An alternate crawl space plan which separates the Kitchen and Breakfast nook with counters and cabinets

■ Bedrooms that include ample closet space and easy access to the large hall bath

FIRST FLOOR — 1,092 SQ. FT.

TOTAL LIVING AREA:
1,092 SQ. FT.

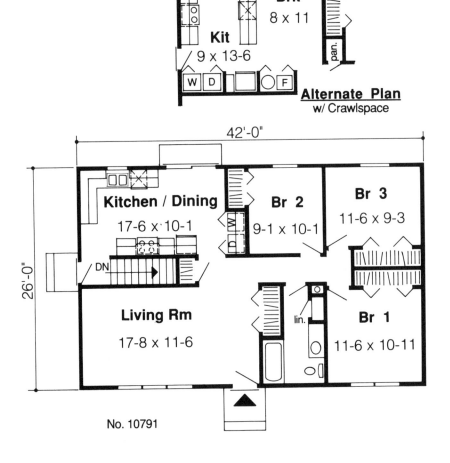

Alternate Plan
w/ Crawlspace

No. 10791

No. 20504

Octagon-Shaped Study Adds Interest

■ This plan features:

— Two or three bedrooms

— Three full baths

■ Decorative ceilings in the Living Room, Study and Master Suite

■ Luxurious Master Suite with spacious compartmented Master Bath and two walk in closets

■ Palladium windows from floor to ceiling in the octagon shaped Study

■ An efficient gourmet Kitchen including a cooktop island and eating bar, corner double sink and ample counter and cabinet space

MAIN AREA — 1,958 SQ. FT.
GARAGE — 405 SQ. FT.

**TOTAL LIVING AREA:
1,958 SQ. FT.**

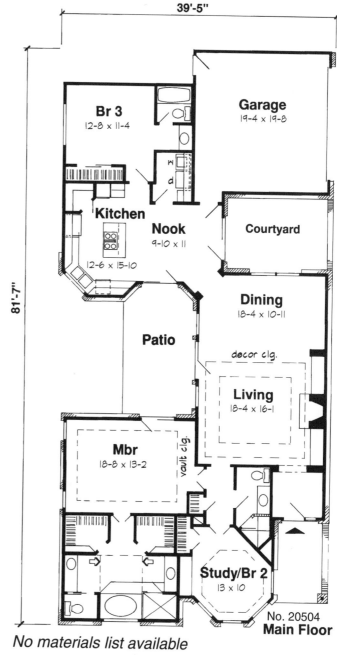

39'-5"

81'-7"

Br 3
12-8 x 11-4

Garage
19-4 x 19-8

Kitchen

Nook
9-10 x 11

Courtyard

12-6 x 15-10

Dining
18-4 x 10-11

Patio

decor clg.

Living
18-4 x 16-1

Mbr
18-8 x 13-2

vault clg.

Study/Br 2
13 x 10

No. 20504
Main Floor

No materials list available

No. 1074
Design Features Six Sides

■ This plan features:

— Three bedrooms

— Two full baths

■ Active living areas centrally located between two quiet bedroom and bath areas

■ A Living Room that can be closed off from bedroom wings giving privacy to both areas

■ A bath located behind a third bedroom

■ A bedroom complete with washer/dryer facilities.

FIRST FLOOR — 1,040 SQ. FT.
STORAGE — 44 SQ. FT.
DECK — 258 SQ. FT.
CARPORT — 230 SQ. FT.

TOTAL LIVING AREA:
1,040 SQ. FT.

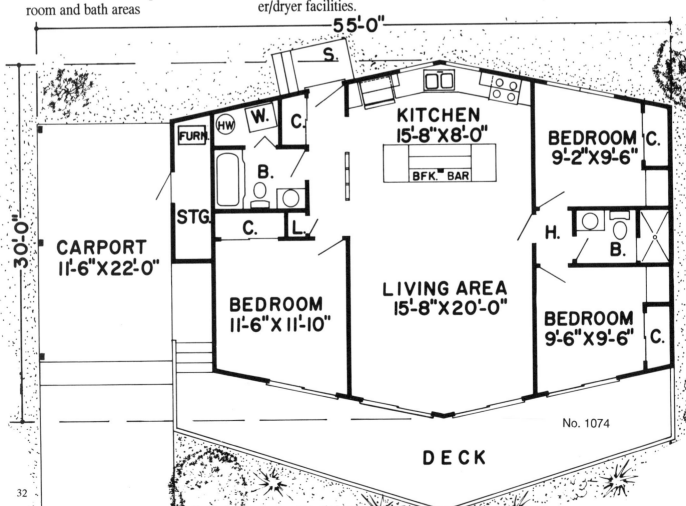

32

No. 24554
Traditional Interior

■ This plan features:

— Four bedrooms

— Three full and one half baths

■ An appealing symmetrical facade providing a sheltered entrance into open, contemporary living spaces

■ A unique railing defining formal Living Room space with double doors leading to the Family Room

■ A Family Room with a cozy fireplace and triple window view of backyard opens to Kitchen area

■ An ideally located Kitchen with a center work island adjoins the Breakfast bay, formal Dining Room, laundry area, and Garage

■ A comfortable Master Suite with a vaulted ceiling includes a walk-in closet, a private Bath with an oval, window tub, double vanity and separate shower

■ Three additional bedrooms with oversized closets, sharing a full hall bath

FIRST FLOOR — 1,063 SQ. FT.
SECOND FLOOR — 979 SQ. FT.

TOTAL LIVING AREA:
2,042 SQ. FT.

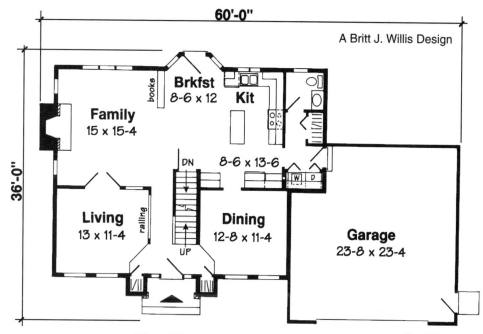

A Britt J. Willis Design

60'-0"

36'-0"

books

Brkfst
8-6 x 12

Kit

Family
15 x 15-4

DN

8-6 x 13-6

W D

Living
13 x 11-4

railing

UP

Dining
12-8 x 11-4

Garage
23-8 x 23-4

First Floor

No. 24554

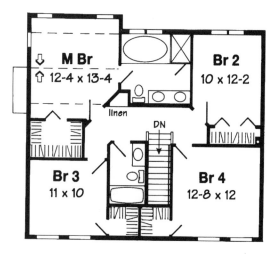

M Br
12-4 x 13-4

Br 2
10 x 12-2

linen

DN

Br 3
11 x 10

Br 4
12-8 x 12

Second Floor

No. 20175
Friendly Facade

■ This plan features:

— Four bedrooms

— Two full and one half baths

■ Columns separating the Living and Dining Rooms so that the fireplace in the Living Room can be enjoyed by both rooms

■ A well-appointed and efficiently arranged Kitchen with peninsula counter and opening to the Breakfast room

■ A first-floor Master Suite with walk-in closet and private Master Bath

■ Three additional bedrooms, two with walk-in closets, that share a full hall bath

FIRST FLOOR — 1,800 SQ. FT.
SECOND FLOOR — 790 SQ. FT.
BASEMENT — 1,800 SQ. FT.
GARAGE — 559 SQ. FT.

TOTAL LIVING AREA:
2,590 SQ. FT.

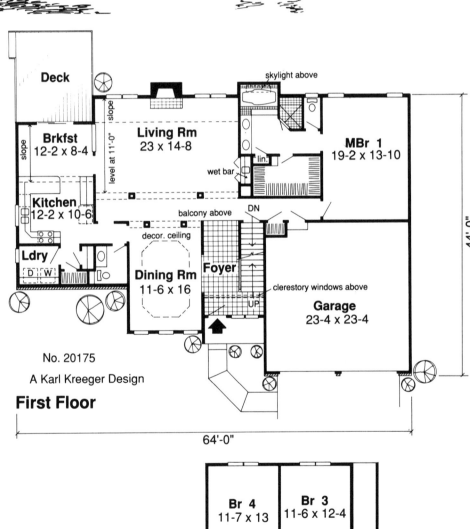

No. 20175

A Karl Kreeger Design

First Floor

64'-0"

Second Floor

No. 20209

Zoned for Harmony

■ This plan features:

— Three bedrooms

— Two and one half baths

■ A lofty vaulted ceiling over the entire living level

■ A spacious, efficient Kitchen with a peninsula counter separating it from the Breakfast Room

■ A formal Living and Dining Room that efficiently flow into each other for ease in entertaining

■ A Family Room with a fireplace and built-in bookshelves

■ A Master Suite with a romantic window seat, a large walk-in closet and a lavish Master Bath

■ Two additional bedrooms, with walk-in closets, that share a full hall bath

FIRST FLOOR — 1,861 SQ. FT.
LOWER FLOOR — 526 SQ. FT.
BASEMENT — 874 SQ. FT.
GARAGE — 574 SQ. FT.

TOTAL LIVING AREA: 2,387 SQ. FT.

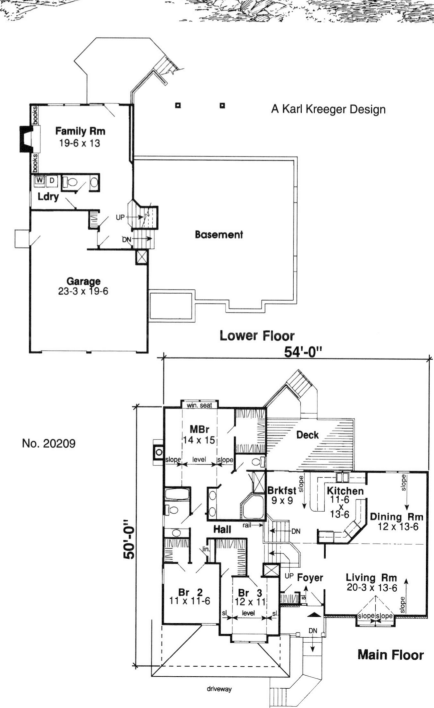

A Karl Kreeger Design

No. 20209

No. 34027

Enticing Two-Story Traditional

■ This plan features:

— Four bedrooms

— Two and one half baths

■ A porch serving as a wonderful, relaxing area to enjoy the outdoors

■ A Dining Room including a decorative ceiling and easy access to the Kitchen

■ A Kitchen/Utility area with access to the Garage

■ A Living Room with double doors into the Family Room which features a fireplace and access to the patio

■ A Master Bedroom with two enormous walk-in closets, as well as a dressing area and private bath

FIRST FLOOR — 925 SQ. FT.
SECOND FLOOR — 975 SQ. FT.
GARAGE — 484 SQ. FT.

No. 34027

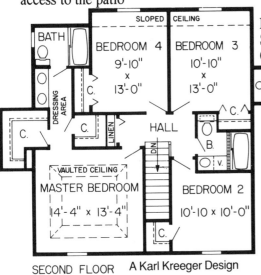

SLOPED CEILING

BATH

BEDROOM 4
9'-10"
x
13'-0"

BEDROOM 3
10'-10"
x
13'-0"

DRESSING AREA

C.

C.

C.

LINEN

HALL

DN

C.

B.

V.

VAULTED CEILING

MASTER BEDROOM
14'-4" x 13'-4"

BEDROOM 2
10'-10 x 10'-0"

C.

SECOND FLOOR   A Karl Kreeger Design

TOTAL LIVING AREA:
1,900 SQ. FT.

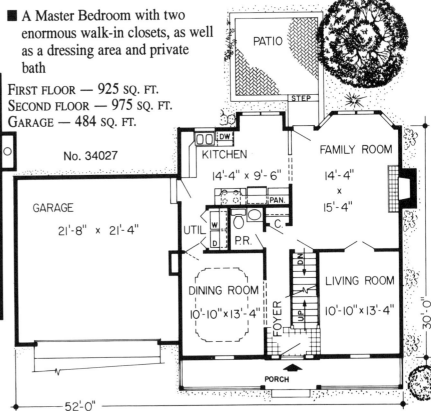

PATIO

STEP

KITCHEN
14'-4" x 9'-6"

FAMILY ROOM
14'-4"
x
15'-4"

DW

PAN.

GARAGE
21'-8" x 21'-4"

UTIL

W
D

P.R.

C.

DINING ROOM
10'-10"x13'-4"

FOYER

DN

UP

LIVING ROOM
10'-10" x 13'-4"

PORCH

30'-0"

52'-0"

No. 20195

Cozy and Restful

■ This plan features:

— Three bedrooms

— One and one half baths

■ A decorative ceiling in the Master Bedroom with private access to the full hall sky-lit bath

■ A convenient laundry center near the bedrooms

■ An efficient Kitchen with ample counter and cabinet space and a double sink under a window

■ A Dining/Living Room combination that flows into each other for easy entertaining

■ A Family Room with a cozy fireplace and convenient half bath

FIRST FLOOR — 1,139 SQ. FT.
BASEMENT — 288 SQ. FT.
GARAGE — 598 SQ. FT.

TOTAL LIVING AREA:
1,427 SQ. FT.

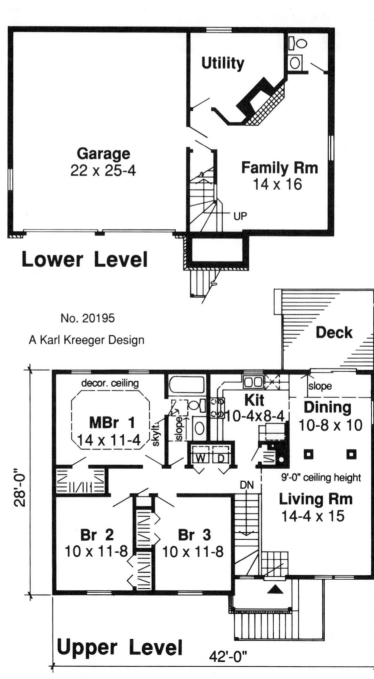

No. 20195

A Karl Kreeger Design

Lower Level

Garage
22 x 25-4

Utility

Family Rm
14 x 16

UP

Deck

decor. ceiling

MBr 1
14 x 11-4

Kit
10-4x8-4

Dining
10-8 x 10

W D

9'-0" ceiling height

DN

Living Rm
14-4 x 15

Br 2
10 x 11-8

Br 3
10 x 11-8

28'-0"

Upper Level

42'-0"

No. 20083
One-Level with a Twist

■ This plan features:

— Three bedrooms

— Two full baths

■ Wide-open active areas that are centrally located

■ A spacious Dining, Living, and Kitchen area

■ A Master Suite at the rear of the house with a full bath

■ Two additional bedrooms that share a full hall bath and the quiet atmosphere that results from an intelligent design

FIRST FLOOR — 1,575 SQ. FT.
BASEMENT —1,575 SQ. FT.
GARAGE —475 SQ. FT.

TOTAL LIVING AREA:
1,575 SQ. FT.

A Karl Kreeger Design

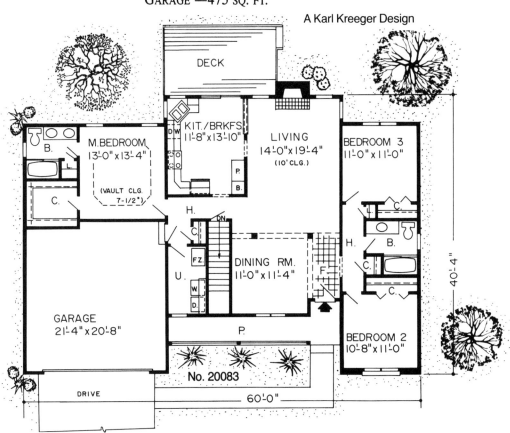

No. 20198

Dramatic Ranch

■ This plan features:

— Three bedrooms

— Two full baths

■ A large Living Room with a stone fireplace and decorative beamed ceiling

■ A Kitchen/Dining Room arrangement which makes the rooms seem more spacious

■ A Laundry with large pantry located close to the bedrooms and the Kitchen

■ A Master Bedroom with walk-in closet and private Master Bath

■ Two additional bedrooms, one with a walk-in closet, that share the full hall bath

FIRST FLOOR — 1,792 SQ. FT.
BASEMENT — 864 SQ. FT.
GARAGE — 928 SQ. FT.

TOTAL LIVING AREA:
1,792 SQ. FT.

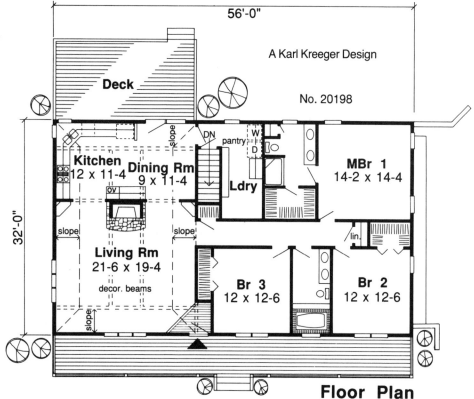

A Karl Kreeger Design

No. 20198

56'-0"

32'-0"

Deck

Kitchen
12 x 11-4

Dining Rm
9 x 11-4

pantry

Ldry

MBr 1
14-2 x 14-4

Living Rm
21-6 x 19-4

decor. beams

slope

Br 3
12 x 12-6

Br 2
12 x 12-6

lin.

DN

W
D

ov

Floor Plan

No. 20080

Window Graces Parlor

■ This plan features:

— Three bedrooms

— Two and one half baths

■ A brick and stucco facade with rustic wood trim

■ A Family Room with a massive fireplace and ten-foot ceilings

■ An island Kitchen and Breakfast Nook adjacent to a gracious formal Dining Room

■ A first floor Master Suite with a private bath and an abundance of closet space

FIRST FLOOR — 1,859 SQ. FT.
SECOND FLOOR — 556 SQ. FT.
BASEMENT — 1,844 SQ. FT.
GARAGE — 598 SQ. FT.

TOTAL LIVING AREA: 2,415 SQ. FT.

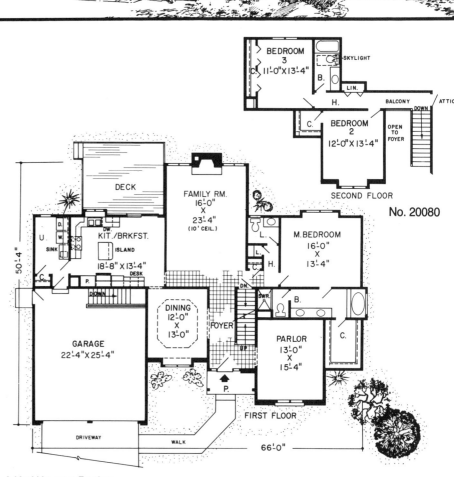

BEDROOM 3
11'-0"X13'-4"

BEDROOM 2
12'-0"X13'-4"

SECOND FLOOR

No. 20080

FAMILY RM.
16'-0" X 23'-4"
(10' CEIL.)

KIT./BRKFST.
18'-8" X 13'-4"

M. BEDROOM
16'-0" X 13'-4"

DINING
12'-0" X 13'-0"

PARLOR
13'-0" X 15'-4"

GARAGE
22'-4" X 25'-4"

FOYER

FIRST FLOOR

DRIVEWAY   WALK   66'-0"

A Karl Kreeger Design

40

No. 24309

Rustic Retreat

■ This plan features:

— Two bedrooms

— One full bath

■ A wrap-around deck equipped with a built-in bar-b-que for easy outdoor living

■ An entry, in a wall of glass opens the Living area to the outdoors

■ A large fireplace in the Living area opens into an efficient Kitchen, with a built-in pantry, that serves the Nook area

■ Two bedrooms share a centrally-located full bath with a window tub

■ A loft area ready for multiple uses

MAIN FLOOR — 897 SQ. FT.

MAIN LIVING AREA:
897 SQ. FT.

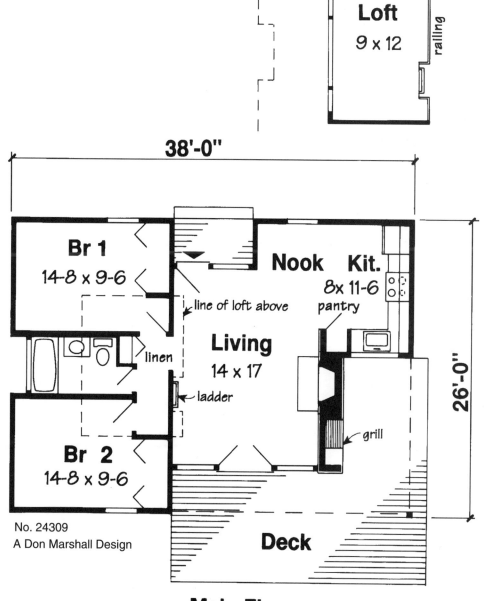

Loft
9 x 12
railing

38'-0"

26'-0"

Br 1
14-8 x 9-6

Nook **Kit.**
8x 11-6

line of loft above

pantry

Living
14 x 17

linen

ladder

grill

Br 2
14-8 x 9-6

No. 24309
A Don Marshall Design

Deck

Main Floor

No. 20143
Stunning Split Entry

■ This plan features:

— Three bedrooms

— Two full baths

■ A Recreation Room with built-in bar, powder room, and storage space

■ A Master suite featuring a walk-in closet, double vanitied bath, and decorative ceilings

■ The Dining Room also features decorative ceilings and columns

UPPER FLOOR — 1,599 SQ. FT.
LOWER FLOOR — 346 SQ. FT.
GARAGE — 520 SQ. FT.

TOTAL LIVING AREA:
1,945 SQ. FT.

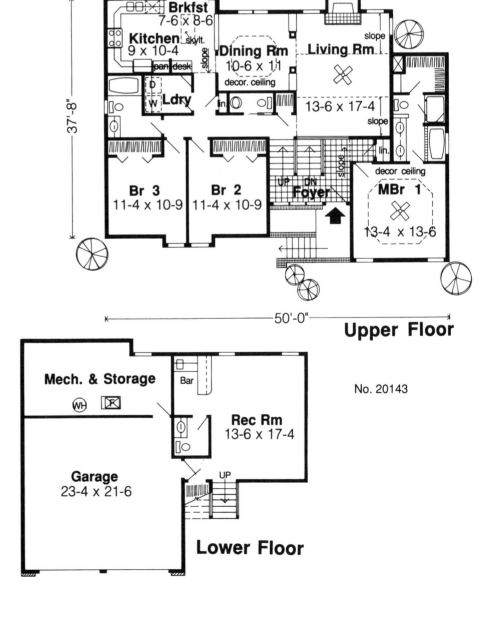

A Karl Kreeger Design

Deck

Brkfst
7-6 x 8-6

Kitchen
9 x 10-4

skylt.

Dining Rm
10-6 x 11
decor. ceiling

Living Rm
13-6 x 17-4
slope

Ldry
D
W

Foyer
UP DN

Br 3
11-4 x 10-9

Br 2
11-4 x 10-9

MBr 1
13-4 x 13-6
decor ceiling

37'-8"

50'-0"

Upper Floor

Mech. & Storage
WH

Bar

Rec Rm
13-6 x 17-4

No. 20143

Garage
23-4 x 21-6

UP

Lower Floor

No. 20196

Gorgeous and Livable

■ This plan features:

— Four bedrooms

— Three full baths

■ A bay window that enhances the Living Room with natural light

■ A decorative ceiling accentuating the formal Dining Room

■ A Breakfast room with an incredible shape

■ An island Kitchen with an efficient layout and in close proximity to both the formal Dining Room and the informal Breakfast Room

■ A spacious Family Room that is warmed by a cozy fireplace

■ A fantastic Master Suite with a decorative ceiling, private Master Bath and a large walk-in closet

■ Three additional bedrooms with walk-in closets, that share a full hall bath

FIRST FLOOR — 1,273 SQ. FT.
SECOND FLOOR — 1,477 SQ. FT.
BASEMENT — 974 SQ. FT.
GARAGE — 852 SQ. FT.

TOTAL LIVING AREA:
2,750 SQ. FT.

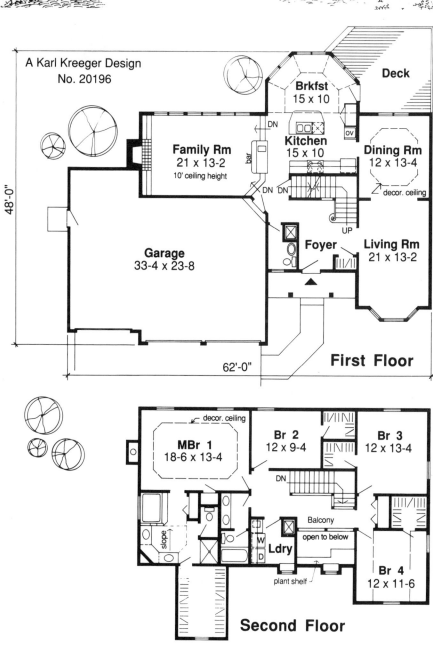

A Karl Kreeger Design
No. 20196

Deck

Brkfst
15 x 10

Family Rm
21 x 13-2
10' ceiling height

Kitchen
15 x 10
ov

Dining Rm
12 x 13-4
decor. ceiling

DN

DN DN

UP

48'-0"

Garage
33-4 x 23-8

Foyer

Living Rm
21 x 13-2

62'-0"

First Floor

decor. ceiling

MBr 1
18-6 x 13-4

Br 2
12 x 9-4

Br 3
12 x 13-4

DN

slope

W D

Ldry

Balcony
open to below

plant shelf

Br 4
12 x 11-6

Second Floor

No. 34075

A Cozy Cabin

■ This plan features:

— Two bedrooms

— One full bath

■ A compact design that can accommodate four to six people comfortably

■ A Living Room connected to the Kitchen and Dining area giving an open feeling

■ A perfect design for a weekend get-away

FIRST FLOOR — 576 SQ. FT.

TOTAL LIVING AREA: 576 SQ. FT.

No. 34075

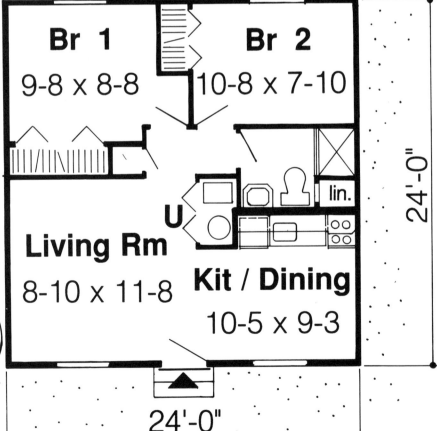

Br 1
9-8 x 8-8

Br 2
10-8 x 7-10

lin.

U

Living Rm
8-10 x 11-8

Kit / Dining
10-5 x 9-3

24'-0"

24'-0"

No. 34055

Ranch Provides Great Floor Plan

■ This plan features:

— Four bedrooms

— Two full baths

■ A large Living Room and Dining Room flowing together into one open space perfect for entertaining

■ A Laundry area, which doubles as a mud room, off the Kitchen

■ A Master Suite including a private bath

■ A two-car Garage

FIRST FLOOR — 1,527 SQ. FT.
BASEMENT — 1,344 SQ. FT.
GARAGE — 425 SQ. FT.

TOTAL LIVING AREA: 1,527 SQ. FT.

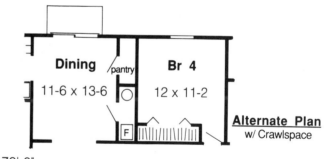

Dining
11-6 x 13-6

pantry

Br 4
12 x 11-2

Alternate Plan
w/ Crawlspace

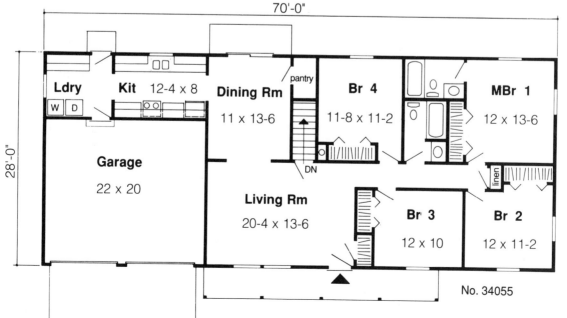

70'-0"

28'-0"

Ldry — W D
Kit 12-4 x 8
Garage 22 x 20
Dining Rm 11 x 13-6
pantry
Living Rm 20-4 x 13-6
DN
Br 4 11-8 x 11-2
Br 3 12 x 10
MBr 1 12 x 13-6
linen
Br 2 12 x 11-2

No. 34055

No. 24263

Family Home with all the Amenities

■ This plan features:

— Four bedrooms

— Two full and one half bath

■ A see-through fireplace between the Living Room and the Family Room

■ A gourmet Kitchen with an island, built-in pantry and double sink

■ A Master Bedroom with a vaulted ceiling

■ A Master Bath with large double vanity, linen closet, corner tub, separate shower, compartmented toilet, and huge walk-in closet

■ Three additional bedrooms, one with a walk-in closet, share a full hall Bath

FIRST FLOOR — 1,241 SQ. FT.
SECOND FLOOR — 1,170 SQ. FT.

TOTAL LIVING AREA: 2,411 SQ. FT.

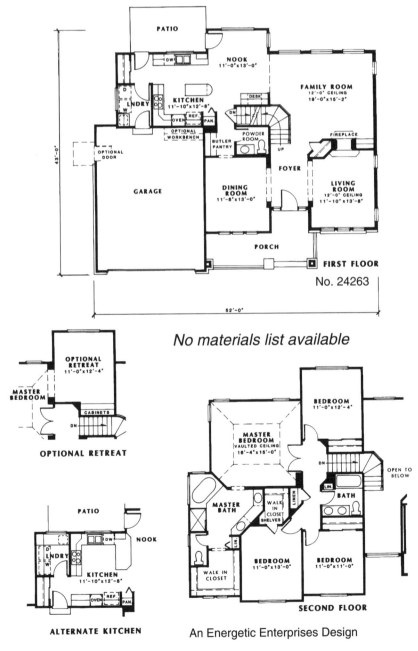

No materials list available

An Energetic Enterprises Design

No. 10663
Perfect for Parties

■ This plan features:

— Three bedrooms

— Three and one half baths

— Two bedroom suites with two full baths adjoining a sitting room on the second floor

— A vaulted Family Room with fireplace and a bay window in the Living Room

— An elegant Dining Room with floor- to-ceiling windows and Study nearby

— A Nook nestled between the Kitchen and the utility room

FIRST FLOOR — 2,310 SQ. FT.
SECOND FLOOR — 866 SQ. FT.
GARAGE — 679 SQ. FT.

**TOTAL LIVING AREA:
3,176 SQ. FT.**

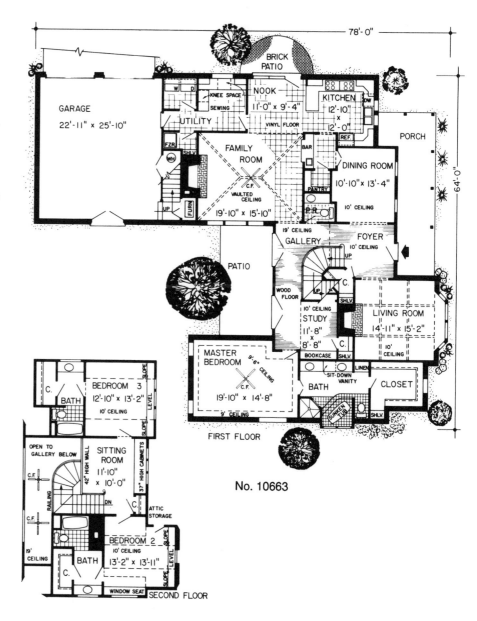

No. 10663

No. 20354

Tudor Grandeur for the Budget-Minded

■ This plan features:

— Three bedrooms

— Two full and one half baths

■ A two-story foyer

■ Window seats in both the Living Room and the Dining Room

■ A convenient range-top island in the spacious Kitchen with built-in pantry and planning desk

■ An open arrangement between the Kitchen, Breakfast area, and the Great Room

■ A Master Suite with sloped ceiling and private Master Bath with spa tub and walk-in closet

■ Two additional bedrooms that share a full hall bath

FIRST FLOOR — 1,346 SQ. FT.
SECOND FLOOR — 1,196 SQ. FT.
BASEMENT — 1,346 SQ. FT.
GARAGE — 840 SQ. FT.

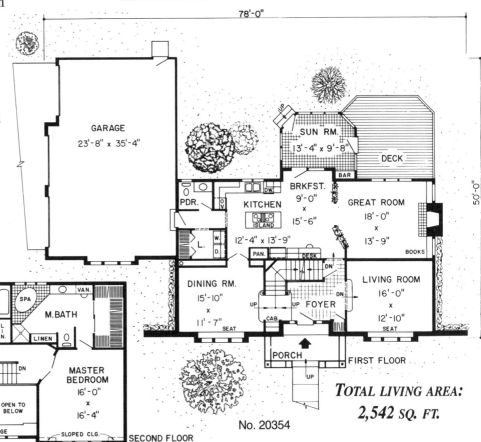

78'-0"

50'-0"

GARAGE
23'-8" x 35'-4"

SUN RM.
13'-4" x 9'-8"

DECK

BRKFST.
9'-0"
x
15'-6"

KITCHEN
ISLAND
12'-4" x 13'-9"

GREAT ROOM
18'-0"
x
13'-9"

BOOKS

PDR.

PAN.

DESK

DINING RM.
15'-10"
x
11'-7"
SEAT

FOYER

LIVING ROOM
16'-0"
x
12'-10"
SEAT

CAB.

PORCH

FIRST FLOOR

BEDRM. 2
12'-6"
x
13'-9"

SPA

M. BATH

VAN.

B.

LIN.

LINEN

BEDRM. 3
12'-4"
x
12'-7"
SLOPED CLG.

OPEN TO
BELOW

DN

MASTER
BEDROOM
16'-0"
x
16'-4"

LEDGE

SLOPED CLG.

SECOND FLOOR

No. 20354

TOTAL LIVING AREA:
2,542 SQ. FT.

48

No. 10754

Sky lit Loft Crowns Updated Traditional

■ This plan features:

— Three bedrooms

— Two and one half baths

■ Rough hewn beams adorning the 11 foot ceilings in the Living Room

■ Elegant recessed ceilings gracing the Master Suite and the formal Dining Room

■ Energy saving fans lend an old fashioned air to the Living Room, Master Suite, and Breakfast area

■ A first floor Master Suite with double vanities, walk-in closets, and a luxurious whirlpool tub

FIRST FLOOR — 1,962 SQ. FT.
SECOND FLOOR — 870 SQ. FT.
BASEMENT — 1,962 SQ. FT.
GARAGE — 611 SQ. FT.

TOTAL LIVING AREA: 2,832 SQ. FT.

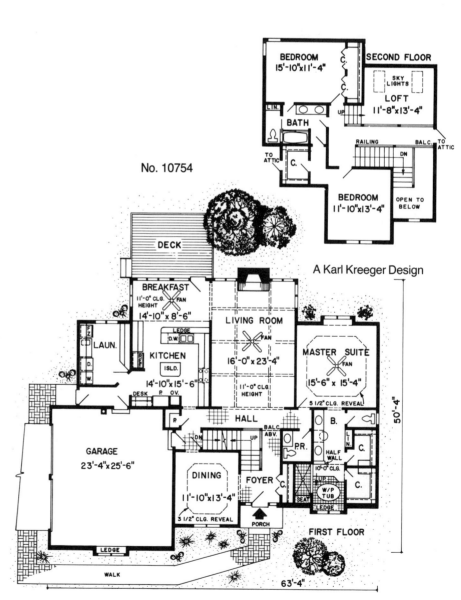

No. 10754

A Karl Kreeger Design

No. 20062

Inexpensive Ranch Design

- ■ This plan features:
- — Three bedrooms
- — Two full baths
- ■ A large picture window brightening the Breakfast area
- ■ A well planned Kitchen
- ■ A Living Room which is accented by an open beam across the sloping ceiling and wood burning fireplace
- ■ A Master Bedroom with an extremely large bath area

FIRST FLOOR — 1,500 SQ. FT.
BASEMENT — 1,500 SQ. FT.
GARAGE — 482 SQ. FT.

TOTAL LIVING AREA: 1,500 SQ. FT.

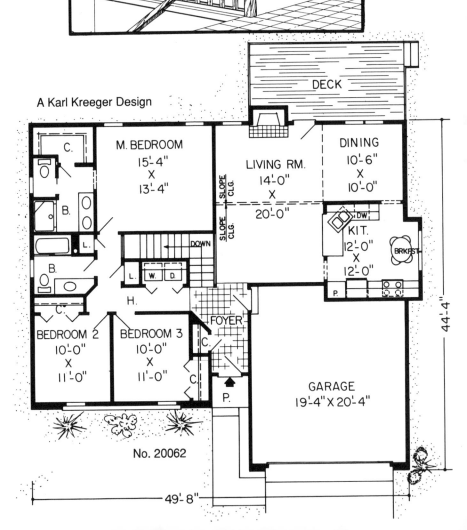

A Karl Kreeger Design

No. 20062

No. 20110

Classic and Convenient

■ This plan features:

— Three bedrooms

— Two full baths

■ Clapboard and brick lending curbside appeal

■ A spacious Living Room dominated by a corner fireplace

■ A hallway off the foyer leading to the two additional bedrooms

■ A formal Dining Room and a sky-lit Breakfast Nook adjoining the Kitchen

■ A rear deck perfect for summer barbecues or relaxing

■ A Master Suite with a double vanity, a raised bath and a walk-in shower

FIRST FLOOR — 1,786 SQ. FT.
BASEMENT — 1,786 SQ. FT.
GARAGE — 484 SQ. FT.

**TOTAL LIVING AREA:
1,786 SQ. FT.**

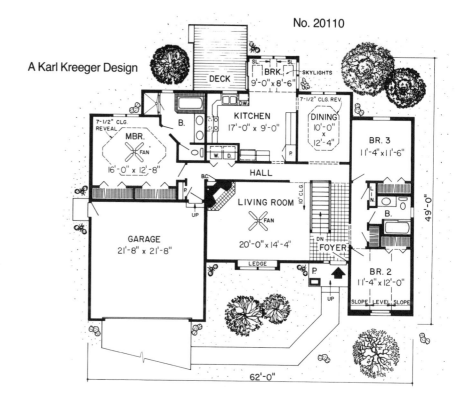

No. 20110

A Karl Kreeger Design

DECK

BRK. 9'-0" x 8'-6" SL SL SKYLIGHTS

7-1/2" CLG. REV.

KITCHEN 17'-0" x 9'-0"

DINING 10'-0" x 12'-4"

7-1/2" CLG. REVEAL

MBR. FAN 16'-0" x 12'-8"

BR. 3 11'-4" x 11'-6"

B.

W. D.

HALL

GARAGE 21'-8" x 21'-8"

LIVING ROOM 20'-0" x 14'-4" FAN

10' CLG.

UP

B.

BR. 2 11'-4" x 12'-0"

LEDGE

DN FOYER

P

UP

SLOPE LEVEL SLOPE

49'-0"

62'-0"

No. 10656

One Level Living is a Breeze

■ This plan features:

— Three bedrooms

— Two and one half baths

■ A Master Bedroom with full bath, walk-in closet and dressing area with access to the deck

■ An airy Kitchen open to the Breakfast Nook and laundry area

■ A Great Room with vaulted ceilings, fireplace, and room for books

FIRST FLOOR — 1,899 SQ. FT.
BASEMENT — 1,890 SQ. FT.
GARAGE — 530 SQ. FT.

TOTAL LIVING AREA:
1,899 SQ. FT.

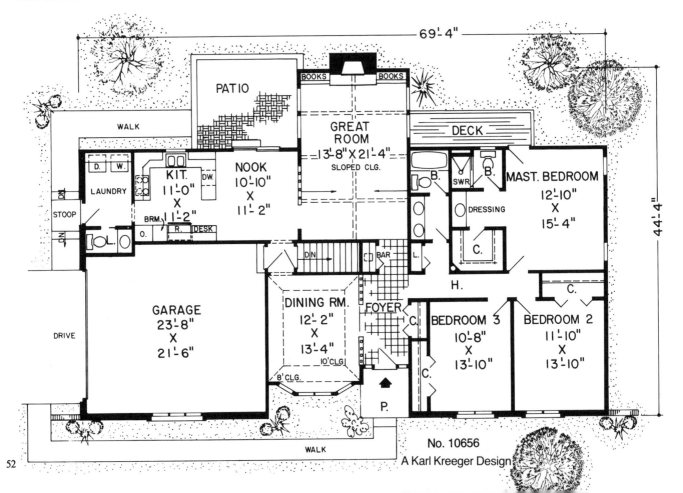

No. 10656
A Karl Kreeger Design

No. 10749

A Celebration of Traditional Elements

■ This plan features:

— Four bedrooms

— Two full and two half baths

■ High ceilings with cooling fans and loads of built-in storage

■ Every bedroom adjoining a bath and the Master Suite enjoying access to the outdoor deck

■ A massive fireplace located the roomy Family Room

■ A Kitchen, Breakfast area, Sewing room, Dining Room and pantry all located within steps of each other for convenience

FIRST FLOOR — 3,438 SQ. FT.
GARAGE — 610 SQ. FT.

TOTAL LIVING AREA: 3,438 SQ. FT.

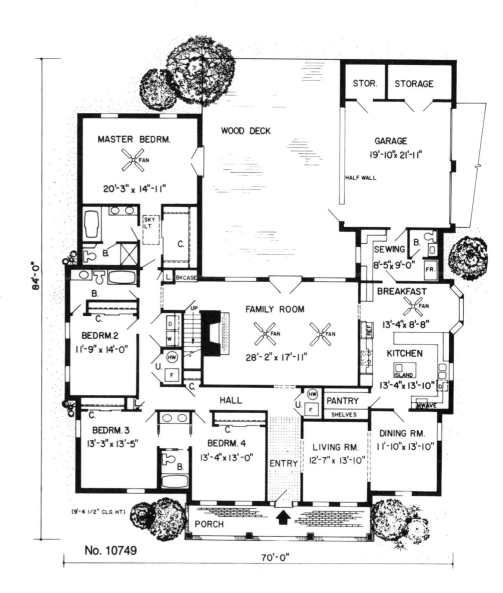

STOR. STORAGE

MASTER BEDRM.
20'-3" x 14"-11"

WOOD DECK

GARAGE
19'-10½" x 21'-11"

HALF WALL

SKY LT.

C.

BKCASE

SEWING
8'-5" x 9'-0"

B.

FR.

BREAKFAST
13'-4" x 8'-8"

FAN

BEDRM. 2
11'-9" x 14'-0"

UP

FAMILY ROOM
28'-2" x 17'-11"

FAN   FAN

REF.

KITCHEN
13'-4" x 13'-10"

ISLAND

D. W. HW U. F. C.

HW U. F.

PANTRY
SHELVES

MWAVE

HALL

BEDRM. 3
13'-3" x 13'-5"

C.

BEDRM. 4
13'-4" x 13'-0"

ENTRY

LIVING RM.
12'-7" x 13'-10"

DINING RM.
11'-10" x 13'-10"

B.

(9'-4 1/2" CLG. HT.)

PORCH

No. 10749

84'-0"

70'-0"

No. 24241

Quiet Summer Hide-A-Way

■ This plan features:

— Three bedrooms

— Two full baths

■ A covered Porch, welcoming visitors

■ A spacious Living Room with a fireplace, adding to the warmth and elegance of the room

■ A formal Dining Room with a convenient, built-in china cabinet

■ Ample cabinets, counters and a built-in pantry in the well-appointed Kitchen

■ A Master Suite with a private bath

■ Two additional bedrooms, one with a walk-in closet, that share a full hall bath

■ A typical bungalow design, allowing the heat to collect in the attic space which keeps the house cool in the summer months

MAIN LIVING AREA — 1,174 SQ. FT.

TOTAL LIVING AREA: 1,174 SQ. FT.

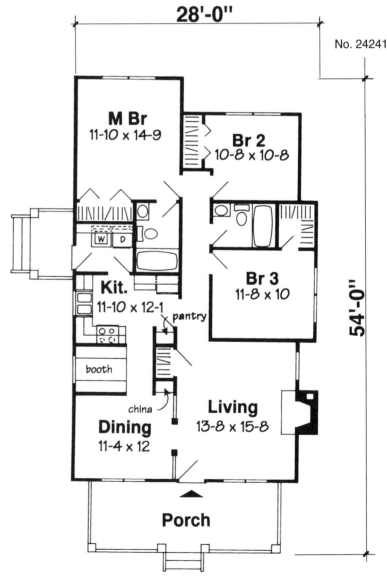

Main Floor

No. 20178

Stone and Stucco Family Home

■ This plan features:

— Three bedrooms

— Two full and one half baths

■ A formal Living Room that is enhanced by a large front window

■ A distinctive formal Dining Room with a decorative ceiling

■ A sloped ceiling and a stunning fireplace in the Hearth Room

■ A range-top island Kitchen having a corner double sink, built-in pantry, ample counter space and a sunny bay window Breakfast nook

■ A first-floor Master Suite equipped with a luxury bath with double vanities, a walk-in closet, and a dressing area

■ Two additional bedrooms that share a full hall bath

FIRST FLOOR — 1,606 SQ. FT.
SECOND FLOOR — 543 SQ. FT.
BASEMENT — 1,606 SQ. FT.
GARAGE — 484 SQ. FT.

TOTAL LIVING AREA: 2,149 SQ. FT.

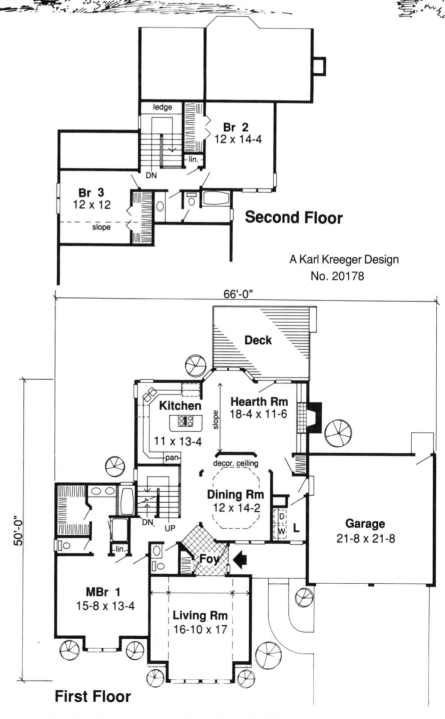

Second Floor

A Karl Kreeger Design
No. 20178

ledge

Br 2
12 x 14-4

lin.

DN

Br 3
12 x 12

slope

66'-0"

50'-0"

Deck

Kitchen
11 x 13-4

pan.

Hearth Rm
18-4 x 11-6

slope

decor. ceiling

DN   UP

lin.

Dining Rm
12 x 14-2

D
W
L

Garage
21-8 x 21-8

Foy

MBr 1
15-8 x 13-4

Living Rm
16-10 x 17

First Floor

No. 10396
Three Levels of Living Space

■ This plan features:

— Three bedrooms

— Three baths

■ A passive solar design suitable for vacation or year round living

■ The southern elevation of the home highlighted by an abundance of decks

■ The Basement level including a large shop, storage, and recreation area plus a bedroom

■ An angled wall lending character to the Kitchen/Dining area

■ A Master Bedroom occupying the entire second floor with its own private bath, walk in closet, and storage nook

FIRST FLOOR — 886 SQ. FT.
SECOND FLOOR — 456 SQ. FT.
BASEMENT — 886 SQ. FT.

TOTAL LIVING AREA: 2,228 SQ. FT.

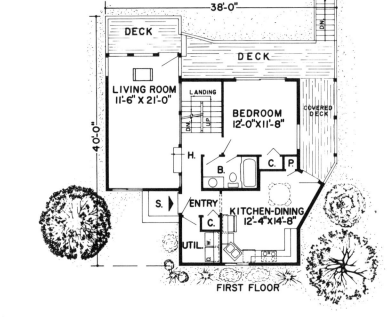

FIRST FLOOR

BASEMENT

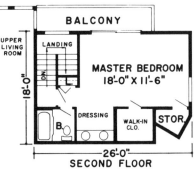

SECOND FLOOR

No. 10396

No. 10673

Bay Windows and Skylights Brighten This Tudor Home

■ This plan features:

— Four bedrooms

— Two and one half baths

■ A Kitchen equipped with a pantry and Breakfast Nook leading onto a brick patio

■ An oversized Living Room with skylights and a fireplace

■ A Master Suite containing a whirlpool tub

FIRST FLOOR — 1,265 SQ. FT.
SECOND FLOOR — 1,210 SQ. FT.
BASEMENT — 1,247 SQ. FT.
GARAGE — 506 SQ. FT.

TOTAL LIVING AREA:
2,475 SQ. FT.

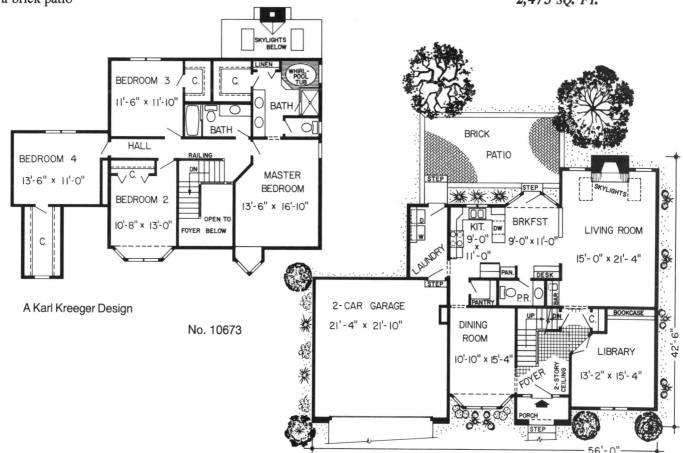

A Karl Kreeger Design

No. 10673

No. 20139
Have it All

■ This plan features:
— Three bedrooms
— Two full baths

■ A classic brick and clapboard exterior adorned with an old-fashioned bay a window

■ An elegant Living Room with a fireplace flowing into a formal Dining Room with sliders to a rear deck

■ A compact Kitchen opening to the Dining Room for a spacious feel

■ A well-appointed Master Suite with ample closet space and a four-piece private bath

FIRST FLOOR — 1,488 SQ. FT.
BASEMENT — 1,488 SQ. FT.
GARAGE — 484 SQ. FT.

TOTAL LIVING AREA:
1,488 SQ. FT.

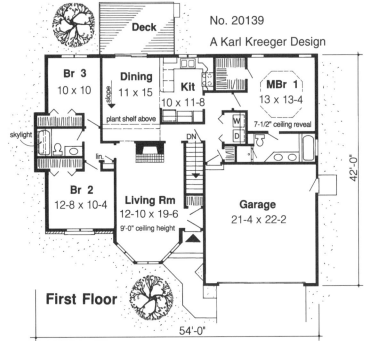

No. 20139

A Karl Kreeger Design

First Floor

No. 10674
Carefree Convenience

■ This plan features:
— Three bedrooms
— Two full baths

■ A galley Kitchen, centrally-located between the Dining, Breakfast and Living Room areas

■ A huge Family Room which exits onto the patio

■ The Master Suite boasts both double closets and double vanities

■ Two additional bedrooms share a full hall bath

MAIN AREA — 1,600 SQ. FT.
GARAGE — 465 SQ. FT.

TOTAL LIVING AREA:
1,600 SQ. FT

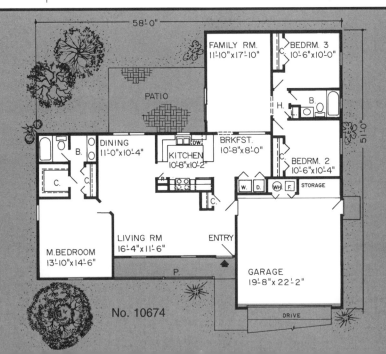

No. 10674

No. 10548
Sloped Ceiling Attractive Feature of Ranch Design

■ This plan features:
— Three bedrooms
— Two and one half baths
■ A fireplace and sloped ceiling in the Living Room
■ A Master Bedroom complete with a full bath, shower and dressing area
■ A decorative ceiling in the Dining Room

FIRST FLOOR — 1,688 SQ. FT.
BASEMENT — 1,688 SQ. FT.
SCREENED PORCH — 120 SQ. FT.
GARAGE — 489 SQ. FT.

TOTAL LIVING AREA:
1,688 SQ. FT.

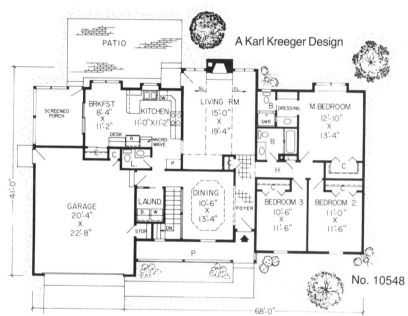

A Karl Kreeger Design

PATIO

SCREENED PORCH

BRKFST.
8'-4"
X
11'-2"

KITCHEN
11'-0"X11'-2"

LIVING RM.
15'-0"
X
19'-4"

DRESSING

M. BEDROOM
12'-10"
X
13'-4"

GARAGE
20'-4"
X
22'-8"

LAUND.

DINING
10'-6"
X
13'-4"

FOYER

BEDROOM 3
10'-6"
X
11'-6"

BEDROOM 2
11'-0"
X
11'-6"

41'-0"

68'-0"

No. 10548

No. 20156
Family Favorite

■ This plan features:
— Three bedrooms
— Two full baths

■ An open arrangement with the Dining Room that combines with ten-foot ceilings to make the Living Room seem more spacious

■ Glass on three sides of the Dining Room overlooking the deck

■ An efficient, compact Kitchen with built-in pantry and peninsula counter

■ A Master Suite with romantic window seat and compartmentalized private bath and walk-in closet

■ Two additional bedrooms that share a full hall closet

FIRST FLOOR — 1,359 SQ. FT.
BASEMENT — 1,359 SQ. FT.
GARAGE — 501 SQ. FT.

TOTAL LIVING AREA:
1,359 SQ. FT.

A Karl Kreeger Design

Floor Plan   58'-0"   No. 20156

No. 20161
Delightful Doll House

■ This plan features:
— Three bedrooms
— Two full baths

■ A sloped ceiling in the Living Room which also has a focal point fireplace

■ An efficient Kitchen with peninsula counter and built-in pantry

■ A decorative ceiling and sliding glass doors to the deck in the Dining Room

■ A Master Suite with a decorative ceiling, ample closet space and a private full bath

■ Two additional bedrooms that share a full hall bath

FIRST FLOOR — 1,307 SQ. FT.
BASEMENT — 1,298 SQ. FT.
GARAGE — 462 SQ. FT.

TOTAL LIVING AREA:
1,307 SQ. FT.

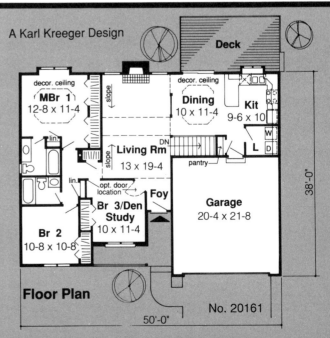

A Karl Kreeger Design

Floor Plan   50'-0"   No. 20161

No. 20154
Fabulous Facade

■ This plan features:
— Three Bedrooms
— Two full baths

■ A spacious Living Room with a sloped ceiling and a large fireplace

■ A decorative ceiling and bow window in the Dining Room which has an open floor plan to the Kitchen

■ An efficient and well-appointed Kitchen having a built-in pantry and double sink located under a window

■ An ornamental ceiling in the Master Suite which is equipped with a walk-in closet and sky-lit private bath

■ Two additional bedrooms sharing a full hall bath

FIRST FLOOR — 1,420 SQ. FT.
BASEMENT — 1,392 SQ. FT.
GARAGE — 442 SQ. FT.

TOTAL LIVING AREA:
1,420 SQ. FT.

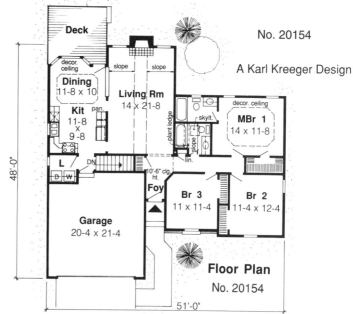

No. 20154

A Karl Kreeger Design

Deck

decor. ceiling
slope | slope

Dining 11-8 x 10

Living Rm 14 x 21-8

Kit 11-8 x 9-8 pan.

MBr 1 14 x 11-8 decor. ceiling

skylt.
plant ledge
lin.

L
D W
DN
10'-6" clg. ht.

Foy

Garage 20-4 x 21-4

Br 3 11 x 11-4

Br 2 11-4 x 12-4

48'-0"

51'-0"

Floor Plan No. 20154

No. 20086
Gardener's Dream House

- This plan features:
- — Three bedrooms
- — Two full baths
- Unlimited opportunities for entry gardening
- A vaulted ceiling in the Living Room and Dining Room
- An island Kitchen with a Breakfast area
- A Master Bedroom with a sky-lit Master Bath and a walk-in closet

FIRST FLOOR — 1,628 SQ. FT.
BASEMENT — 1,628 SQ. FT.
GARAGE — 434 SQ. FT.

TOTAL LIVING AREA:
1,628 SQ. FT.

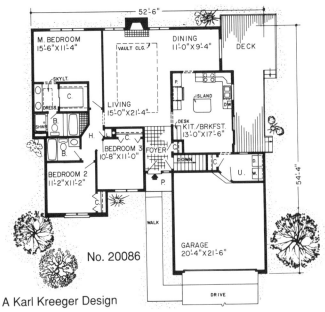

No. 20086

A Karl Kreeger Design

No. 22014
Charming Traditional Emphasizes Living Areas

- This plan features:
- — Three bedrooms
- — Two and one half baths
- A 20-ft. Family Room with a large fireplace and access to the patio
- A formal Dining Room and a Game Room which can function as a formal Living Room if necessary
- Each of the three bedrooms adjoining a full bath
- A Master Bedroom with a luxurious his and hers bath and walk-in closets

FIRST FLOOR — 2,118 SQ. FT.
GARAGE — 448 SQ. FT.

TOTAL LIVING AREA:
2,118 SQ. FT.

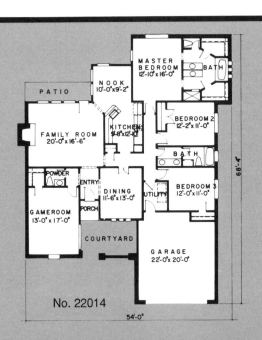

No. 22014

No. 34150
Simple Lines Enhanced by Elegant Window Treatment

■ This plan features:
— Three bedrooms
— Two full baths

■ Huge, arched window which floods the front room with natural light

■ A homey, well-lit Office or Den

■ Compact, efficient use of space

■ An efficient Kitchen with easy access to Dining Room

■ A fireplaced Living Room with sloping ceiling and window wall

■ A Master Bedroom sporting a private Master Bath with roomy walk-in closet

FIRST FLOOR — 1,492 SQ. FT.
BASEMENT — 1,486 SQ. FT.
GARAGE — 462 SQ. FT.

TOTAL LIVING AREA:
1,492 SQ. FT.

No. 34150

optional DECK

DINING
10'-8"
X
11'-4"

LIVING ROOM
14'-8"
X
21'-0"
SLOPED CLG

DESK

DW

KITCHEN
10'-8"
X
10'-0"

GARAGE
20'-4"
X
21'-4"

FOYER

DEN/BR 3
10'-4"
X
11'-10"

MBR 1
13'-4"
X
13'-8"

BR 2
13'-10"
X
11'-4"

C. B.

48'-0"

56'-0"

A Karl Kreeger Design

Slab/Crawlspace Option

No. 10456
Sunlight Streams into Many Windows

■ This plan features:
— Four bedrooms
— Two baths
■ A Living Room graced by twelve-foot beamed ceilings
■ A Dining Room defined by a lower ceiling and enhanced by an oversized bay window of leaded glass
■ A spacious Kitchen including many cabinets, a walk-in pantry, and a center work island
■ A Master Bedroom with a five piece bath, and an extra large walk-in closet

FIRST FLOOR — 2,511 SQ. FT.
GARAGE — 517 SQ. FT.

TOTAL LIVING AREA: 2,511 SQ. FT.

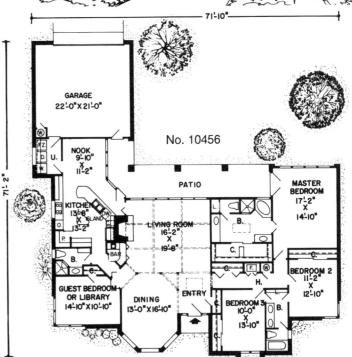

No. 10465
Beamed Ceiling Accents Family Room

■ This plan features:
— Four bedrooms
— Three baths
■ A Family Room accentuated by a beamed ceiling, built-in bookcase, and a large fireplace
■ A Dining Room easily accessible from the efficient Kitchen
■ A Master Bedroom located along the opposite side of the home with its own bath and spacious walk-in closets

FIRST FLOOR — 2,144 SQ. FT.
GARAGE — 483 SQ. FT.

TOTAL LIVING AREA: 2,144 SQ. FT.

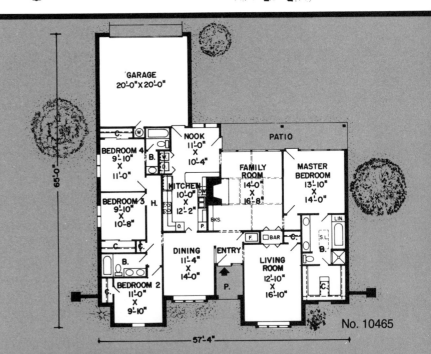

No. 10455
Compact Home Design

■ This plan features:
— Three bedrooms
— Two full baths
■ An airlock entry which saves energy
■ A Living Room with a window wall, fireplace, built-in bookcases, and a wet bar
■ A step-saver Kitchen with an abundance of storage and a convenient peninsula
■ A Master Bedroom with separate vanities and walk-in closets

FIRST FLOOR — 1,643 SQ. FT.
GARAGE — 500 SQ. FT.

TOTAL LIVING AREA: 1,643 SQ. FT.

50'-2"

49'-0"

PATIO

LIVING ROOM
19'-4" X 16'-0"

BAR

C.

B.

C.

KITCHEN
11'-2"
X
13'-9"

DW

O

DINING
10'-4"
X
10'-10"

BKS.

MAST. BEDROOM
16'-10" X 13'-0"

C.

F.

H.

W

U.

W

BEDROOM 2
10'-10" X 10'-6"

GARAGE
22'-0" X 20'-0"

AIR LOCK
ENTRY

C.

B.

C.

C.

BEDROOM 3
10'-2" X 10'-8"

DRIVEWAY

No. 10455

No. 20150
Sunshine Special

■ This plan features:
— Three bedrooms.
— Two full baths.

■ A Living Room with a large fireplace and sloped ceiling.

■ A walk-in closet in each bedroom

■ A Master Suite including a luxury bath and decorative ceilings.

FIRST FLOOR — 1,638 SQ. FT.
BASEMENT — 1,320 SQ. FT.
GARAGE — 462 SQ. FT.

TOTAL LIVING AREA:
1,638 SQ. FT.

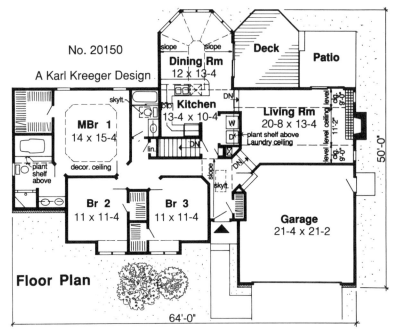

No. 20150

A Karl Kreeger Design

Dining Rm 12 x 13-4
Deck
Patio
Kitchen 13-4 x 10-4
MBr 1 14 x 15-4
Living Rm 20-8 x 13-4
decor. ceiling
Br 2 11 x 11-4
Br 3 11 x 11-4
Garage 21-4 x 21-2

Floor Plan

64'-0"
50'-0"

No. 10745
Light and Airy

■ This plan features:
— Three bedrooms
— Two full baths

■ An open plan with cathedral ceilings

■ A fireplaced Great Room flowing into the Dining Room

■ A Master Bedroom with a private Master Bath

■ An efficient Kitchen with Laundry area and pantry at close proximity

FIRST FLOOR — 1,643 SQ. FT.
BASEMENT — 1,643 SQ. FT.
GARAGE — 484 SQ. FT.

TOTAL LIVING AREA:
1,643 SQ. FT.

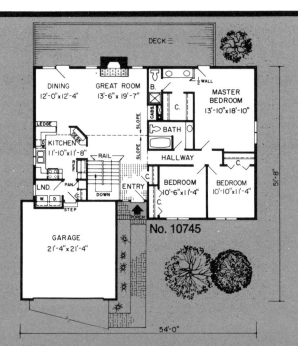

DECK

DINING 12'-0"x12'-4"
GREAT ROOM 13'-6" x 19'-7"
MASTER BEDROOM 13'-10"x18'-10"
KITCHEN 11'-10"x11'-8"
BATH
HALLWAY
BEDROOM 10'-6"x11'-4"
BEDROOM 10'-10"x11'-4"
ENTRY
GARAGE 21'-4"x21'-4"
No. 10745

54'-0"
51'-8"

No. 20092
Surrounded with Sunshine

■ This plan features:
— Three bedrooms
— Two full baths
■ A Garage and front entry open to the central foyer
■ A sky-lit Dining Room with sliders to the deck
■ A U-shaped Kitchen with an area for laundry facilities
■ A Master Suite with a private bath and plenty of closet space
■ A large Living Room with a fireplace

FIRST FLOOR — 1,693 SQ. FT.
BASEMENT — 1,693 SQ. FT.
GARAGE — 484 SQ. FT.

TOTAL LIVING AREA: 1,693 SQ. FT.

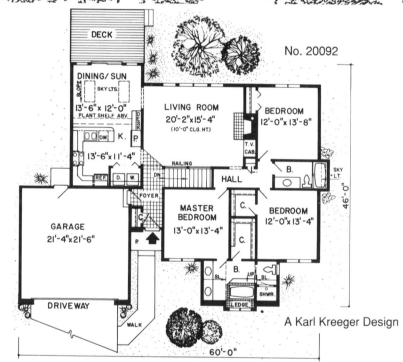

No. 20092

A Karl Kreeger Design

No. 20065
Storage Space Galore in Garage

■ This plan features:
— Three bedrooms
— Two and one half baths

■ A spacious Living Room with wood burning fireplace

■ A Breakfast Room with access to large outdoor wooden deck

■ A large amount of storage space available in two car Garage

FIRST FLOOR — 936 SQ. FT
SECOND FLOOR — 777 SQ. FT.
GARAGE/STORAGE — 624 SQ. FT.

TOTAL LIVING AREA: 1,713 SQ. FT.

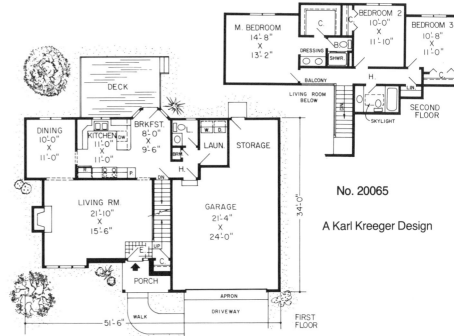

No. 20065

A Karl Kreeger Design

No. 20099
One-Floor Living

■ This plan features:
— Three bedrooms
— Two and one half baths

■ Angular windows and recessed ceilings separating the two dining areas from the adjoining island Kitchen

■ A window wall flanking the fireplace in the soaring, sky-lit Living Room

■ A Master Suite with a bump-out window and a double-vanity bath

FIRST FLOOR — 2,020 SQ. FT.
BASEMENT — 2,020 SQ. FT.
GARAGE — 534 SQ. FT.

TOTAL LIVING AREA: 2,020 SQ. FT.

A Karl Kreeger Design

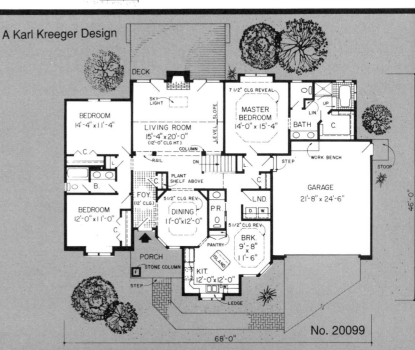

No. 20099

No. 24266

A Fireplace in the Master Suite

■ This plan features:
— Three or four bedrooms
— Three full baths

■ Vaulted ceilings in both the Family Room and the Master Bedroom

■ An elegant sunken formal Living Room

■ A first floor study/guest room with closet space and accessibility to a full hall bath

■ A spacious Family Room with a fireplace and an open layout into the eating Nook and Kitchen

■ A private Master Suite with a fireplace and a lavish Master Bath

■ Two additional bedrooms that share a full hall bath

FIRST FLOOR — 1,574 SQ. FT.
SECOND FLOOR — 1,098 SQ. FT.
GARAGE — 522 SQ. FT.

TOTAL LIVING AREA:
2,672 SQ. FT.

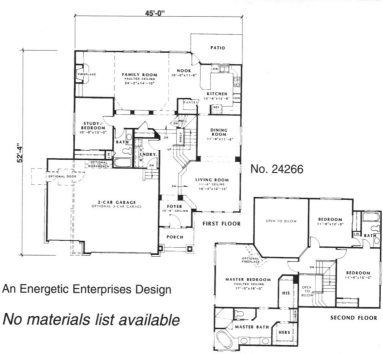

No. 24266

An Energetic Enterprises Design

No materials list available

No. 20058
Ranch with Character

- This plan features:
- — Three bedrooms
- — Two and one half baths
- A Master Bedroom with walk-in closet, individual shower, full tub and two-sink basin
- A large island Kitchen with its own Breakfast area
- A fireplaced Living Room
- Two additional bedrooms sharing a full bath
- A two-car Garage providing excellent additional storage

FIRST FLOOR — 1,787 SQ. FT.
BASEMENT — 1,787 SQ. FT.
GARAGE — 484 SQ. FT.

TOTAL LIVING AREA:
1,787 SQ. FT.

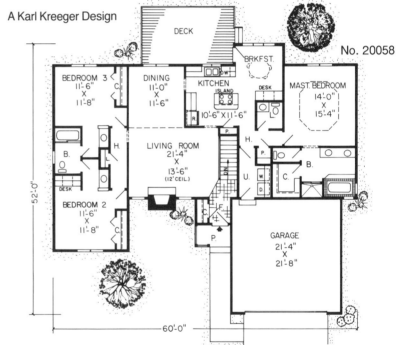

A Karl Kreeger Design

No. 20058

No. 20180
Classic Arches

- This plan features:
- — Three bedrooms
- — Two full baths
- Twin arched windows and a friendly covered porch
- An angled entry adding intrigue to the sunny, soaring Kitchen-Breakfast Room combination accented by a rangetop island and built-in pantry
- Living and Dining Rooms at rear of the house flowing together

FIRST FLOOR — 1,592 SQ. FT.
GARAGE — 487 SQ. FT.
BASEMENT — 1,592 SQ. FT.

TOTAL LIVING AREA:
1,592 SQ. FT.

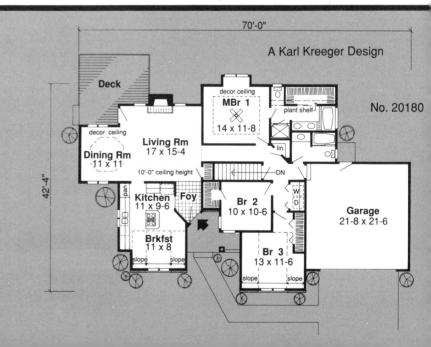

A Karl Kreeger Design

No. 20180

No. 20164
Easy Living

■ This plan features:
— Three bedrooms
— Two full baths

■ Dramatic sloped ceiling and massive fireplace in the Living Room

■ A Dining Room crowned by sloping ceiling and a plant shelf also having sliding doors to the deck

■ A U-shaped Kitchen with abundant cabinets, a window over the sink and a walk-in pantry

■ A Master Suite with a private full bath, decorative ceiling and walk-in closet

■ Two additional bedrooms that share a full bath

FIRST FLOOR — 1,456 SQ. FT.
BASEMENT — 1,448 SQ. FT.
GARAGE — 452 SQ. FT.

TOTAL LIVING AREA:
1,456 SQ. FT.

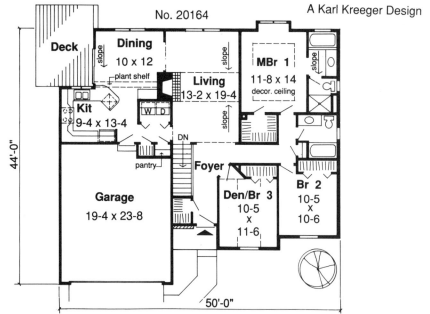

A Karl Kreeger Design

No. 20164

Deck

Dining 10 x 12
plant shelf

Kit 9-4 x 13-4
W D
pantry

Living 13-2 x 19-4
DN

Foyer

Garage 19-4 x 23-8

MBr 1 11-8 x 14
decor. ceiling

Den/Br 3 10-5 x 11-6

Br 2 10-5 x 10-6

44'-0"

50'-0"

No. 20160
Streetside Appeal

■ This plan features:
— Three bedrooms
— Two full and one half baths

■ An elegant Living and Dining Room combination that is divided by columns

■ A Family/Hearth Room with a two-way fireplace to the Breakfast room

■ A well-appointed Kitchen with built-in pantry, peninsula counter and double corner sink

■ A Master Suite with decorative ceiling, walk-in closet and private bath

■ Two additional bedrooms that share a full hall bath

First floor — 1,590 sq. ft.
Second floor — 567 sq. ft.
Basement — 1,576 sq. ft.
Garage — 456 sq. ft.

Total Living Area:
2,157 sq. ft.

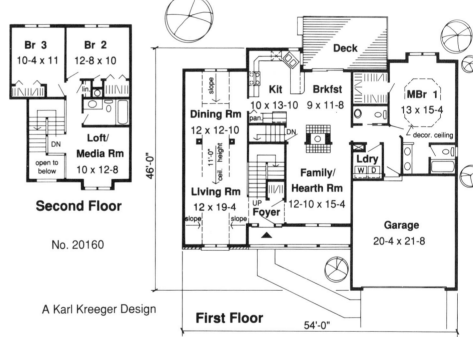

Second Floor

No. 20160

A Karl Kreeger Design

First Floor

No. 10468
Greenhouse Adds Charm

■ This plan features:
— Three bedrooms
— Two baths

■ A well-placed solar greenhouse located on the lower level

■ Sliding glass doors opening into the greenhouse from the Family Room

■ A Master Bedroom with access to the elevated deck through sliding doors

■ A Living Room warmed by a hearth fireplace

First floor — 1,294 sq. ft.
Family room level — 292 sq. ft.
Garage — 608 sq. ft.
Greenhouse — 164 sq. ft.

Total Living Area:
1,586 sq. ft.

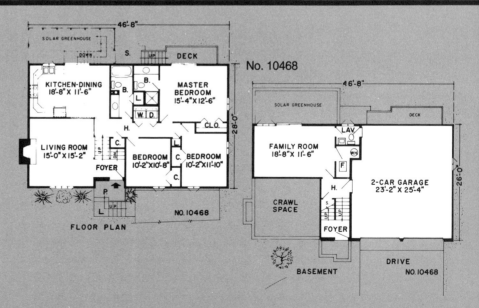

No. 10468

No. 10567
Comfort Expressed in Contemporary Design

■ This plan features:

— Three bedrooms

— Two baths

■ A Kitchen with an open, non-partitioned Dining Area

■ A Living Room with a skylight adding more natural light to the room

■ A secluded Master Bedroom with a sitting room, walk-in closets, and a full bath

FIRST FLOOR — 1,046 SQ. FT.

SECOND FLOOR — 375 SQ. FT.

BASEMENT — 1,046 SQ. FT.

GARAGE — 472 SQ. FT.

TOTAL LIVING AREA:
1,421 SQ. FT.

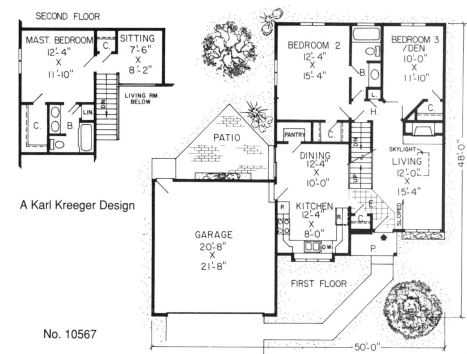

A Karl Kreeger Design

No. 10567

No. 10758
Front Bedroom Features Corner Window Seat

■ This plan features:
— Three bedrooms
— Three full and one half bath
■ Soaring ceilings to create an airy atmosphere
■ Open railings and single steps separating the Family and Living Rooms from the entry and Dining areas
■ A private Master Suite with a private deck and sky-lit spa area

FIRST FLOOR — 2,027 SQ. FT.
SECOND FLOOR — 1,476 SQ. FT.
GARAGE — 650 SQ. FT.

TOTAL LIVING AREA:
3,503 SQ. FT.

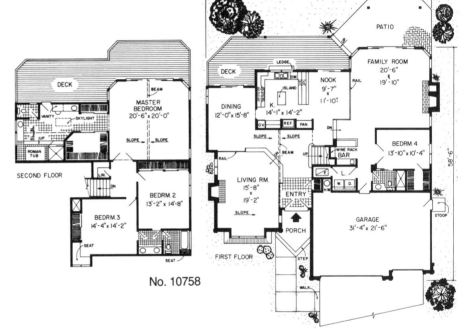

No. 10758

No. 9332
A Stately Home

This plan features:
— Three bedrooms
— Two and one half baths

■ A charming Tudor adaptation with a contemporary floor plan
■ A wood burning fireplace in both the Living Room and Family Room
■ A formal Dining Room with sliding glass doors opening onto an elevated wood deck
■ A square bay window in the Living Room and an ornamental iron railing running along the stairway and the entry
■ Seven foot long closets in all three large bedrooms

FIRST FLOOR — 1,633 SQ. FT.
SECOND FLOOR — 858 SQ. FT.
GARAGE & SHOP — 718 SQ. FT.

TOTAL LIVING AREA:
2,491 SQ. FT.

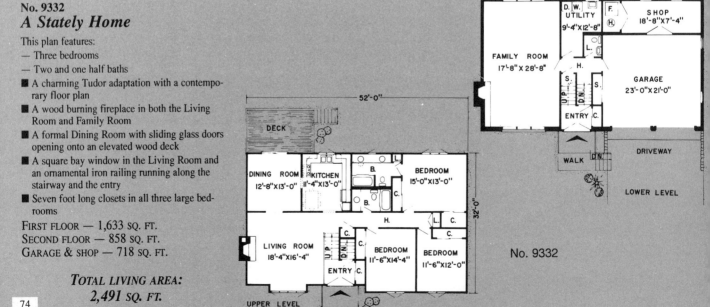

No. 9332

No. 20089
Carefree Living on One Level

■ This plan features:
— Three bedrooms
— Two full baths

■ A full basement and oversized two car Garage

■ A spacious Master Suite with walk-in closet

■ A fireplaced Living Room, an open Dining Room and Kitchen for convenience

FIRST FLOOR — 1,588 SQ. FT.
BASEMENT — 780 SQ. FT.
GARAGE — 808 SQ. FT.

TOTAL LIVING AREA:
1,588 SQ. FT.

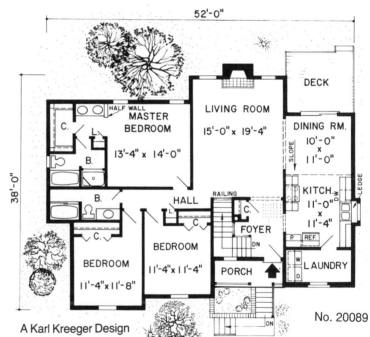

52'-0"

38'-0"

HALF WALL
C.
MASTER BEDROOM
13'-4" x 14'-0"
B.
B.
C.

LIVING ROOM
15'-0" x 19'-4"

DECK

DINING RM.
10'-0"
x
11'-0"

SLOPE

KITCH.
11'-0"
x
11'-4"

LEDGE

HALL
RAILING
C.
FOYER
DN
P REF.
W
D
LAUNDRY

BEDROOM
11'-4" x 11'-8"

BEDROOM
11'-4" x 11'-4"

PORCH
DN

No. 20089

A Karl Kreeger Design

No. 20094
You Deserve this Classic Beauty

■ This plan features:
— Four bedrooms
— Three and one half baths

■ Sturdy stucco, fieldstone, and rough-hewn timbers, lending a distinguished air to this Tudor Classic

■ A Master Suite with an elegant recessed ceiling, a raised tub and a spacious dressing area

■ An island Kitchen with wetbar service to the Living Room

■ A book-lined Library/Study to relax in after a long day

FIRST FLOOR — 2,065 SQ. FT.
SECOND FLOOR — 970 SQ. FT.
BASEMENT — 2,047 SQ. FT.
GARAGE — 524 SQ. FT.

TOTAL LIVING AREA:
3,035 *SQ. FT.*

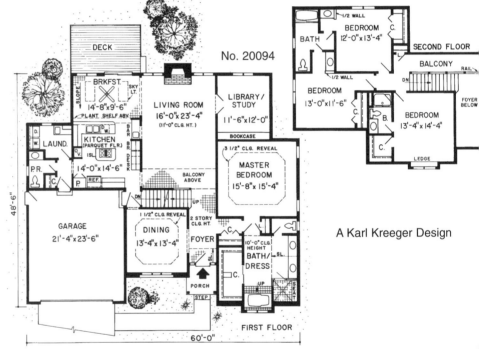

No. 20094

A Karl Kreeger Design

No. 24257
Welcoming Porch

■ This plan features:
— Three Bedrooms
— Two full baths

■ Vaulted ceilings in the Living Room, Dining Room, Family Room and Eating Nook

■ A U-shaped Kitchen with an island, a built-in pantry and a peninsula eating bar

■ A spacious, open layout

■ Two bedrooms with a full hall bath

FIRST FLOOR — 2,108 SQ. FT.
GARAGE — 462 SQ. FT.
OPTIONAL DEN — 121 SQ. FT.

TOTAL LIVING AREA:
2,108 *SQ. FT.*

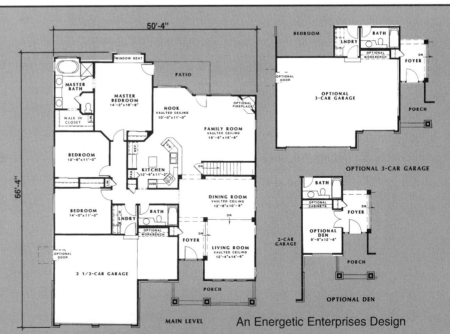

An Energetic Enterprises Design

No. 20128
Skylit Breakfast Room With Plant Shelf Above

■ This plan features:
— Three bedrooms
— Two full baths

■ A Kitchen with a range peninsula that separates the Kitchen from a sunny, sky-lit Breakfast Nook

■ A fireplaced Living Room which adjoins the formal Dining Room

■ A Master Suite with his-and-her walk-in closets and a private bath

FIRST FLOOR — 942 SQ. FT.
SECOND FLOOR — 895 SQ. FT.
BASEMENT — 942 SQ. FT.
GARAGE — 484 SQ. FT.

TOTAL LIVING AREA:
1,837 SQ. FT.

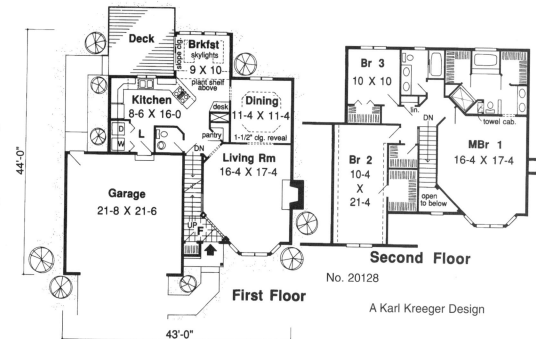

First Floor

Deck

Brkfst
skylights
9 X 10
plant shelf above

Kitchen
8-6 X 16-0

D
W
L

desk

Dining
11-4 X 11-4
1-1/2" clg. reveal

pantry

DN

Living Rm
16-4 X 17-4

Garage
21-8 X 21-6

UP
F

44'-0"

43'-0"

Second Floor

No. 20128

A Karl Kreeger Design

Br 3
10 X 10

lin.

DN

towel cab.

Br 2
10-4
X
21-4

MBr 1
16-4 X 17-4

open to below

No. 34328
Compact Ranch Loaded with Living Space

■ This plan features:
— Three bedrooms
— One full bath

■ A central entrance opening to the Living Room with ample windows

■ A Kitchen featuring a dining area with sliding doors to the backyard and optional deck

■ An optional slab or crawl space foundation — please specify when ordering

FIRST FLOOR — 1,092 SQ. FT.
BASEMENT — 1,092 SQ. FT.

TOTAL LIVING AREA:
1,092 SQ. FT.

ALTERNATE FLOOR PLAN
for Crawl Space

No. 34328

No. 34328

Kit 9-8 x 10-1
Brkfst 8-4 x 10-1
Br 3 9-1 x 10-1
Br 2 11-6 x 9-3
DN
Living Rm 17-0 x 11-6
lin
MBr 1 11-6 x 10-11
26'-0"
42'-0"

No. 34054
Ranch Provides Great Kitchen Area

■ This plan features:
— Three bedrooms
— Two full baths

■ A Dining Room with sliding glass doors to backyard

■ Access to the Garage through the laundry room

■ A Master Bedroom with private full bath

■ An optional two car Garage

■ An optional basement or crawl space foundation available — please specify when ordering

FIRST FLOOR — 1,400 SQ. FT.
BASEMENT — 1,400 SQ. FT.
GARAGE — 528 SQ. FT.

TOTAL LIVING AREA:
1,400 SQ. FT.

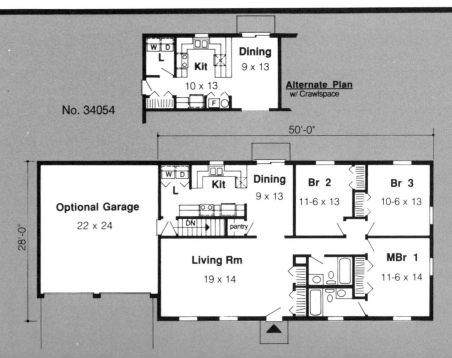

No. 34054

W D
L
Kit 10 x 13
Dining 9 x 13
F
Alternate Plan w/ Crawlspace

No. 34054

50'-0"
28'-0"

Optional Garage 22 x 24

W D
L
Kit
Dining 9 x 13
Br 2 11-6 x 13
Br 3 10-6 x 13
DN
pantry
Living Rm 19 x 14
MBr 1 11-6 x 14

No. 20204
Abundance of Closet Space

■ This plan features:
— Three bedrooms
— Two full baths

■ Roomy walk-in closets in all bedrooms

■ A Master Bedroom with decorative ceiling and a private full bath

■ A fireplaced Living Room with sloped ceilings and sliders to the deck

■ An efficient Kitchen with plenty of cupboard space and a pantry

FIRST FLOOR —1,532 SQ. FT.
GARAGE — 484 SQ. FT.

TOTAL LIVING AREA:
1,532 SQ. FT.

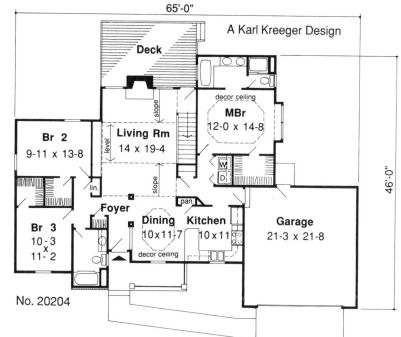

65'-0"

A Karl Kreeger Design

Deck

decor ceiling

Br 2
9-11 x 13-8

Living Rm
14 x 19-4

MBr
12-0 x 14-8

lin.

Br 3
10-3
x
11-2

Foyer

Dining
10x11-7

Kitchen
10 x 11

Garage
21-3 x 21-8

pan.

decor ceiling

46'-0"

No. 20204

No. 34800
Two Story Design Ideal for Small Lot

■ This plan features:
— Three bedrooms
— Two and one half baths
■ Individual dressing areas adjacent to upstairs bath
■ A large Master Bedroom including walk-in closet
■ An inviting two-story foyer
■ A Kitchen including a pantry, space for a dinette set, and direct access to rear deck

FIRST FLOOR — 1,187 SQ. FT.
SECOND FLOOR — 597 SQ. FT.
BASEMENT — 1,169 SQ. FT.
GARAGE — 484 SQ. FT.

TOTAL LIVING AREA: 1,784 SQ. FT.

A Karl Kreeger Design

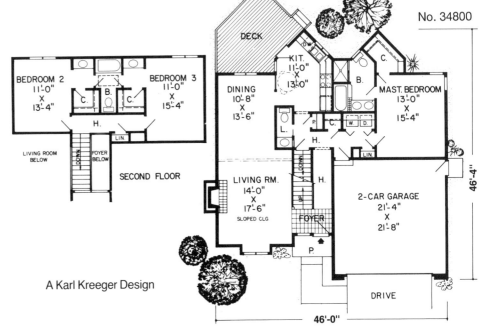

No. 10518
Compact Design, Ample Space

■ This plan features:
— Three bedrooms
— Two baths
■ A combined Living/Dining Room opening to a deck
■ A Kitchen easily accessible from the entry
■ A Master Bedroom with its own private bath

FIRST FLOOR — 864 SQ. FT.
SECOND FLOOR — 307 SQ. FT.

TOTAL LIVING AREA: 1,171 SQ. FT.

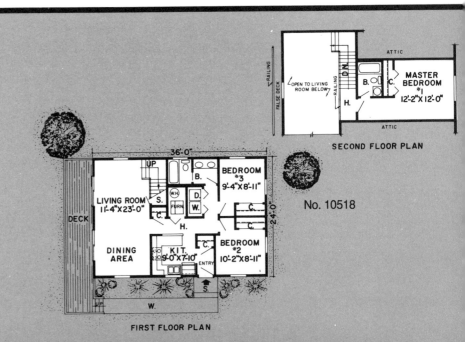

No. 9964
Recreation Room Houses Fireplace

■ This plan features:
— Four bedrooms
— Two full baths

■ A wood-burning fireplace warming the Living/Dining Room, which is accessible to the large wooden sun deck

■ Two first-floor bedrooms with access to a full hall bath

■ Two ample-sized second floor bedrooms

■ A Recreation Room with a cozy fireplace and convenient half bath

FIRST FLOOR — 896 SQ. FT.
SECOND FLOOR — 457 SQ. FT.
BASEMENT — 864 SQ. FT.

TOTAL LIVING AREA:
1,353 SQ. FT.

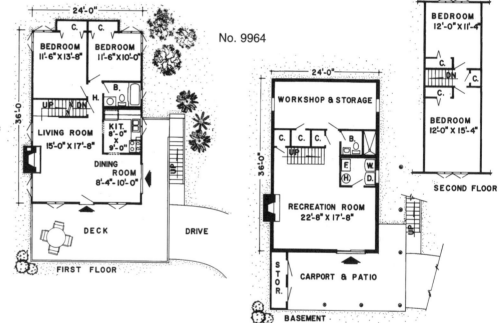

No. 9964

FIRST FLOOR

24'-0"
36'-0"

BEDROOM 11'-6" X 13'-8"
BEDROOM 11'-6" X 10'-0"
C. C.
B.
H.
KIT. 8'-0" X 9'-0"
LIVING ROOM 15'-0" X 17'-8"
UP DN
DINING ROOM 8'-4"-10'-0"
UP
DECK
DRIVE

BASEMENT

24'-0"
36'-0"

WORKSHOP & STORAGE
C. C. C. B.
UP F W.
H. D.
RECREATION ROOM 22'-8" X 17'-8"
STOR.
CARPORT & PATIO
UP

SECOND FLOOR

BEDROOM 12'-0" X 11'-4"
C.
DN
C.
C.
BEDROOM 12'-0" X 15'-4"

No. 10376
Underground Delight

■ This plan features:
— Three bedrooms
— Two full baths

■ A design that aids against the high cost of living through many energy-saving features including the use of passive solar energy

■ Sliding glass doors leading to the front lawn from all three bedrooms

■ A large eat in Kitchen open to the Family Room and near the Utility Room

■ Added features including a greenhouse, Sewing Room and Jacuzzi in the Master Bathroom

FIRST FLOOR — 2,086 SQ. FT.

TOTAL LIVING AREA:
2,086 SQ. FT.

No. 10376

No. 10619
Deck Doubles Outdoor Living Space

■ This plan features:
— Three bedrooms
— Three baths

■ A design made for the sun lover with a front deck and patio

■ A sunken Living Room with three window walls and a massive fireplace.

■ A hot tub with skylight, a vaulted Master Suite and a utility area

FIRST FLOOR — 2,352 SQ. FT.
BASEMENT — 2,352 SQ. FT.
GARAGE — 696 SQ. FT.

TOTAL LIVING AREA:
2,352 SQ. FT.

A Karl Kreeger Design

No. 10619

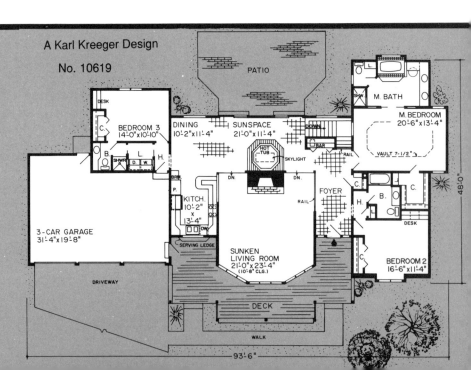

No. 5035
Dormer Windows Accent
Unique Cape

■ This plan features:
— Three bedrooms
— One full and one half bath

■ A detailed Entry leading to an expansive Living Room with a hearth fireplace and decorative windows on three sides

■ An efficient eat-in Kitchen with a peninsula counter and easy access to both the Dining Room and the Garage

■ A comfortable Master Bedroom with two closets, and offering decorative windows on three sides

■ Two additional bedrooms sharing a full hall bath

FIRST FLOOR — 725 SQ. FT.
SECOND FLOOR — 651 SQ. FT.
BASEMENT — 725 SQ. FT.
GARAGE — 265 SQ. FT.

TOTAL LIVING AREA:
1,376 SQ. FT.

No. 5035

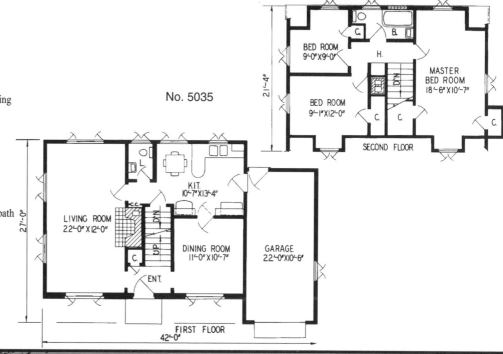

No. 20134
Classic Beauty

■ This plan features:
— Three bedrooms
— Two and one half baths

■ Generous, well-placed windows and angular ceilings giving every room a cheery atmosphere

■ The Living and Dining Rooms flowing together off the foyer

■ Family areas at the rear of the home including a cozy Hearth Room adjoining the efficient Kitchen

■ A Master Suite located over the Garage, enhanced by a sky-lit bath, cozy sitting area, and a room-size closet

First floor — 1,361 sq. ft.
Second floor — 1,122 sq. ft.
Basement — 1,361 sq. ft.
Garage — 477 sq. ft.

Total living area:
2,483 sq. ft.

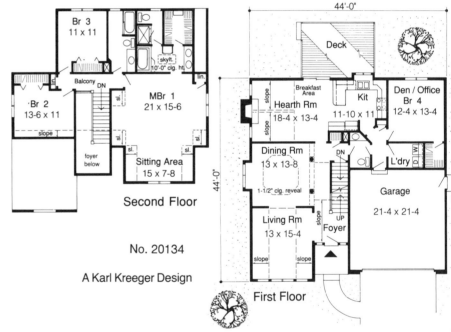

Second Floor

No. 20134

A Karl Kreeger Design

First Floor

No. 20060
Master Bedroom at Entry Level

■ This plan features:
— Three bedrooms
— Two and a half baths

■ A sloping, open beam ceiling in the fireplaced Living Room

■ A Master Bedroom with a dressing area, walk-in closet and full bath

■ A Kitchen centered perfectly between the Breakfast area and the formal Dining Room

First floor — 1,279 sq. ft.
Second floor — 502 sq. ft.
Basement — 729 sq. ft.
Garage — 470 sq. ft.

Total living area:
1,781 sq. ft.

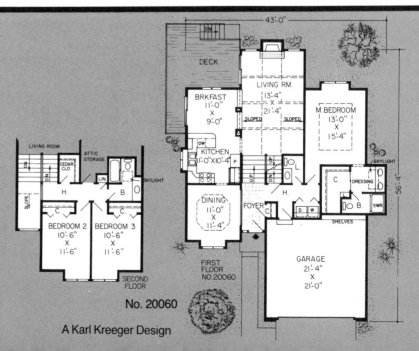

No. 20060

A Karl Kreeger Design

No. 20055
Outdoor-Lovers Dream

■ This plan features:
— Three bedrooms
— Two and one half baths
■ Sloped ceilings
■ An efficient Kitchen with cooktop peninsula and easy access to Breakfast Bay or Dining Room
■ A Master Suite featuring soaring ceilings and private dressing area flanked by full bath and walk-in closet
■ A large Living room that adjoins a deck

FIRST FLOOR — 928 SQ. FT.
SECOND FLOOR — 773 SQ. FT.
BASEMENT — 910 SQ. FT.
GARAGE — 484 SQ. FT.

TOTAL LIVING AREA:
1,701 SQ. FT.

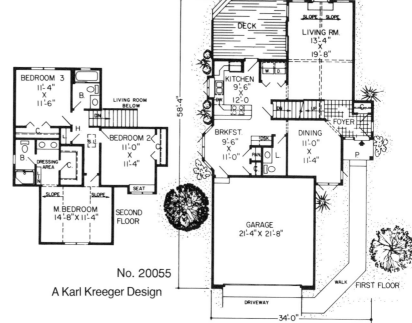

No. 20055

A Karl Kreeger Design

No. 9714
Excellent Choice for Sloping Lot

- ■ This plan features:
- — Three bedrooms
- — Three full baths
- ■ A Family Room on the lower level facing the front, and opening onto the lower level
- ■ A sun deck on the upper level adjoining the Living and Dining Rooms
- ■ A tiled country Kitchen with a cooking island and a built-in laundry room

FIRST FLOOR — 1,748 SQ. FT.
SECOND FLOOR — 932 SQ. FT.
GARAGE — 768 SQ. FT.

**TOTAL LIVING AREA:
2,680 SQ. FT.**

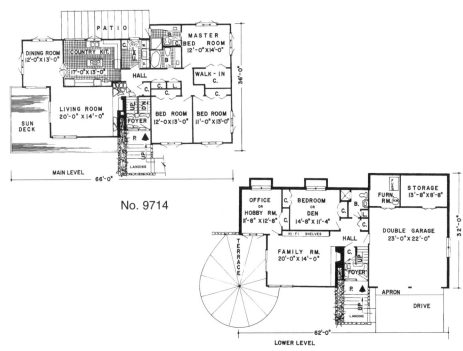

No. 9714

No. 20211
Inspired by Country Porches of Old

- ■ This plan features:
- — Three bedrooms
- — Two full baths
- ■ Decorative and sloped ceilings
- ■ A large Kitchen with a central island, a double sink, a pantry, as well as ample cabinet and counter space
- ■ A Master Suite with a decorative ceiling, and a walk-in closet
- ■ A decorative ceiling in the Dining Room
- ■ A central, focal-point fireplace and sloped ceilings in the Living Room
- ■ Two additional bedrooms that share use of a full hall bath

MAIN AREA — 1,609 SQ. FT.

**TOTAL LIVING AREA:
1,609 SQ. FT.**

A Karl Kreeger Design

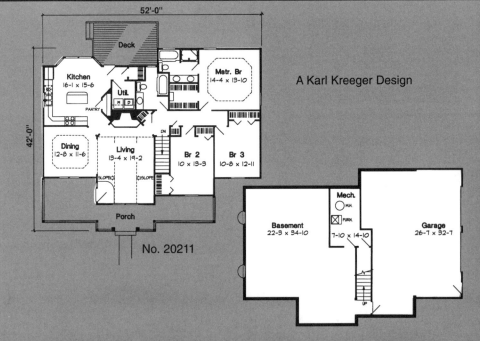

No. 20211

No. 20148
Hillside Haven

■ This plan features:
— Three bedrooms
— Two full baths

■ A well-appointed Kitchen that adjoins a cheerful, six-sided Breakfast Room with access to the wrap-around deck

■ A decorative ceiling in the formal Dining Room which flows into the Living Room

■ A sky-lit Living Room with a built-in wetbar and a fireplace

■ A Master Suite with a decorative ceiling, a window seat, a walk-in closet, and a private Master Bath

■ Two additional bedrooms with ample closet space that share a full hall bath

First floor — 1,774 sq. ft.
Basement — 1,399 sq. ft.
Garage — 551 sq. ft.

Total living area:
1,774 sq. ft.

Slab/Crawl Space Option

No. 20148

A Karl Kreeger Design

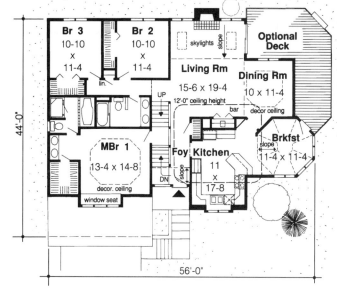

No. 9812
Mudroom Separates Garage, Kitchen

■ This plan features:
— Three bedrooms
— Two full baths
■ An open Kitchen flowing into the Family Room
■ A Master Bedroom with private bath and ample closet space
■ A spacious, formal Living Room
■ A double Garage and storage closet in the Mudroom adding to storage area

FIRST FLOOR — 1,396 SQ. FT.
BASEMENT — 1,396 SQ. FT.
GARAGE — 484 SQ. FT.

TOTAL LIVING AREA:
1,396 SQ. FT.

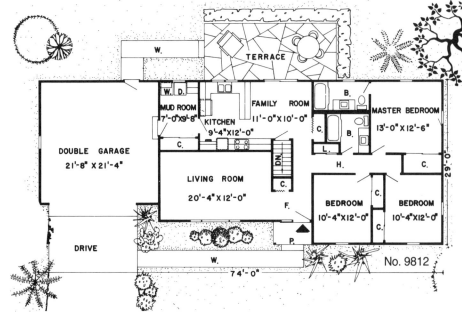

No. 10270
Master Bedroom Merits Deck

■ This plan features:
— Three bedrooms
— Two and one half baths
■ A large eat in Kitchen with easy access to a step saving Laundry Room
■ A Work Shop for the hobbyist
■ Two appealing rear decks and a basement terrace

FIRST FLOOR — 2,202 SQ. FT.
BASEMENT — 2,016 SQ. FT.
GARAGE & WORKSHOP — 677 SQ. FT.

TOTAL LIVING AREA:
2,202 SQ. FT.

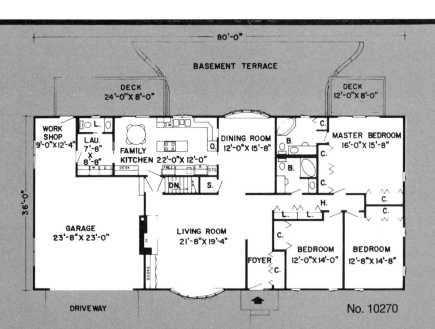

No. 20451
Dramatic Impressions

■ This plan features:
— Three bedrooms
— Two and one half baths

■ A soaring Living Room off the vaulted sky-lit foyer

■ A cozy Family Room that shares the backyard view with the glass-walled Breakfast room

■ A Kitchen that easily serves every area, including the elegant formal Dining Room at the front of the house

■ A Master Suite tucked behind the Garage, including private deck access, and a magnificent bath with a garden tub

FIRST FLOOR — 2,084 SQ. FT.

**TOTAL LIVING AREA:
2,084 SQ. FT.**

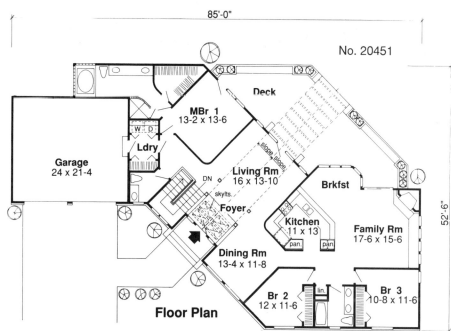

No. 20451

85'-0"

52'-6"

Garage
24 x 21-4

Ldry
W D

MBr 1
13-2 x 13-6

Deck

Living Rm
16 x 13-10

Brkfst

DN

skylts.

Foyer

Kitchen
11 x 13

pan.   pan.

Family Rm
17-6 x 15-6

Dining Rm
13-4 x 11-8

Br 2
12 x 11-6

lin.

Br 3
10-8 x 11-6

Floor Plan

No. 20054
Striking Entryway

■ This plan features:
— Two bedrooms, possible 3rd bedroom/den
— Two full baths
■ A cathedral ceiling gracing the Living Room
■ A large Master Bedroom with ample closet and full Master Bath
■ A Dining Room with decorative ceiling
■ A modern Kitchen flowing into the Breakfast area
■ Conveniently located laundry area

MAIN AREA — 1,461 SQ. FT.
BASEMENT — 1,458 SQ. FT.
GARAGE — 528 SQ. FT.

**TOTAL LIVING AREA:
1,461 SQ. FT.**

A Karl Kreeger Design

FIRST FLOOR
No. 20054

No. 10569
Ranch Offers Attractive Window Facade

■ This plan features:
— Four bedrooms
— Three full baths
■ A Living Room with sloping, open beamed ceilings and a fireplace with built-in bookshelves
■ A Dining Room with a vaulted ceiling adding a feeling of spaciousness
■ A Master Bath with ample closet space and a private bath
■ A two-car Garage

FIRST FLOOR — 1,840 SQ. FT
BASEMENT — 1,803 SQ. FT
GARAGE — 445 SQ. FT.

**TOTAL LIVING AREA:
1,840 SQ. FT.**

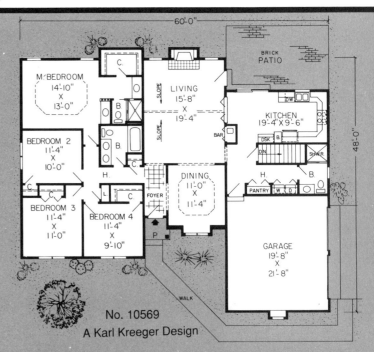

No. 10569
A Karl Kreeger Design

No. 20187
Ranch with Everything

■ This plan features:
— Three bedrooms
— Two full baths

■ A decorative ceiling in the elegant formal Dining Room

■ A well-appointed Kitchen with built-in pantry, ample counter space and peninsula island that separates the Kitchen from the Breakfast room

■ A Living Room made cozy by a fireplace and with easy access to the deck

■ A Master Bedroom with private Master Bath and walk-in closet

■ Two additional bedrooms that share a full hall bath

FIRST FLOOR — 1,416 SQ. FT.
BASEMENT — 1,416 SQ. FT.
GARAGE — 484 SQ. FT.

TOTAL LIVING AREA:
1,416 SQ. FT.

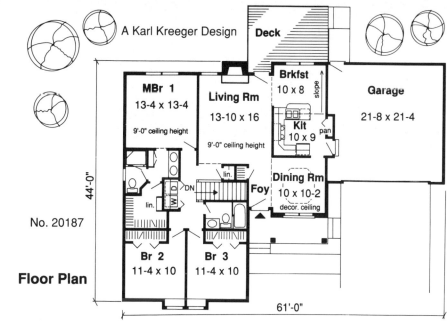

A Karl Kreeger Design

No. 20187

Floor Plan

Deck

MBr 1
13-4 x 13-4
9'-0" ceiling height

Living Rm
13-10 x 16
9'-0" ceiling height

Brkfst
10 x 8

Garage
21-8 x 21-4

Kit
10 x 9

Dining Rm
10 x 10-2
decor. ceiling

Foy

44'-0"

Br 2
11-4 x 10

Br 3
11-4 x 10

61'-0"

No. 10531
Luxury is Always Popular

■ This plan features:
— Three bedrooms
— Three full and one half bath

■ A sunken Great Room, a spectacular Breakfast Nook, and a bridge-like balcony on the second floor

■ A Master Suite highlighted by two huge walk-in closets, a five piece bath, and a sitting room with bay window

■ A Great Room accented by a bar, fireplace, and built-in cabinets for the television and stereo

■ Cathedral ceilings in the Dining Room and foyer

FIRST FLOOR — 2,579 SQ. FT.
SECOND FLOOR — 997 SQ. FT.
BASEMENT — 2,579 SQ. FT.
GARAGE & STORAGE — 1,001 SQ. FT.

**TOTAL LIVING AREA:
3,576 SQ. FT.**

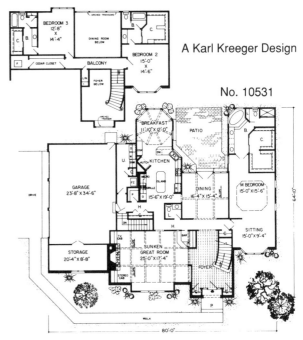

A Karl Kreeger Design

No. 10531

No. 10568
Family Preferred Features in Tudor Design

■ This plan features:
— Three bedrooms
— Two and one half baths

■ An energy-efficient foyer leading into a Great Room including a large fireplace

■ A Master Bedroom with its own private deck, and a bath area with a two-way shower

■ An efficient Kitchen with a large Breakfast Nook

FIRST FLOOR — 2,167 SQ. FT.
SECOND FLOOR — 755 SQ. FT.
BASEMENT — 2,224 SQ. FT.
GARAGE — 1,020 SQ. FT.

**TOTAL LIVING AREA:
2,922 SQ. FT.**

Total living area — 2,922 sq. ft.

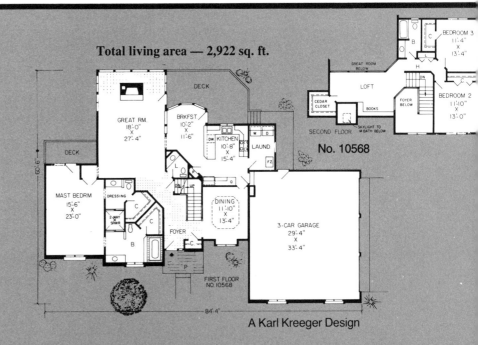

No. 10568

A Karl Kreeger Design

No. 20071
Traditional Energy Saver

■ This plan features:

— Four bedrooms

— Three and one half baths

■ A heat storing floor in the sun room adjoining the Living Room and Breakfast Room

■ A Living Room with French doors and a massive fireplace

■ A balcony overlooking the soaring two-story foyer and Living Room

■ An island Kitchen centrally located between the formal and informal Dining Rooms

FIRST FLOOR — 2,186 SQ. FT.

SECOND FLOOR — 983 SQ. FT.

BASEMENT — 2,186 SQ. FT.

GARAGE — 704 SQ. FT.

TOTAL LIVING AREA: 3,169 SQ. FT.

A Karl Kreeger Design

No. 20071

No. 20090
Family Living on Two Levels

■ This plan features:
— Four bedrooms
— Two and one half baths

■ A stacked window gracing the facade of this spacious, four-bedroom classic

■ A formal Parlor and Dining Room with decorative ceilings off the foyer

■ Family areas at the rear of the house arranged for convenient access to the Kitchen

■ A sky-lit Breakfast room with a surrounding outdoor deck

■ A cozy fireplace in the Family Room

■ A first floor Master Suite with double vanities, a walk-in closet, and an elegant recessed ceiling

FIRST FLOOR — 1,933 SQ. FT.
SECOND FLOOR — 918 SQ. FT.
BASEMENT — 1,933 SQ. FT.
GARAGE— 484 SQ. FT.

TOTAL LIVING AREA: 2,851 SQ. FT.

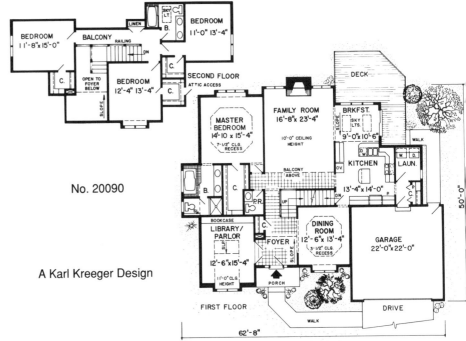

No. 20090

A Karl Kreeger Design

No. 20199
The Perfect Home

■ This plan features:
— Four bedrooms
— Three and one half baths

■ A stunning fireplace in the Breakfast/Hearth Room with built-in TV cabinet and plant shelf

■ A spacious Living Room with ten-foot ceiling height

■ A decorative ceiling enhancing the elegant Dining Room

■ An efficient Kitchen with all the amenities

■ A sloped ceiling in the Master Suite and a private full bath with walk-in closet

■ Three additional bedrooms, one with a private bath and two with walk-in closets

FIRST FLOOR — 1,760 SQ. FT.
SECOND FLOOR — 785 SQ. FT.
BASEMENT — 1,760 SQ. FT.
GARAGE — 797 SQ. FT.

TOTAL LIVING AREA: 2,545 SQ. FT.

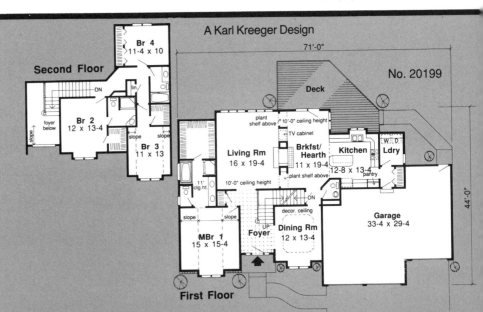

A Karl Kreeger Design

No. 20199

No. 20105
Timeless Elegance

■ This plan features:
— Four bedrooms
— Three and one half baths

■ A handsome Tudor exterior

■ A foyer flanked by a formal Dining Room and a Library

■ A massive Living Room enhanced by high ceilings, abundant windows, and access to a rear deck

■ The Living and Hearth Rooms sharing a fireplace and wetbar creating a convenient atmosphere for entertaining

■ A Kitchen with a handy breakfast bar and pantry

■ A first-floor Master Suite with recessed ceilings, twin walk-in closets, and a luxurious bath

FIRST FLOOR — 2,080 SQ. FT.
SECOND FLOOR — 1,051 SQ. FT.
BASEMENT — 2,080 SQ. FT.
GARAGE — 666 SQ. FT.

TOTAL LIVING AREA: 3,131 SQ. FT.

A Karl Kreeger Design

No. 20105

No. 10805
Today's Features, Yesterday's Old-Fashioned Charm

■ This plan features:
— Three bedrooms
— Two and one half baths

■ Wide corner boards, clapboard siding, and a full-length covered porch lending a friendly air to this classic home

■ A central entry opening to a cozy Den on the right, a sunken Living Room with adjoining Dining Room on the left

■ An informal Dining Nook accented by bay windows

■ A Master Suite spanning the rear of the home including a huge, walk-in closet, a private bath with double vanities, and a whirlpool tub

FIRST FLOOR — 1,622 SQ. FT.
SECOND FLOOR — 1,156 SQ. FT.

TOTAL LIVING AREA:
2,778 SQ. FT.

Second Floor

First Floor
No. 10805

No. 10649
Room for Family Activities

■ This plan features:
— Three bedrooms
— Two and one half baths

■ A Family Room warmed with a fireplace, lots of windows, French doors, wet bar and access to the covered porch

■ A Kitchen centered between a bay window breakfast nook and a formal Dining Room

■ Window seats adorning the front bedrooms

FIRST FLOOR — 1,285 SQ. FT.
SECOND FLOOR — 930 SQ. FT.
GARAGE — 492 SQ. FT.

TOTAL LIVING AREA:
2,215 SQ. FT.

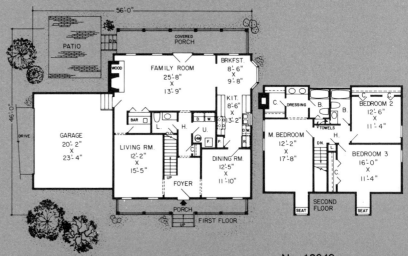

No. 10649

No. 24260
Spacious Great Room Provides Center of Activity

■ This plan features:
— Three bedrooms
— Two full baths

■ A spacious Great Room which dominates the center of the home with a built-in entertainment center and a fireplace

■ A secluded Master Suite including a private Master Bath with a double vanity, a corner oval tub, a separate shower and a large walk-in closet

■ An efficient Kitchen with a built-in pantry, a peninsula eating bar and an eating Nook

■ A formal Dining Room with a butler's pantry located at the entrance of the room

■ Two additional bedrooms that share a full hall bath

FIRST FLOOR — 2,010 SQ. FT.
GARAGE — 482 SQ. FT.

TOTAL LIVING AREA: 2,010 SQ. FT.

No materials list available

An Energetic Enterprises Design

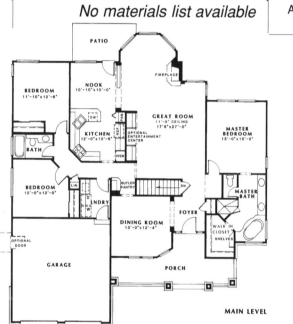

56'-0"

PATIO

BEDROOM
11'-10"x12'-8"

NOOK
10'-10"x10'-0"

FIREPLACE

GREAT ROOM
11'-0" CEILING
17'8"x27'-0"

MASTER BEDROOM
13'-0"x15'-0"

KITCHEN
12'-0"x10'-8"

OPTIONAL ENTERTAINMENT CENTER

BATH

BEDROOM
12'-0"x12'-0"

LIN

LNDRY

BUTLER PANTRY

DN

MASTER BATH

DINING ROOM
13'-0"x12'-4"

FOYER

WALK IN CLOSET SHELVES

OPTIONAL DOOR

GARAGE

PORCH

61'-8"

MAIN LEVEL

OPTIONAL DEN
12'-0"x12'-0"

LIN

OPTIONAL CABINETS

No. 24260

No. 20526
Exciting Ceilings and Terraces

■ This plan features:

— Three bedrooms

— Two full baths

■ A foyer leading into the Family Room with sloped ceilings

■ A U-shaped Kitchen with space for informal meals

■ A Dining Room separated from the Living Room, but with the warmth from the fireplace reaching the table

■ A Dining Room with access to the terrace through sliding doors

■ A Master Bedroom with a high tray ceiling, a private bath, and sliders to a private terrace

FIRST FLOOR — 1,633 SQ. FT.

BASEMENT — 1,633 SQ. FT.

GARAGE — 423 SQ. FT.

TOTAL LIVING AREA:
1,633 SQ. FT.

Terrace · Terrace

Dining Rm 10 x 12-4
slope

MBr 1 16 x 12
9'-0" ceiling height
tray ceiling

Living Rm 15-2 x 15
11'-8" ceiling height

Br 2 12 x 11

Kit / Nook 9 x 18
slope · slope

Family Rm 11 x 14

Br 3 10-8 x 10

Foyer L

Garage 20-2 x 20

DN

55'-0"

50'-0"

Floor Plan

No. 20526

No. 20104
Easy One Level Living

■ This plan features:

— Three bedrooms

— Two full baths

■ A sky-lit Kitchen

■ Ample closet space

■ Built-in storage areas in Kitchen

■ A Master bath with twin vanities, raised tub, and walk in shower

FIRST FLOOR — 1,686 SQ. FT.

BASEMENT — 1,677 SQ. FT.

GARAGE — 475 SQ. FT.

TOTAL LIVING AREA:
1,686 SQ. FT.

A Karl Kreeger Design

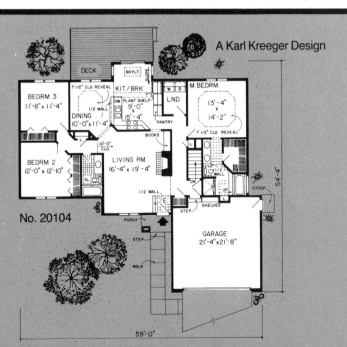

DECK · SKYLT.

BEDRM. 3 11'-8" x 11'-4"

KIT./BRK. 9'-0" x 15'-4"

M. BEDRM. 13'-4" x 14'-2"

DINING 10'-0" x 11'-4"

BEDRM. 2 12'-0" x 12'-10"

LIVING RM. 16'-4" x 19'-4"

PANTRY · BOOKS

W · D · LND.

PORCH · STEP · WALK · STOOP

GARAGE 21'-4" x 21'-8"

54'-4"

59'-0"

No. 20104

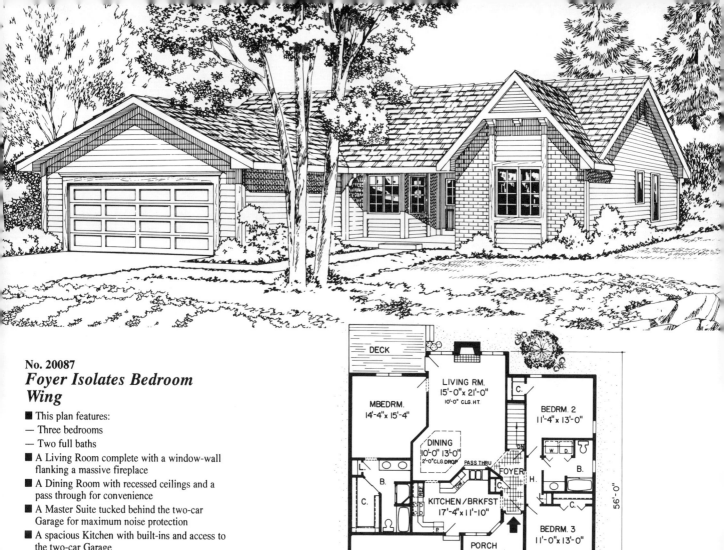

No. 20087
Foyer Isolates Bedroom Wing

■ This plan features:
— Three bedrooms
— Two full baths

■ A Living Room complete with a window-wall flanking a massive fireplace

■ A Dining Room with recessed ceilings and a pass through for convenience

■ A Master Suite tucked behind the two-car Garage for maximum noise protection

■ A spacious Kitchen with built-ins and access to the two-car Garage

FIRST FLOOR —1,568 SQ. FT.
BASEMENT — 1,568 SQ. FT.
GARAGE — 484 SQ. FT.

TOTAL LIVING AREA: 1,568 SQ. FT.

DECK

LIVING RM.
15'-0" x 21'-0"
10'-0" CLG. HT.

MBEDRM.
14'-4" x 15'-4"

BEDRM. 2
11'-4" x 13'-0"

DINING
10'-0" 13'-0"
2'-0" CLG. DROP

PASS THRU

FOYER

KITCHEN/BRKFST
17'-4" x 11'-10"

BEDRM. 3
11'-0" x 13'-0"

PORCH

GARAGE
21'-8" x 21'-6"

56'-0"

DRIVE

WALK

48'-0"

No. 20087

Karl Kreeger Design

No. 10394
Master Suite Crowns Plan

■ This plan features:
— Three bedrooms
— Two full baths
■ A Master Bedroom which occupies the entire
second level
■ A passive solar design
■ A Living Room which rises two stories in the
front
■ Skylights in the sloping ceilings of the Kitchen
and Master Bath

FIRST FLOOR — 1,306 SQ. FT.
SECOND FLOOR — 472 SQ. FT.
GARAGE — 576 SQ. FT.

TOTAL LIVING AREA:
1,778 SQ. FT.

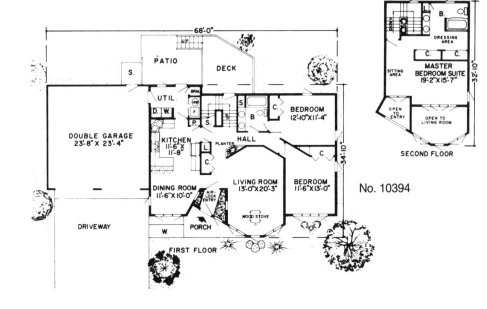

No. 10394

No. 1078
Vacation Retreat or Year Round Living

■ This plan features:
— Two bedrooms
— One full bath
■ A long hallway dividing bedrooms and living
areas assuring privacy
■ A centrally located utility room and bath
■ An open Living/Dining Room area with exposed
beams, sloping ceilings and optional fireplace

FIRST FLOOR — 1,024 SQ. FT.
CARPORT & STORAGE — 387 SQ. FT.
DECK — 411 SQ. FT.

TOTAL LIVING AREA:
1,024 SQ. FT.

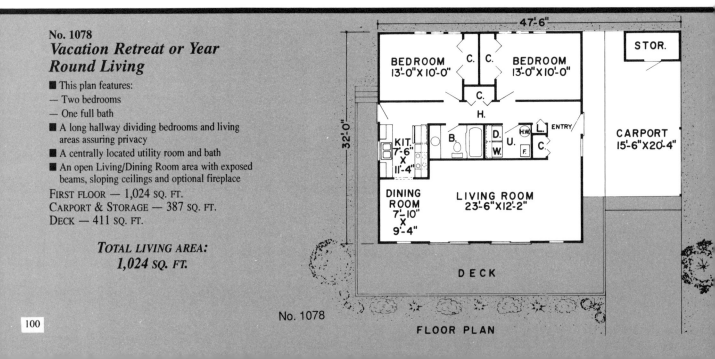

No. 1078

FLOOR PLAN

No. 84058
Well Planned Saltbox has Rustic Charm

■ This plan features:
— Three bedrooms
— Two full baths
■ Efficient use of living space creating a spacious feeling
■ A Living/Dining area occupying more than half of the lower level
■ A central chimney accommodating a built-in fireplace
■ An optional deck
■ An optional basement, slab or crawl space foundation available — please specify when ordering

FIRST FLOOR — 779 SQ. FT.
SECOND FLOOR — 519 SQ. FT.

TOTAL LIVING AREA: 1,298 SQ. FT.

No materials list available

27'-6"

optional **Deck**

Living/ Dining Rm
20-5 x 16-4
open to above

UP   DN

28'-4"

Kit
11-5 x 11-8

MBr 1
12-8 x 9-5

W   D

No. 84058
First Floor

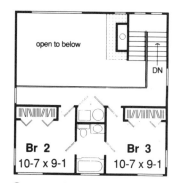

Second Floor

open to below

DN

Br 2
10-7 x 9-1

Br 3
10-7 x 9-1

opt. slab/crawl space

No. 10445
Morning Room Accents

■ This plan features:
— Three bedrooms
— Two and one half baths
■ Tiled floors unifying the dining and food preparation areas
■ A Morning Room located off the well-organized Kitchen
■ A Family Room employing more tile accents which opens to the patio
■ A secluded Master Bedroom which includes a sunken tub, small greenhouses, and ample closet space

FIRST FLOOR — 2,466 SQ. FT.
GARAGE — 482 SQ. FT.

TOTAL LIVING AREA:
2,466 SQ. FT.

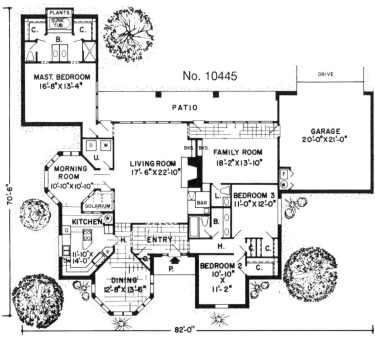

No. 20353
Window-Studded Brick Facade Communicates Success

■ This plan features:
— Three bedrooms
— Three full and one half bath
■ A sky-lit Foyer with a balcony above
■ A formal Dining Room made spacious by a vaulted ceiling
■ A large island Kitchen with peninsula counter that serves a glass-walled Breakfast area equipped with an adjoining pantry
■ A built-in bar in the huge Family Room with cozy fireplace that is just steps away from the elegant Parlor
■ A magnificent Master Suite with pan vault ceiling, fireplace, circular spa, two-way access to a private deck and large walk-in closet
■ Two additional bedrooms each with a full bath

FIRST FLOOR — 1,807 SQ. FT.
SECOND FLOOR — 1,359 SQ. FT.
BASEMENT — 1,807 SQ. FT.
GARAGE — 840 SQ. FT.

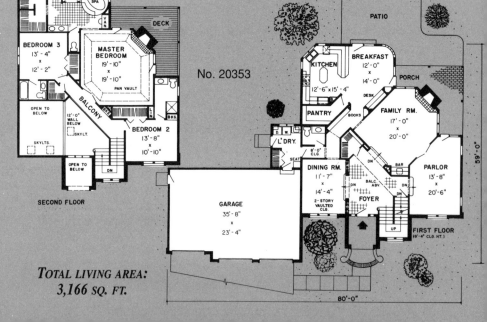

TOTAL LIVING AREA:
3,166 SQ. FT.

No. 20359
Intelligent Plan Separates Formal from Family Areas

■ This plan features:
— Four bedrooms
— Three and one half baths

■ A sunken Study with large front window illuminating the room

■ A sunken Living Room with a stunning fireplace and opened to the Dining Room

■ An island Kitchen with walk-in pantry, built-in desk and sky-lit Breakfast room

■ A Family Room made spacious by a vaulted ceiling and cozy by a corner fireplace

■ A Master Suite with a tray ceiling, private deck, walk-in closet and private Master Bath

■ A Guest Room with a private full bath

■ Two additional bedrooms that have shared access to the full hall bath with double vanities

FIRST FLOOR — 2,516 SQ. FT.
SECOND FLOOR — 1,602 SQ. FT.
BASEMENT — 2,516 SQ. FT.
GARAGE — 822 SQ. FT.

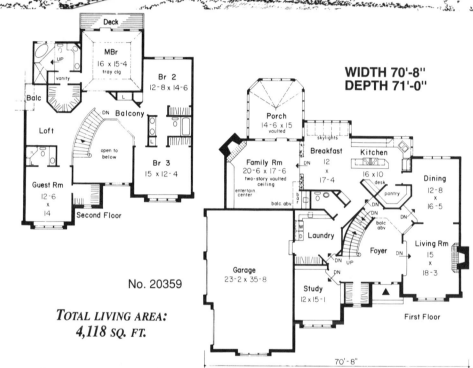

WIDTH 70'-8"
DEPTH 71'-0"

No. 20359

TOTAL LIVING AREA:
4,118 SQ. FT.

Deck

MBr
16 x 15-4
tray clg

Br 2
12-8 x 14-6

Balc

DN Balcony

Loft

open to below

Guest Rm
12-6 x 14

Br 3
15 x 12-4

Second Floor

Porch
14-6 x 15
vaulted

Breakfast
12 x 17-4

Kitchen
16 x 10

Family Rm
20-6 x 17-6
two-story vaulted ceiling
entertain center

Dining
12-8 x 16-5

Laundry

pantry

Foyer

Living Rm
15 x 18-3

Garage
23-2 x 35-8

Study
12 x 15-1

First Floor

70'-8"

No. 24314
Rambling Ranch

■ This plan features:
— Three bedrooms
— Two full baths

■ A Living Room that flows into an elegant Dining
Room

■ A Kitchen that includes a double sink and a
walk-in pantry

■ A Family Room with direct access to the rear
yard

■ A Master Suite with a lavish private bath and a
walk-in closet

■ Two additional bedrooms that share a full hall
bath

FIRST FLOOR — 1,850 SQ. FT.

TOTAL LIVING AREA:
1,850 SQ. FT.

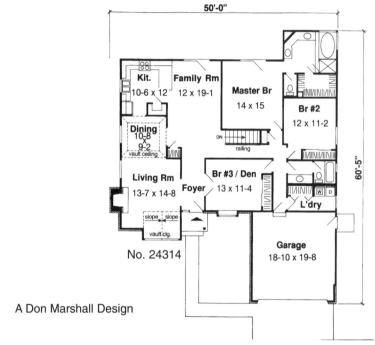

No. 24314

A Don Marshall Design

No. 24264
Warm and Inviting

■ This plan features:
— Four bedrooms
— Two full and one half bath

■ A see-through fireplace

■ A Kitchen with an island, a built-in pantry, and a
double sink

■ A Master Bedroom with a vaulted ceiling, a
double vanity, a corner tub, a separate shower, a
compartmented toilet, and a huge walk-in closet

■ Three bedrooms, one with walk-in closet share
full hall Bath

FIRST FLOOR — 1,241 SQ. FT.
SECOND FLOOR — 1,170 SQ. FT.

TOTAL LIVING AREA:
2,411 SQ. FT.

No. 24264

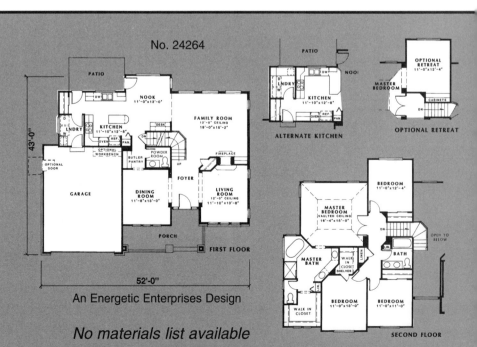

An Energetic Enterprises Design

No materials list available

No. 10328
Living Room Focus of Spacious Home

■ This plan features:
— Three bedrooms
— One and one half baths
■ A well planned traffic pattern connecting the Dining Area, the Kitchen, the laundry niche and the bath
■ A second floor balcony overlooking the open Living Room on the
■ Sliding glass doors opening to the deck, a fireplace and a sizable Living Room

FIRST FLOOR — 1,024 SQ. FT.
SECOND FLOOR — 576 SQ. FT.
BASEMENT — 1,024 SQ. FT.

TOTAL LIVING AREA:
1,600 SQ. FT.

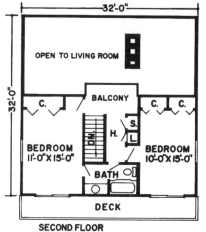

SECOND FLOOR
No. 10328

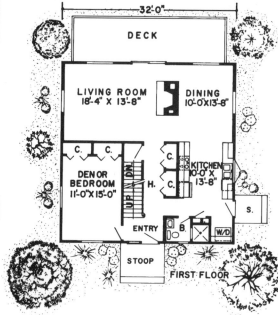

No. 26111
Sunny Beauty

■ This plan features:

— Two bedrooms

— Two full baths

■ A wooden deck skirting most of the three sides of the plan

■ A Living Room which can be reached through sliders from the deck or several steps down from the main living level

■ A low balcony overlooking the entry way and Dining Room

FIRST FLOOR — 769 SQ. FT.
SECOND FLOOR — 572 SQ. FT.
BASEMENT — 546 SQ. FT.

TOTAL LIVING AREA:
1,341 SQ. FT.

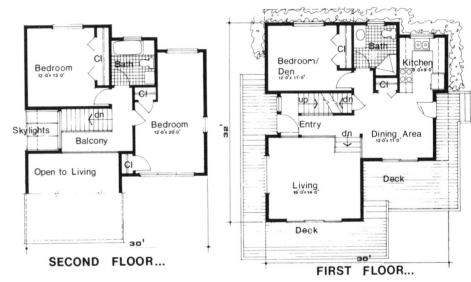

No. 26111

No. 26112
Contemporary Design Features Sunken Living Room

■ This plan features:

— Two bedrooms, with possible third bedroom/den

— One and one half baths

■ A solar design with southern glass doors, windows, and an air-lock entry

■ R-26 insulation used for floors and sloping ceilings

■ A deck rimming the front of the home

■ A Dining Room separated from the Living Room by a half wall

■ An efficient Kitchen with an eating bar

FIRST FLOOR — 911 SQ. FT.
SECOND FLOOR — 576 SQ. FT.
BASEMENT — 911 SQ. FT.

TOTAL LIVING AREA:
1,487 SQ. FT.

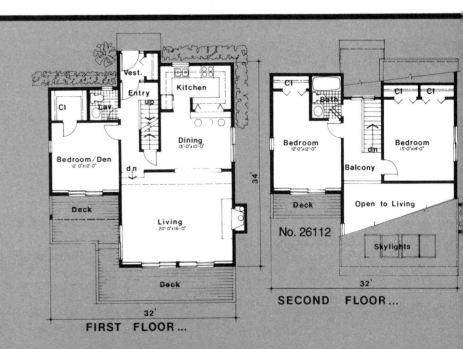

No. 26110
Passive Solar and Contemporary Features

■ This plan features:

— Two bedrooms (with possible third bedroom/den)

— One and one half baths

■ Numerous glass doors, windows, and a greenhouse

■ 2 x 6 studs, R-19 insulation in the exterior walls, and R-33 insulation in all sloping ceilings

■ A Living Room with a concrete slab floor for solar gain

■ A sky-lit Living Room ceiling which slants two stories

FIRST FLOOR — 902 SQ. FT.

SECOND FLOOR — 567 SQ. FT.

TOTAL LIVING AREA: 1,469 SQ. FT.

Second Floor...

No. 26110

First Floor...

No. 20526

Exciting Ceilings and Terraces

■ This plan features:
— Three bedrooms
— Two full baths
■ A foyer leading into the Family Room with sloped ceilings
■ A U-shaped Kitchen with space for informal meals
■ A Dining Room separated from the Living Room, with the warmth from the fireplace reaching the table
■ A Dining Room with access to the terrace through sliding doors
■ A Master Bedroom with a high tray ceiling, a private bath, and sliders to a private terrace

FIRST FLOOR — 1,633 SQ. FT.
BASEMENT — 1,633 SQ. FT.
GARAGE — 423 SQ. FT.

TOTAL LIVING AREA:
1,633 SQ. FT.

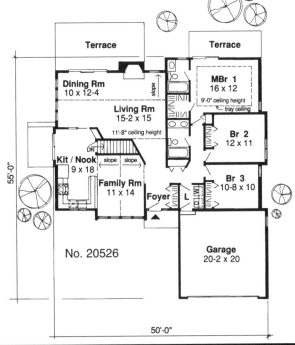

No. 10600

A New Angle Home
■ This plan features:
–- Three bedrooms
— Two full baths
■ A rustic facade with a sheltered entry leading to a tiled Foyer
■ A Living Room with a fieldstone fireplace and a sloped ceiling
■ A bay windowed Breakfast Nook
■ A U-shaped Kitchen with a double sink, ample counter and storage space
■ A lovely Master Suite with a bay window area, access to the patio and a double vanitied Bath

MAIN AREA — 1,219 SQ. FT.
GARAGE — 410 SQ. FT.

TOTAL LIVING AREA:
1,219 SQ. FT.

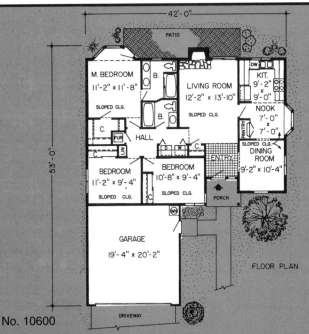

No. 10492

Distinctive Design

■ This plan features:

— Three/four bedrooms

— Three full baths

■ A Television Room, Den, Family Room and a Sitting Room

■ A well-equipped Kitchen with double bay windows, a separate dining Nook, and adjoining the formal Dining Room

■ A private Deck and Master Bath with a Roman tub and a walk-in closet enhance the Master Suite

■ Two smaller bedrooms connecting to a walk-through, full bath

FIRST FLOOR — 2,409 SQ. FT.

SECOND FLOOR — 2,032 SQ. FT.

GARAGE — 690 SQ. FT.

TOTAL LIVING AREA:
4,441 SQ. FT.

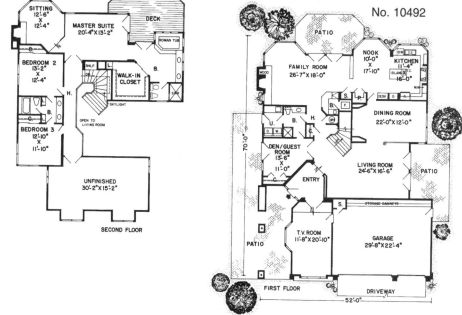

No. 20303
Good Things Come in Small Packages

■ This plan features:
— Three bedrooms
— Two full baths

■ An air-lock vestibule entry that keeps the chill outside

■ A cozy sitting nook in the Living Room

■ A well-equipped Kitchen with a Breakfast nook

■ A sky-lit hall bath shared by two of the bedrooms

■ A Master Suite with his-n-her closets and a private, sky-lit full bath

FIRST FLOOR — 885 SQ. FT.
SECOND FLOOR — 368 SQ. FT.
BASEMENT — 715 SQ. FT.

TOTAL LIVING AREA:
1,253 SQ. FT.

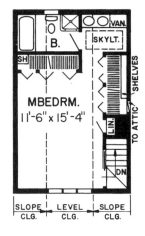

SECOND FLOOR

No. 20303

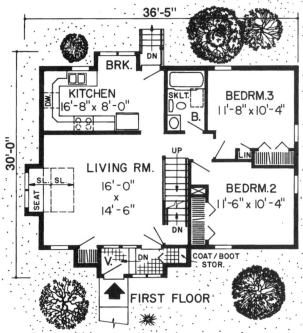

No. 34851
Traditional Gem

■ This plan features:
— Three bedrooms
— Two full and one half baths

■ A sloped-ceiling Living/Dining Room combination

■ A Family Room with a fireplace

■ A Kitchen with a built-in pantry

■ A Master Suite with a sloped ceiling, and a private Master Bath

■ Two additional bedrooms with direct access to a full bath

FIRST FLOOR — 1,056 SQ. FT.
SECOND FLOOR — 874 SQ. FT.
BASEMENT — 1,023 SQ. FT.
GARAGE — 430 SQ. FT.

TOTAL LIVING AREA:
1,930 SQ. FT.

Second Floor

Slab/Crawlspace Option

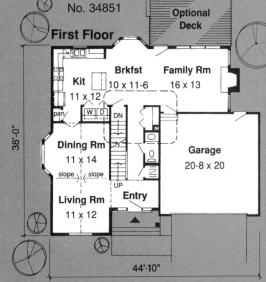

No. 20203
Contemporary with a Country Flair

- This plan features:
— Three bedrooms
— Two and a half baths

- A fireplaced Living Room flowing easily into the Dining Room which boasts a decorative ceiling

- A Master Suite with a walk-in closet and a private Master Bath

- Two additional bedrooms sharing a full sky-lit bath

FIRST FLOOR — 1,229 SQ. FT.
SECOND FLOOR — 515 SQ. FT.
GARAGE — 452 SQ. FT.

TOTAL LIVING AREA:
1,744 SQ. FT.

A Karl Kreeger Design

No. 20203

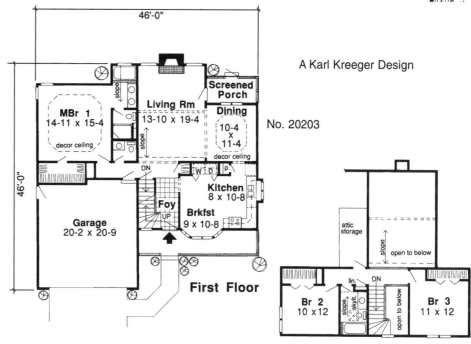

First Floor

46'-0"

46'-0"

MBr 1
14-11 x 15-4
decor ceiling

Living Rm
13-10 x 19-4

Screened Porch

Dining
10-4 X 11-4
decor ceiling

DN

W D

p.

Kitchen
8 x 10-8

Garage
20-2 x 20-9

Foy
UP

Brkfst
9 x 10-8

Second Floor

attic storage

slope
open to below

Br 2
10 x 12

lin.

DN

skylt.

open to below

Br 3
11 x 12

No. 10012
Rustic Design Blends into Hillside

■ This plan features:
— Three bedrooms
— Two and one half baths
■ A redwood deck that adapts equally to both lake and ocean settings
■ A Family Room measuring 36 feet long and leading out to a shaded patio
■ Fireplaces in both the Living Room and the Family Room
■ An open Kitchen with a laundry room for convenience

FIRST FLOOR — 1,198 SQ. FT.
BASEMENT — 1,198 SQ. FT.

TOTAL LIVING AREA: 1,198 SQ. FT.

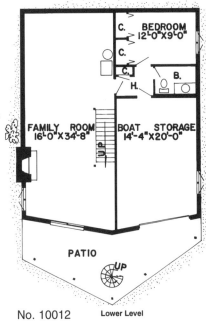

BEDROOM
12'-0"X9'-0"

C.
C.
C.
B.
H.

FAMILY ROOM
16'-0"X34'-8"

BOAT STORAGE
14'-4"X20'-0"

UP

PATIO   UP

No. 10012   **Lower Level**

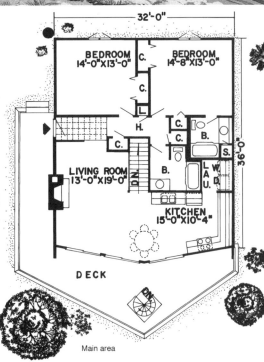

32'-0"

BEDROOM
14'-0"X13'-0"   BEDROOM
14'-8"X13'-0"

C.
C.
C.
L.
H.
C.
B.
S.

LIVING ROOM
13'-0"X19'-0"

DN   B.   LAU.   W. D.

KITCHEN
15'-0"X10'-4"

36'-0"

DECK   Main area

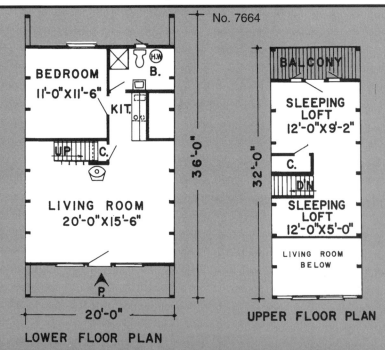

No. 7664
Easy to Build A-Frame

■ This plan features:
— Three bedrooms
— One full bath
■ A large deck expanding the living space to enjoy the outdoors
■ A two-story Living Room with an entry surrounded by windows, and a rustic interior with exposed beams
■ A galley Kitchen offering efficiency and easy access
■ A first floor bedroom convenient to a full bath
■ Two Loft areas for multiple uses

FIRST FLOOR — 560 SQ. FT.
SECOND FLOOR — 240 SQ. FT.

TOTAL LIVING AREA: 800 SQ. FT.

No. 7664

BEDROOM
11'-0"X11'-6"   B.   H.W

KIT.

UP   C.

LIVING ROOM
20'-0"X15'-6"

36'-0"

20'-0"

LOWER FLOOR PLAN

BALCONY

SLEEPING LOFT
12'-0"X9'-2"

C.

DN

SLEEPING LOFT
12'-0"X5'-0"

LIVING ROOM BELOW

32'-0"

UPPER FLOOR PLAN

No. 10108
Double Doors and Arches Give a Spanish Welcome

■ This plan features:
— Three bedrooms
— Two full and one half baths
■ Massive double doors opening to the foyer
■ A 27-foot Living Room to the right of the foyer
■ A large Master Bedroom with a walk-in closet and a private full bath

FIRST FLOOR — 1,176 SQ. FT.
SECOND FLOOR — 1,176 SQ. FT.
BASEMENT — 1,176 SQ. FT.
GARAGE — 576 SQ. FT.

TOTAL LIVING AREA: 2,352 SQ. FT.

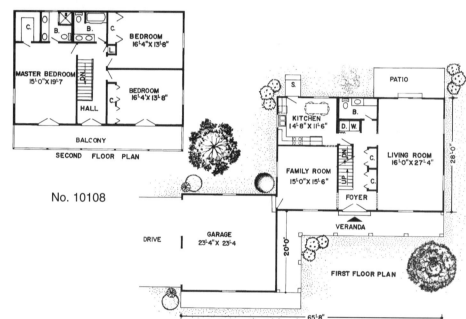

No. 10108

SECOND FLOOR PLAN

MASTER BEDROOM 15'-0" X 19'-7"
BEDROOM 16'-4" X 13'-8"
BEDROOM 16'-4" X 13'-8"
HALL
BALCONY

FIRST FLOOR PLAN

KITCHEN 14'-8" X 11'-6"
PATIO
LIVING ROOM 16'-0" X 27'-4"
FAMILY ROOM 15'-0" X 15'-6"
FOYER
VERANDA
GARAGE 23'-4" X 23'-4"
DRIVE

65'-8"

No. 10677
Arches Grace Classic Facade

■ This plan features:
— Three bedrooms
— Two and one half baths
■ Built-in planters and half walls to define rooms
■ A balcony that connects three upstairs bedrooms
■ Double sinks and built-in vanities in the Master Bath
■ Ample closet space

FIRST FLOOR — 932 SQ. FT.
SECOND FLOOR — 764 SQ. FT.
GARAGE — 430 SQ. FT.
BASEMENT — 920 SQ. FT.

TOTAL LIVING AREA:
1,696 SQ. FT.

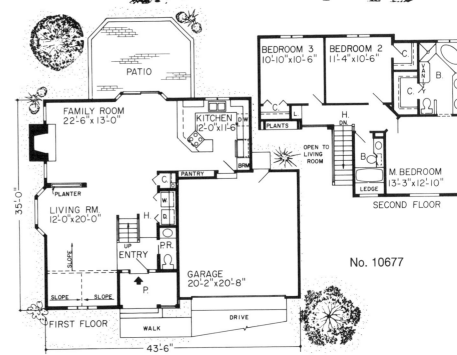

No. 10677

No. 20070
Sheltered Porch is an Inviting Entrance

■ This plan features:
— Three bedrooms
— Two and one half baths
■ A dramatic two-story entry
■ A fireplaced Living Room
■ A modern Kitchen flowing easily into a sunny Breakfast Nook
■ A formal Dining Room with elegant decorative ceiling
■ A Master Bedroom highlighted by a sky lit bath

FIRST FLOOR — 877 SQ. FT.
SECOND FLOOR — 910 SQ. FT.
BASEMENT — 877 SQ. FT.
GARAGE — 458 SQ. FT.

TOTAL LIVING AREA:
1,787 SQ. FT.

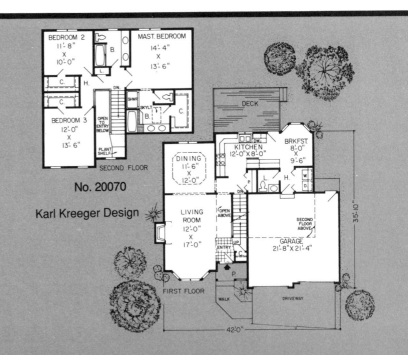

No. 20070

Karl Kreeger Design

No. 20102
Multi-Level Excitement

■ This plan features:
— Four bedrooms
— Two and a half baths

■ A sky-lit Breakfast Room with sliders to a rear deck

■ A sunken, fireplaced Living Room

■ An island Kitchen that serves both the formal Dining Room and the Breakfast Room easily

■ A spacious Master Suite with private bath and walk-in closet

■ A third floor containing the fourth Bedroom with a walk-in closet and sloping ceiling

First floor — 1,003 sq. ft.
Second floor — 808 sq. ft.
Third floor — 241 sq. ft.
Basement — 573 sq. ft.
Garage — 493 sq. ft.

TOTAL LIVING AREA:
2,052 sq. ft.

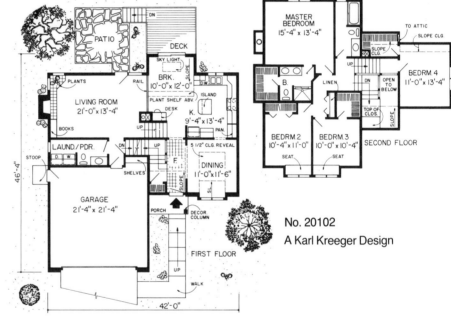

No. 20102

A Karl Kreeger Design

No. 20075
Compact and Appealing

■ This plan features:
— Three bedrooms
— Two full baths
■ A fireplaced Living Room and formal Dining Room with extra wide doorways
■ A centrally located Kitchen for maximum convenience
■ A Master Bedroom with vaulted ceiling and private Master Bath and walk-in closet

FIRST FLOOR — 1,682 SQ. FT.
BASEMENT — 1,682 SQ. FT.
GARAGE — 484 SQ. FT.

TOTAL LIVING AREA:
1,682 SQ. FT.

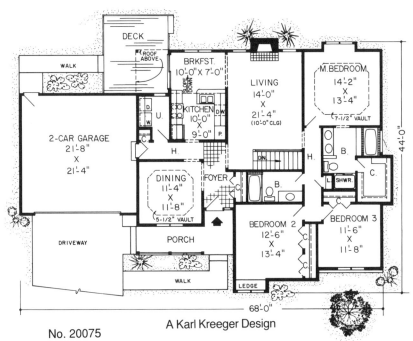

No. 20075

A Karl Kreeger Design

No. 20100
Wide Open and Convenient

A Karl Kreeger Design

■ This plan features:
— Three bedrooms
— Two full baths
■ Vaulted ceilings in the Dining Room and Master Bedroom
■ A sloped ceiling in the fireplaced Living Room
■ A skylight illuminating the Master Bath
■ A large Master Bedroom with walk-in closet

FIRST FLOOR — 1,727 SQ. FT.
BASEMENT — 1,727 SQ. FT.
GARAGE — 484 SQ. FT.

TOTAL LIVING AREA:
1,727 SQ. FT.

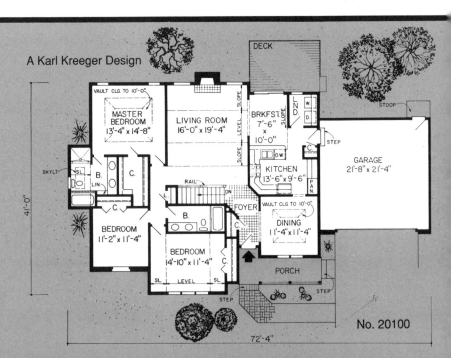

No. 20100

No. 10610
Entertaining is No Problem

■ This plan features:
— Three bedrooms
— Two and one half baths

■ A Master Bedroom privately set with a sitting area, full bath and walk-in closet

■ An island Kitchen centered between the Dining Room and Breakfast area

■ A sunken Living Room with vaulted ceilings and a two-way fireplace

■ A covered porch and enormous deck

FIRST FLOOR — 1,818 SQ. FT.
SECOND FLOOR — 528 SQ. FT.
BASEMENT — 1,818 SQ. FT.

TOTAL LIVING AREA:
2,346 SQ. FT.

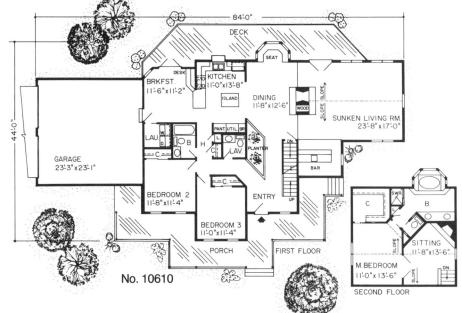

No. 10610

No. 24316
First Floor Master Suite

■ This plan features:
— Four bedrooms
— Two full and one half baths

■ A formal Living Room, with a distinctive boxed window, stepping down from an open Foyer and formal Dining Room

■ A bright, efficient Kitchen with a corner double sink, a bay window area for informal eating and open access to the Family Room and Patio

■ Unique corner fireplace in the Family Room serving as a cozy focal point

■ A first floor Master Suite featuring a double closet and a private Bath with a double vanity and a raised window tub

■ Three additional bedrooms on the second floor sharing a full hall bath

FIRST FLOOR — 1,400 SQ. FT.
SECOND FLOOR — 540 SQ. FT.

TOTAL LIVING AREA:
1,940 SQ. FT.

No. 24316

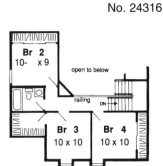

Second Floor

A Don Marshall Design

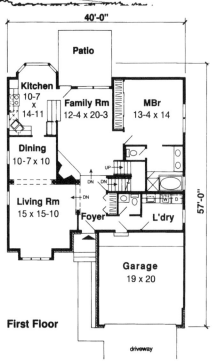

First Floor

No. 10839
Perfect Compact Ranch

■ This plan features:
— Two bedrooms
— Two full baths

■ A large, sunken Great Room with a cozy fireplace

■ A Master Bedroom with an unforgettable skylit Bathroom

■ A three-car Garage, with a work area for the family carpenter

■ A Kitchen with a Breakfast Nook for family gatherings

FIRST FLOOR — 1,738 SQ. FT.
BASEMENT — 1,083 SQ. FT.
GARAGE — 796 SQ. FT.

TOTAL LIVING AREA:
1,738 SQ. FT.

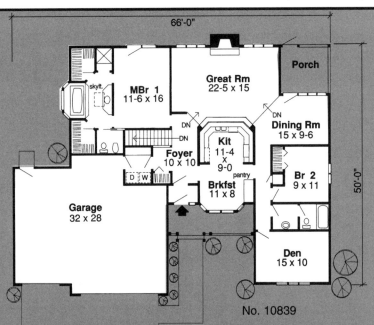

No. 10839

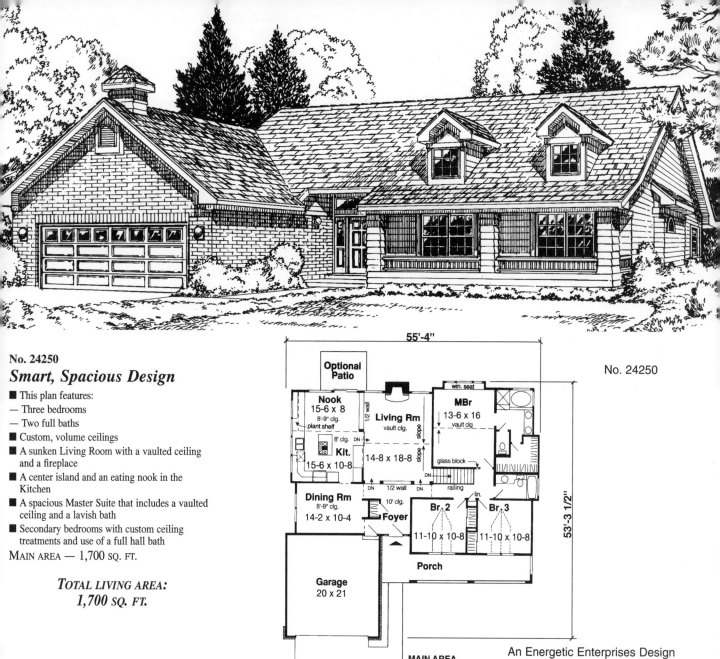

No. 24250
Smart, Spacious Design

■ This plan features:
— Three bedrooms
— Two full baths

■ Custom, volume ceilings

■ A sunken Living Room with a vaulted ceiling and a fireplace

■ A center island and an eating nook in the Kitchen

■ A spacious Master Suite that includes a vaulted ceiling and a lavish bath

■ Secondary bedrooms with custom ceiling treatments and use of a full hall bath

MAIN AREA — 1,700 SQ. FT.

TOTAL LIVING AREA:
1,700 SQ. FT.

No. 24250

Optional Patio

Nook
15-6 x 8
8'-9" clg.
plant shelf

1/2 wall

Living Rm
vault clg.

MBr
13-6 x 16
vault clg.

win. seat

8' clg.

Kit.
15-6 x 10-8

14-8 x 18-8

slope

DN

glass block

DN

DN

railing

1/2 wall

Dining Rm
8'-9" clg.
14-2 x 10-4

10' clg.

Foyer

Br. 2
11-10 x 10-8

lin.

Br. 3
11-10 x 10-8

Garage
20 x 21

Porch

55'-4"

53'-3 1/2"

MAIN AREA

An Energetic Enterprises Design

No. 10652
Two-Way Fireplace

■ This plan features:
— Three bedrooms
— Two and one half baths
■ A large Kitchen with cook-top island and a breakfast area opening to the deck
■ Built-in cedar closets and spacious bedrooms
■ A Master Suite loaded with a walk-in closet, skylight, double vanities and a sunken tub
■ A vaulted formal Dining Room and ceiling fans in the Kitchen and Living Room

FIRST FLOOR — 1,789 SQ. FT.
SECOND FLOOR — 568 SQ. FT.
BASEMENT — 1,789 SQ. FT.
GARAGE — 529 SQ. FT.

TOTAL LIVING AREA:
2,357 SQ. FT.

No. 10652
A Karl Kreeger Design

No. 10494
Window Dominates Facade

■ This plan features:
— Three bedrooms
— Two and one half baths
■ A large Fireplaced Living Room
■ A formal Dining Room
■ A large Kitchen with peninsula cooktop flowing into Breakfast Nook
■ A first floor Master Bedroom with private bath

FIRST FLOOR — 1,584 SQ. FT.
SECOND FLOOR — 599 SQ. FT.
BASEMENT — 1,584 SQ. FT.
GARAGE — 514 SQ. FT.

TOTAL LIVING AREA:
2,183 SQ. FT.

No. 10494

A Karl Kreeger Design

No. 10737

Modern Tudor is Hard to Resist

■ This plan features:
— Four bedrooms
— Three and one half baths
■ A seven-sided Breakfast room, an island Kitchen adjoining the Formal Dining Room
■ A beamed Family Room with private Study
■ A Master Suite complete with sauna, whirlpool, double vanity and fireplace

FIRST FLOOR — 2,457 SQ. FT.
SECOND FLOOR — 1,047 SQ. FT.
BASEMENT — 2,457 SQ. FT.
GARAGE — 837 SQ. FT.
SUN ROOM — 213 SQ. FT.

TOTAL LIVING AREA:
3,504 SQ. FT.

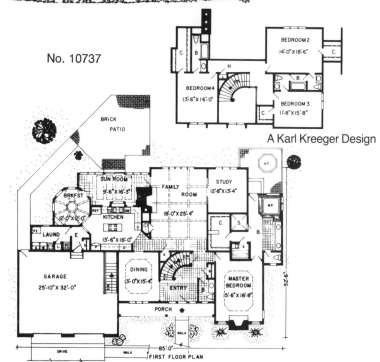

No. 10737

A Karl Kreeger Design

No. 20108
Windows Add Light and Space

■ This plan features:
— Three bedrooms
— Two full and one half bath

■ Shutters, round-cut shingles, and an attractive railed porch adding classic charm to the Traditional exterior of this home

■ A central entry leading to the formal Living Room and also to the informal Family Room

■ Elegant ceiling treatment and a room-size walk-in closet in the Master Suite

■ A Kitchen with a range-top island, bump-out window and a strategic location between the Family and Dining Rooms

FIRST FLOOR — 2,120 SQ. FT.
BASEMENT — 2,120 SQ. FT.
GARAGE — 576 SQ. FT.

TOTAL LIVING AREA:
2,120 SQ. FT.

A Karl Kreeger Design

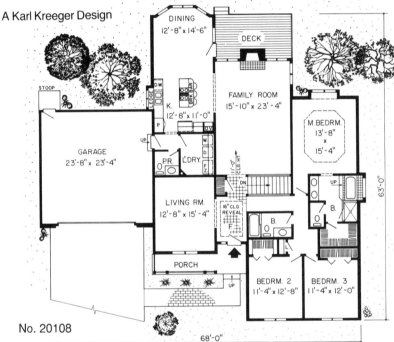

No. 20108

No. 34029
Skylight Brightens Master Bedroom

■ This plan features:
— Three bedrooms
— Two full baths

■ A covered-porch entry

■ A foyer separating the Dining Room from the Breakfast area and Kitchen

■ A Living Room enhanced by a vaulted beam ceiling and a fireplace

■ A Master Bedroom with a decorative ceiling and a skylight in the private bath

■ An optional deck accessible through sliding doors off the Master Bedroom

FIRST FLOOR — 1,698 SQ. FT.
GARAGE — 484 SQ. FT.

TOTAL LIVING AREA:
1,698 SQ. FT.

No. 34029

A Karl Kreeger Design

124

No. 20111
High Impact Family Home

- This plan features:
  — Four bedrooms
  — Two and one half baths
- A balcony linking the upstairs bedrooms and sky-lit bath dividing a two-story foyer
- A massive fireplace in the open Living Room
- A well-situated Kitchen handy to both the formal Dining Room and sunny Breakfast area
- A convenient, private first-floor Master Suite with a garden tub, step-in shower, and walk-in closet

First floor — 1,680 sq. ft.
Second floor — 514 sq. ft.
Basement — 1,045 sq. ft.
Garage — 635 sq. ft.

**Total living area:
2,194 sq. ft.**

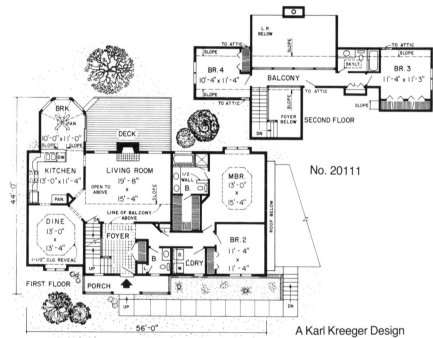

No. 20111

A Karl Kreeger Design

No. 9998
Exterior Promise of Luxury Fulfilled

■ This plan features:
— Three bedrooms
— Two full and one half baths
■ A Master Bedroom with a Lounge and a walk-in closet
■ A formal Living Room with exposed rustic beams and a cathedral ceiling
■ A Family Room equipped with a wood-burning fireplace
■ A Kitchen/Dinette with a built-in pantry and a peninsula counter

FIRST FLOOR — 2,333 SQ. FT.
BASEMENT — 2,333 SQ. FT.
GARAGE — 559 SQ. FT.

TOTAL LIVING AREA:
2,333 SQ. FT.

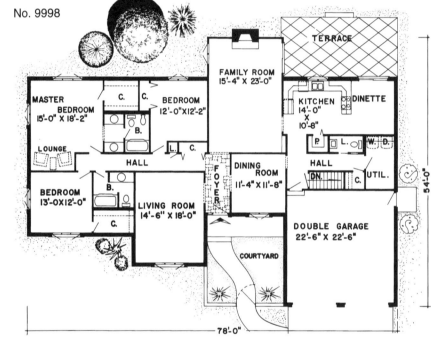

No. 9998

TERRACE

FAMILY ROOM
15'-4" X 23'-0"

MASTER BEDROOM
15'-0" X 18'-2"

C. C.

BEDROOM
12'-0" X 12'-2"

KITCHEN
14'-0" X 10'-8"

DINETTE

B.

LOUNGE

L. C.

HALL

P. L. W.D.

FOYER

DINING ROOM
11'-4" X 11'-8"

HALL

DN. C. UTIL.

BEDROOM
13'-0 X 12'-0"

B.

LIVING ROOM
14'-6" X 18'-0"

DOUBLE GARAGE
22'-6" X 22'-6"

C.

COURTYARD

54'-0"

78'-0"

No. 24262
Attractively Styled Roof

■ This plan features:
— Four bedrooms
— Two full and one half bath
■ A see-through fireplace between the Living and Family Rooms
■ A Kitchen with an island, built-in pantry, and double sink
■ A Master Bedroom with a vaulted ceiling, a double vanity, a linen closet, a corner tub, a separate shower, compartmented toilet, and huge walk-in closet
■ Three bedrooms, one with walk-in closet, share full hall Bath

FIRST FLOOR — 1,241 SQ. FT.
SECOND FLOOR — 1,170 SQ. FT.

TOTAL LIVING AREA:
2,411 SQ. FT.

An Energetic Enterprises Design

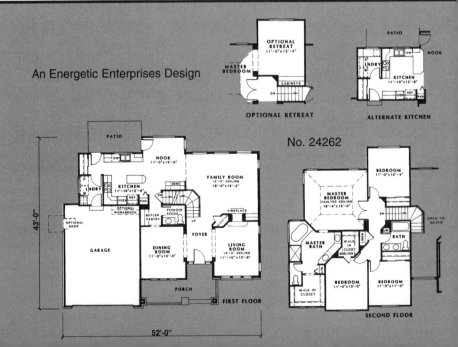

OPTIONAL RETREAT
11'-0" X 12'-4"

MASTER BEDROOM

CABINETS

OPTIONAL RETREAT

PATIO

NOOK

LNDRY

KITCHEN
11'-10" X 13'-8"

ALTERNATE KITCHEN

No. 24262

PATIO

NOOK
11'-0" X 13'-0"

KITCHEN
11'-10" X 13'-8"

FAMILY ROOM
13'-0" X 18'-0" CEILING

DESK

BEDROOM
11'-0" X 12'-4"

LNDRY

OPTIONAL WORKBENCH

BUTLER PANTRY

POWDER ROOM

UP

FIREPLACE

MASTER BEDROOM
VAULTED CEILING
16'-4" X 18'-0"

WALK IN CLOSET SHELVES

BATH

OPTIONAL DOOR

GARAGE

DINING ROOM
11'-8" X 13'-0"

FOYER

LIVING ROOM
11'-10" X 13'-8" CEILING

MASTER BATH

OPEN TO BELOW

PORCH

FIRST FLOOR

WALK IN CLOSET

BEDROOM
11'-0" X 13'-0"

BEDROOM
11'-0" X 11'-0"

SECOND FLOOR

43'-0"

52'-0"

126

No. 10593
Victorian Details

■ This plan features:
— Four bedrooms
— Two and one half baths

■ A large country Kitchen in full view of a breakfast area

■ A fireplace shared by the cozy Living Room and the Family Room containing a bar and access to the patio

■ Octagonal recessed ceilings in the formal Dining Room

■ Walk-in closets enhancing all the bedrooms

FIRST FLOOR — 1,450 SQ. FT.
SECOND FLOOR — 1,341 SQ. FT.
BASEMENT — 1,450 SQ. FT.
GARAGE — 629 SQ. FT.
COVERED PORCH — 144 SQ. FT.
WOOD STORAGE — 48 SQ. FT.

TOTAL LIVING AREA:
2,791 SQ. FT.

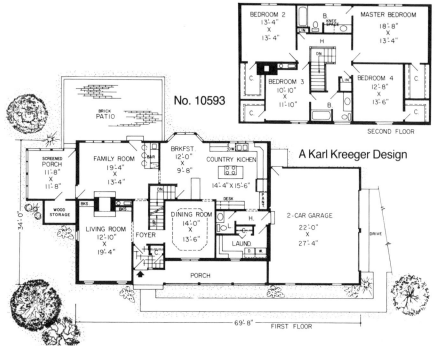

No. 10593

A Karl Kreeger Design

No. 10386
Modified Cape with Passive Solar Features

■ This plan features:
— Three bedrooms
— Two baths

■ A solar greenhouse on the south side of the home employing energy storage rods and water to capture the sun's warmth

■ Triple glazed windows for energy efficiency

■ A Living Room accentuated by a heat circulating fireplace

■ Sliding doors leading from the sitting area of the Master Bedroom to a private patio

■ A Garage with a large storage area

FIRST FLOOR — 1,164 SQ. FT.
SECOND FLOOR — 574 SQ. FT.
BASEMENT — 1,164 SQ. FT.
GARAGE & STORAGE AREA — 574 SQ. FT.
GREENHOUSE — 238 SQ. FT.

TOTAL LIVING AREA:
1,738 SQ. FT.

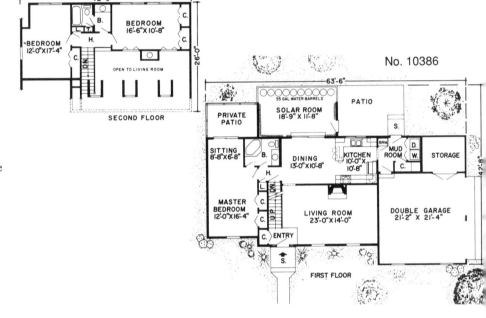

No. 20146
Family Favorite

■ This plan features:
— Three bedrooms
— Two full baths

■ A sky-lit breakfast bay

■ A Dining Room with recessed ceilings

■ A Master Suite featuring double vanitied bath and walk-in closet

FIRST FLOOR — 1,352 SQ. FT.
SECOND FLOOR — 736 SQ. FT.
BASEMENT — 1,340 SQ. FT.
GARAGE — 490 SQ. FT.

TOTAL LIVING AREA:
2,088 SQ. FT.

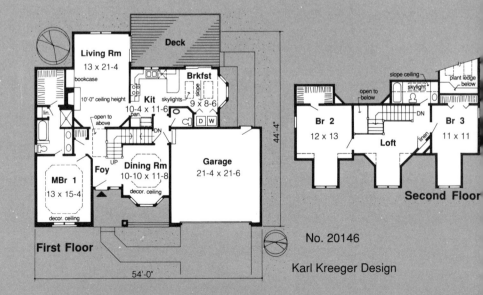

No. 20146

Karl Kreeger Design

No. 10533
Master Suite Dominates Second Floor

■ This plan features:
— Three bedrooms
— Two and one half baths

■ A Master Suite including a sitting room plus individual walk-in closets and baths

■ A formal Parlor and Dining Room

■ A Great Room with a massive fireplace and a bar

■ A convenient laundry area accessing the three car Garage

FIRST FLOOR — 1,669 SQ. FT.
SECOND FLOOR — 1,450 SQ. FT.
BASEMENT — 1,653 SQ. FT.
GARAGE — 823 SQ. FT.

TOTAL LIVING AREA: 3,119 SQ. FT.

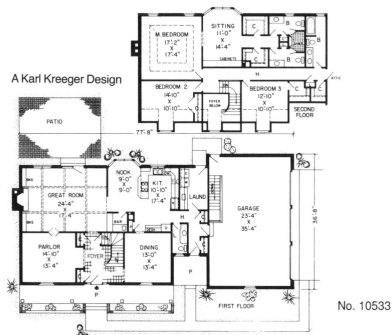

A Karl Kreeger Design

No. 10533

No. 10689
Elegant and Inviting

■ This plan features:
— Five bedrooms
— Three and one half baths
■ Wrap-around veranda's and a three-season porch
■ An elegant Parlor with a parquets floor and formal Dining Room separated by a half-wall
■ An adjoining Kitchen with a Breakfast bar and nook
■ A Gathering Room with a fireplace, soaring ceilings and access to the porch

FIRST FLOOR — 1,580 SQ. FT.
SECOND FLOOR — 1,164 SQ. FT.
BASEMENT — 1,329 SQ. FT.
GARAGE — 576 SQ. FT.

TOTAL LIVING AREA:
2,744 SQ. FT.

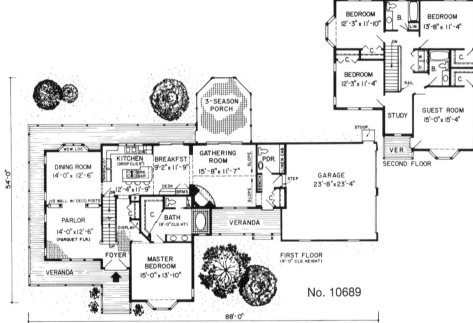

No. 10690
Gingerbread Charm

■ This plan features:
— Three bedrooms
— Two and one half baths
■ A wrap-around porch and rear deck adding lots of extra living space
■ A formal Parlor and Dining Room just off the central entry
■ A Family Room with a fireplace
■ A Master Suite complete with five-sided sitting nook, walk-in closets and a sunken tub

FIRST FLOOR — 1,260 SQ. FT.
SECOND FLOOR — 1,021 SQ. FT.
BASEMENT — 1,186 SQ. FT.
GARAGE — 840 SQ. FT.

TOTAL LIVING AREA:
2,281 SQ. FT.

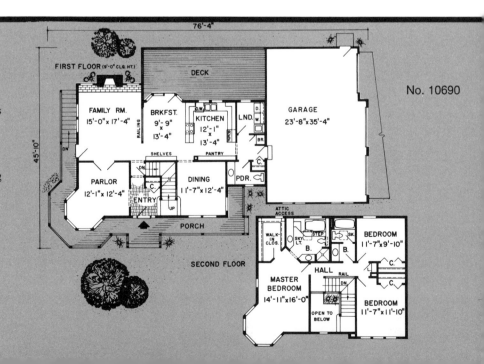

No. 20212
Vaulted Ceilings Add Architectural Interest

■ This plan features:
— Four bedrooms
— Three full baths
■ A formal Living Room with a cozy fireplace
■ An elegant formal Dining Room with a vaulted ceiling
■ A gourmet Kitchen with a center island, a double sink and ample cabinet and counter space
■ A Master Suite with a vaulted ceiling, master bath and walk-in closet
■ Two additional bedrooms on the main floor share a full bath
■ A Recreation Room and fourth bedroom with a walk-in closet on the lower floor

MAIN FLOOR — 1,923 SQ. FT.
LOWER FLOOR — 777 SQ. FT.
GARAGE — 1,046 SQ. FT.
BASEMENT — 684 SQ. FT.

TOTAL LIVING AREA:
2,700 SQ. FT.

No. 20212

A Karl Kreeger Design

No materials list available

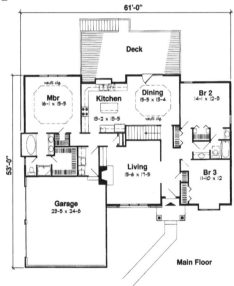

No. 10536
Covered Drive and Entrance Add Touch of Elegance to Spanish Ranch

■ This plan features:
— Four bedrooms
— Four and two half baths

■ An impressive covered entry leading to the tiled foyer

■ Two patios offering ample space for outdoor entertaining

■ A spacious Hearth Room accented by a massive fireplace and a bar

■ A roomy Kitchen with the convenience of an island and plenty of cabinet space

■ A scenic garden court dividing bedrooms three and four

FIRST FLOOR — 3,972 SQ. FT.
BASEMENT — 3,972 SQ. FT.
GARAGE — 924 SQ. FT.

TOTAL LIVING AREA: 3,972 SQ. FT.

Karl Kreeger Design

No. 10536

No. 9828
Superior Comfort and Privacy

■ This plan features:
— Four bedrooms
— Three full baths

■ A natural stone exterior with slate floors in the foyer and leading to the private patio off the Master Bedroom

■ A two way fireplace between the Living Room and Family Room

■ A breakfast nook with a large bow window facing the terrace and pool

■ Four bedrooms grouped in one wing for privacy

FIRST FLOOR — 2,679 SQ. FT.
BASEMENT — 2,679 SQ. FT.
GARAGE — 541 SQ. FT.

TOTAL LIVING AREA: 2,679 SQ. FT.

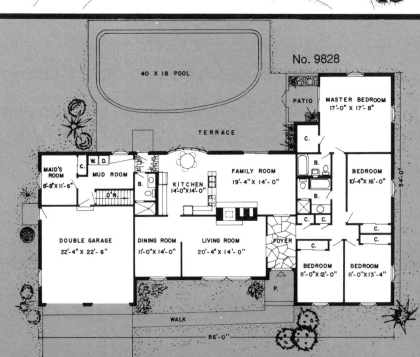

No. 9828

No. 10507
Central Courtyard Features Pool

■ This plan features:
— Three bedrooms
— Two baths

■ A central courtyard complete with a pool

■ A secluded Master Bedroom accented by a sky light, spacious walk-in closet, and private bath

■ A convenient Kitchen easily serving the patio for comfortable outdoor entertaining

■ A detached two-car Garage

FIRST FLOOR — 2,194 SQ. FT.
GARAGE — 576 SQ. FT.

TOTAL LIVING AREA:
2,194 SQ. FT.

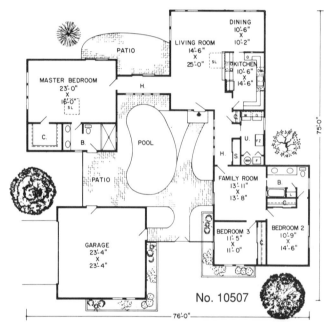

No. 10507

No. 34705
Colonial Home with All the Traditional Comforts

■ This plan features:
— Four bedrooms
— Two and one half baths

■ A formal Living Room and Dining Room flanking a spacious entry

■ Family areas flowing together into an open space at the rear of the home

■ An island Kitchen with a built-in pantry centrally located for easy service to the Dining Room and Breakfast area

■ A Master Suite including large closets and double vanities in the bath

FIRST FLOOR — 1,090 SQ. FT.
SECOND FLOOR — 1,134 SQ. FT.
BASEMENT — 1,090 SQ. FT.
GARAGE — 576 SQ. FT.

TOTAL LIVING AREA:
2,224 SQ. FT.

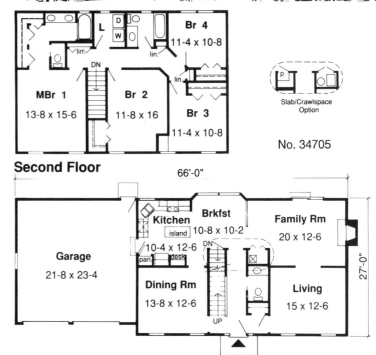

Second Floor

No. 34705

No. 270
Family Living for the Budget Minded

■ This plan features:
— Four bedrooms
— Three baths

■ A large efficient U-shaped Kitchen with double sink, ample cabinet and storage space and a peninsula counter dividing it from the Dining Room

■ A lovely Dining Room with access to a balcony and built-in china cabinet

■ A Master Suite with access to the balcony and a full private bath

■ Two additional first floor bedrooms, with ample closet space, that share a full hall bath

■ A lower floor equipped with Recreation Room, Hobby Room, Workshop and a bedroom with private bath

FIRST FLOOR — 1,456 SQ. FT.
LOWER FLOOR — 1,456 SQ. FT.
GARAGE — 528 SQ. FT.

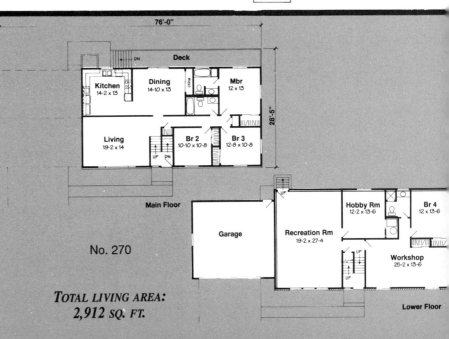

No. 270

TOTAL LIVING AREA:
2,912 SQ. FT.

No. 20149
Colonial Classic

■ This plan features:
— Four bedrooms
— Two and one half baths
■ A range-top island Kitchen which has double sinks, and built-in desk
■ A built-in bar in the Family Room with decorative beamed ceiling, and a fireplace
■ A decorative ceiling in the Breakfast area with access to an expansive deck
■ A second-floor Master Suite with his and hers walk-in closets, luxury sky-lit bath and elegant decorative ceilings
■ Three additional bedrooms, each with walk-in closets, that share a full bath

FIRST FLOOR — 1,508 SQ. FT.
SECOND FLOOR — 1,722 SQ. FT.
BASEMENT — 1,494 SQ. FT.
GARAGE — 599 SQ. FT.

TOTAL LIVING AREA:
3,230 SQ. FT.

Second Floor

Br 2
13 x 13-4

Br 4
17-6 x 12

MBr 1
15-10 x 18-4

Br 3
12 x 14-8

DN linen

Balcony

decor. ceiling

Deck

Brkfst
10 x 12-8

Kitchen
12 x 13-4

Dining Rm
13-4 x 13-10

Garage
23-8 x 25-4

decor. ceiling

Parlor
15-10 x 18-4

Family Rm
15-10 x 18-4

9'-0" ceiling height

Foyer

decor. beams

DN

UP

balcony above

bar

39'-6"

68'-0"

First Floor

No. 20149

A Karl Kreeger Design

No. 20363
Comfort and Convenience

- This plan features:
- — Three bedrooms
- — Two and one half baths
- Transom windows, skylights, and an open plan combining to make this brick classic a sun-filled retreat
- Soaring ceilings in the foyer
- A Family Room including a fireplace and open access to the Kitchen and Breakfast area
- An island Kitchen with a built-in bar to make mealtime preparation a breeze
- A luxurious Master Suite with a vaulted bath area including a garden spa
- Two good-size bedrooms on the second floor, sharing a full hall bath

FIRST FLOOR — 1,859 SQ. FT.
SECOND FLOOR — 579 SQ. FT.
BASEMENT — 1,859 SQ. FT.
GARAGE — 622 SQ. FT.

TOTAL LIVING AREA:
2,438 SQ. FT.

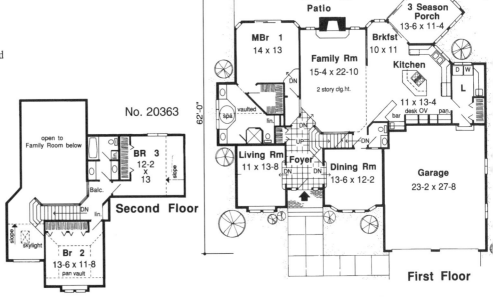

No. 20363

Second Floor

First Floor

No. 10537
Accent on Spiral Staircase

- This plan features:
- — Four bedrooms
- — Four and one half baths
- A roomy kitchen complete with a pantry and lots of cabinet space
- A unique Morning Room complemented by a large fireplace and an entrance to the patio for year round enjoyment
- Four bedrooms, each with walk-in closets and private baths

FIRST FLOOR — 3,282 SQ. FT.
SECOND FLOOR — 956 SQ. FT.
BASEMENT — 3,235 SQ. FT.
GARAGE — 936 SQ. FT.

TOTAL LIVING AREA:
4,238 SQ. FT.

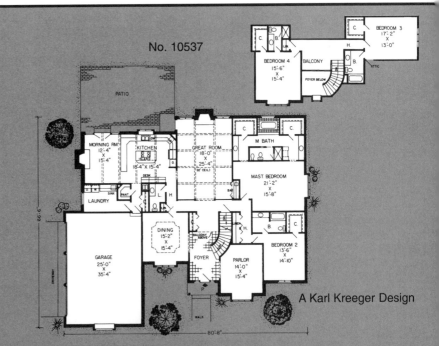

No. 10537

A Karl Kreeger Design

No. 10544
Split Level Tudor Offers Comfort and Versatility

■ This plan features:
— Three bedrooms
— Two full baths

■ A spacious Kitchen adjoining a formal Dining Room

■ A large Family Room on the lower floor enhanced by a large fireplace

■ A bay window in the Dining Room providing a touch of elegance for entertaining

FIRST FLOOR — 1,366 SQ. FT.
LOWER FLOOR — 384 SQ. FT.
BASEMENT — 631 SQ. FT.
GARAGE — 528 SQ. FT.

TOTAL LIVING AREA: 1,750 SQ. FT.

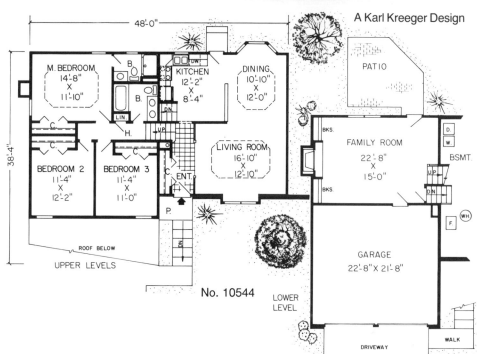

A Karl Kreeger Design

48'-0"

M. BEDROOM
14'-8"
X
11'-10"

KITCHEN
12'-2"
X
8'-4"

DINING
10'-10"
X
12'-0"

38'-4"

BEDROOM 2
11'-4"
X
12'-2"

BEDROOM 3
11'-4"
X
11'-0"

LIVING ROOM
16'-10"
X
12'-10"

ENT.

ROOF BELOW

UPPER LEVELS

No. 10544

PATIO

FAMILY ROOM
22'-8"
X
15'-0"

BSMT.

GARAGE
22'-8" X 21'-8"

LOWER LEVEL

DRIVEWAY

WALK

No. 10451
Secluded Bedroom

■ This plan features:

— Four bedrooms

— Three full and one half bath

■ A secluded Master Bedroom with a charming fireplace, individual dressing areas, and a sky-lit bathroom

■ A court yard effect created by the glassed-in living spaces overlooking the central covered patio

■ A sprawling charm which creates a sense of privacy everywhere you go

FIRST FLOOR — 2,864 SQ. FT.
GARAGE — 607 SQ. FT.

TOTAL LIVING AREA:
2,864 SQ. FT.

No. 10451

No. 10555
Stucco and Stone

■ This plan features:

— Three bedrooms

— Two and one half baths

■ A formal foyer leading through double doors into a well-designed library

■ A Master Bedroom offering vaulted ceilings and a huge bath area

■ An oversized Living Room with a fireplace

■ A utility room and half bath located next to the Garage

FIRST FLOOR — 1,671 SQ. FT.
SECOND FLOOR — 505 SQ. FT.
BASEMENT — 1,661 SQ. FT.
GARAGE — 604 SQ. FT.
SCREENED PORCH — 114 SQ. FT.

TOTAL LIVING AREA:
2,176 SQ. FT.

A Karl Kreeger Design   No. 10555

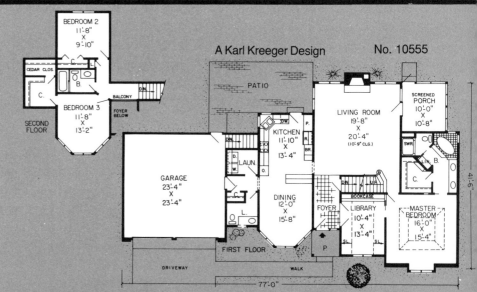

No. 10535

Bridge Over Foyer Introduces Unique Features of Four Bedroom

■ This plan features:
— Four bedrooms
— Two full and two half baths

■ A dramatic two-story foyer opening into a Great Room with a cathedral ceiling

■ A Great Room with a cozy fireplace framed by a bookcase

■ A foyer flanked by a Parlor and the formal Dining Room

■ A spacious Kitchen complete with an octagonal Breakfast nook tucked into a bank of windows

■ A first floor Master Bedroom including a quaint but roomy sitting room

FIRST FLOOR — 2,335 SQ. FT.
SECOND FLOOR — 1,157 SQ. FT.
BASEMENT — 2,281 SQ. FT.
GARAGE — 862 SQ. FT.

TOTAL LIVING AREA: 3,492 SQ. FT.

A Karl Kreeger Design

No. 10535

No. 34600
Rustic Exterior; Complete Home

■ This plan features:
— Three bedrooms
— Two full baths
■ A two-story, fireplaced Living Room with exposed beams add to rustic charm
■ An efficient, modern Kitchen with ample work and storage space
■ Two first floor bedrooms with individual closet space share full bath
■ A Master Bedroom with privacy of second floor and its own full bath
■ A welcoming front Porch adding to living space

FIRST FLOOR — 1,013 SQ. FT.
SECOND FLOOR — 315 SQ. FT.
BASEMENT — 1,008 SQ. FT.

TOTAL LIVING AREA:
1,328 SQ. FT.

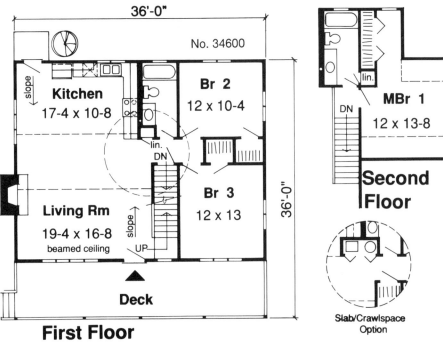

36'-0"

No. 34600

Kitchen
17-4 x 10-8

slope

Br 2
12 x 10-4

lin.

DN

Br 3
12 x 13

36'-0"

Living Rm
19-4 x 16-8
beamed ceiling

slope

UP

Deck

First Floor

MBr 1
12 x 13-8

lin.

DN

Second Floor

Slab/Crawlspace Option

No. 34003
Delightful, Compact Home

■ This plan features:
— Three bedrooms
— Two full baths
■ A fireplaced Living Room brightened by a wonderful picture window
■ A counter island featuring double sinks separating the Kitchen and Dining areas
■ A Master Bedroom including private Master Bath and double closets
■ Two additional bedrooms with ample closet space and share full bath

FIRST FLOOR — 1,146 SQ. FT.

TOTAL LIVING AREA:
1,146 SQ. FT.

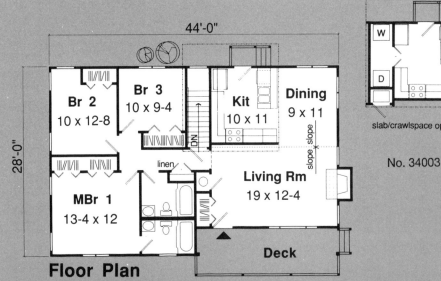

44'-0"

Br 2
10 x 12-8

Br 3
10 x 9-4

Kit
10 x 11

Dining
9 x 11

28'-0"

DN

linen

slope slope

MBr 1
13-4 x 12

Living Rm
19 x 12-4

Deck

Floor Plan

W

D

slab/crawlspace option

No. 34003

No. 20501
Home on a Hill

- ■ This plan features:
  - — Three bedrooms
  - — Two full baths
- ■ Window walls combining with sliders to unite active areas with a huge outdoor deck
- ■ Interior spaces flowing together for an open feeling that is accentuated by the sloping ceilings and towering fireplace in the Living Room
- ■ An island Kitchen with easy access to the Dining Room
- ■ A Master Suite complete with a garden spa, abundant closet space, and a balcony

FIRST FLOOR — 1,316 SQ. FT.
SECOND FLOOR — 592 SQ. FT.

TOTAL LIVING AREA: 1,908 SQ. FT.

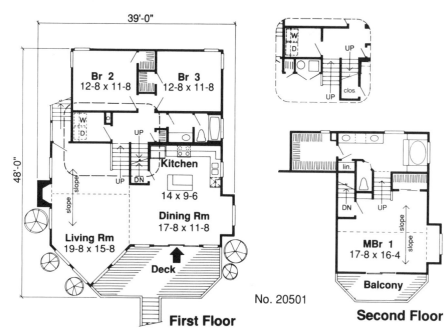

39'-0"

48'-0"

Br 2
12-8 x 11-8

Br 3
12-8 x 11-8

W/D

UP

slope

slope

UP DN

Kitchen
14 x 9-6

Dining Rm
17-8 x 11-8

Living Rm
19-8 x 15-8

Deck

First Floor

No. 20501

W D UP

UP clos

lin.

DN UP

slope
slope

MBr 1
17-8 x 16-4

Balcony

Second Floor

No. 34005
Decorative Detailing Adds Charm

■ This plan features:
— Three bedrooms
— One and one half baths

■ A Living Room with a cozy fireplace and sloped ceiling

■ An efficient Kitchen equipped with a plant shelf and within easy access to the Dining Room

■ A Master Bedroom with a decorative ceiling and a private bath

■ A second bath equipped with a washer and dryer

FIRST FLOOR — 1,441 SQ. FT.

GARAGE — 672 SQ. FT.

TOTAL LIVING AREA:
1,441 SQ. FT.

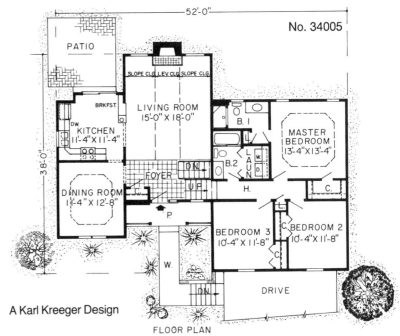

No. 34005

A Karl Kreeger Design

FLOOR PLAN

No. 10493
Raised Ranch Offers Optional Basement Family Room

■ This plan features:
— Three bedrooms
— Two baths (optional future 1/2 bath)

■ A space saving lower level Garage offering the option of finishing the adjacent area at a future date

■ A Master Bedroom including walk-in closets

■ An activity area combining the Living and Dining Rooms into an open living space

■ A compact Kitchen packed with storage and a convenient laundry nook

FIRST FLOOR — 1,152 SQ. FT.

GARAGE — 572 SQ. FT.

BASEMENT — 550 SQ. FT.

TOTAL LIVING AREA:
1,152 SQ. FT.

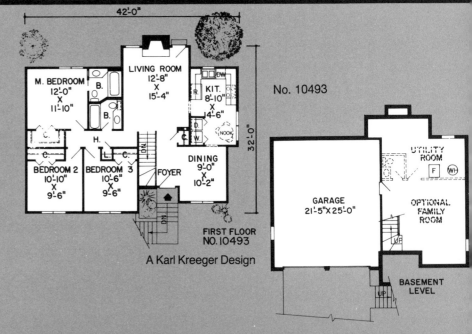

No. 10493

FIRST FLOOR
NO. 10493

A Karl Kreeger Design

BASEMENT LEVEL

144

No. 10643
Low Maintenance, Southwestern Style

■ This plan features:
— Three bedrooms
— Two full baths

■ A cheerful Kitchen with a Breakfast bar and entry onto the patio

■ A sky-lit bath and huge bay window illuminating the Master Suite

■ A spacious Living Room, convenient Dining Room, and a handy utility room

FIRST FLOOR — 1,285 SQ. FT.
GARAGE — 473 SQ. FT.

TOTAL LIVING AREA:
1,285 SQ. FT.

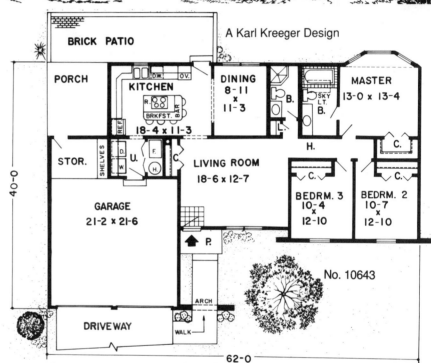

A Karl Kreeger Design

BRICK PATIO

PORCH

KITCHEN
18-4 x 11-3

DINING
8-11
x
11-3

MASTER
13-0 x 13-4

B.

SKY LT.

B.

STOR.

SHELVES

D.
W

U.
F.
H.

C

LIVING ROOM
18-6 x 12-7

H.

C.

C.

C.

C.

GARAGE
21-2 x 21-6

BEDRM. 3
10-4
x
12-10

BEDRM. 2
10-7
x
12-10

P.

40-0

No. 10643

ARCH

DRIVEWAY

WALK

62-0

No. 10292
Airy Design With Decks

- This plan features:
— Two or three bedrooms
— Two and a half baths
- Contemporary styling with cathedral ceilings and gable end windows
- A formal Living Room leading to the formal Dining Room for a smooth transition when entertaining
- An efficient U-shaped Kitchen with a double sink, ample counter and cabinet space and a built-in broom closet
- A sunken Family Room equipped with two closets and sliding doors to the patio
- A Master Bedroom with a full Bath, a walk-in closet and a private deck
- A bright second bedroom with access, through sliding glass doors, to a large sun deck and conveniently near the full hall bath
- A sunny Sitting Room with sliding glass doors to the sun deck, could also be the perfect guest room or study

FIRST FLOOR — 1,145 SQ. FT.
SECOND FLOOR — 864 SQ. FT.
BASEMENT — 1,145 SQ. FT.
GARAGE — 568 SQ. FT.

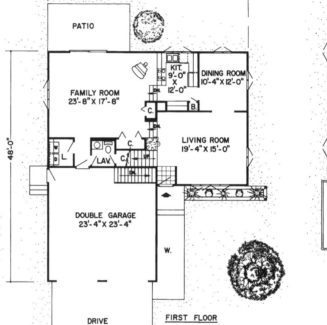

No. 10292

TOTAL LIVING AREA:
2,009 SQ. FT.

No. 10421
Numerous Options Abound

- This plan features:
— Three bedrooms
— Two full and one half baths
- A sheltered entrance leading into an Entry which opens into an expansive Living Room featuring a hearth fireplace, built-in shelves and a wall of windows
- A sunken Dining Room accented by large picture windows and adjacent to Kitchen
- A well-planned Kitchen includes an eating bar and a Nook with easy access to the Laundry area, the Garage and the covered patio
- A Master Suite includes a plush bath and double walk-in closets
- Second floor features two additional bedrooms and a Game Room which share a full hall bath

FIRST FLOOR — 1,605 SQ. FT.
SECOND FLOOR — 732 SQ. FT.
GARAGE — 525 SQ. FT.
PATIO — 395 SQ. FT.

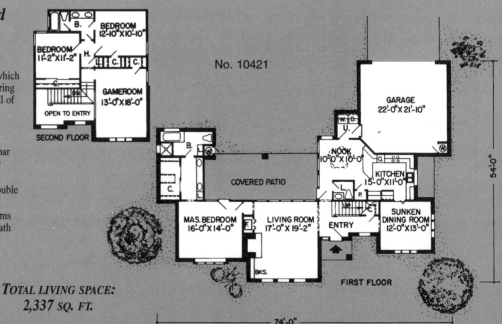

No. 10421

TOTAL LIVING SPACE:
2,337 SQ. FT.

146

No. 24319
Home With Many Views

■ This plan features:

— Three bedrooms

— Two full baths

■ Large Decks and windows taking full advantage of the view

■ A fireplace that divides the Living Room from the Dining Room

■ A Kitchen flowing into the Dining Room

■ A Master Bedroom with full Master Bath

■ A Recreation Room sporting a whirlpool tub and a bar

MAIN FLOOR — 728 SQ. FT.

UPPER FLOOR — 573 SQ. FT.

LOWER FLOOR — 379 SQ. FT.

GARAGE — 240 SQ. FT.

**TOTAL LIVING AREA:
1,680 SQ. FT.**

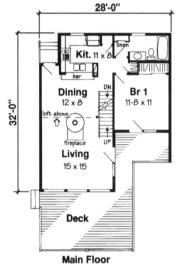

Main Floor

No. 24319

A Don Marshall Design

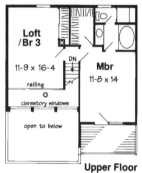

Upper Floor

Lower Floor

No. 20171
Family Home with Flair

■ This plan features:
— Three bedrooms
— Two full baths

■ A classic brick and clapboard exterior

■ A central foyer to an island Kitchen with adjoining formal Dining Room made elegant by floor-to-ceiling window

■ A spacious Living Room with soaring ceilings and sizzling fireplace with sliders to an outdoor deck

FIRST FLOOR — 1,349 SQ. FT.
SECOND FLOOR — 590 SQ. FT.
BASEMENT — 1,342 SQ. FT.
GARAGE — 480 SQ. FT.

**TOTAL LIVING AREA:
1,939 SQ. FT.**

A Karl Kreeger Design

No. 20171
First Floor

Second Floor

No. 20193
Interesting Angles

■ This plan features:
— Three bedrooms
— Two full and one half baths

■ A wrap-around shaped Kitchen with built-in pantry, snack bar counter and double sinks

■ A diamond-shaped Breakfast area that overlooks the deck

■ A spacious Living Room with a wonderful fireplace to add warmth and atmosphere

■ A Master Suite with decorative ceiling and luxury bath with walk-in closet

■ Two additional bedrooms that share a sky-lit full hall bath

FIRST FLOOR — 2,250 SQ. FT.
GARAGE — 573 SQ. FT.
BASEMENT — 2,291 SQ. FT.

**TOTAL LIVING AREA:
2,250 SQ. FT.**

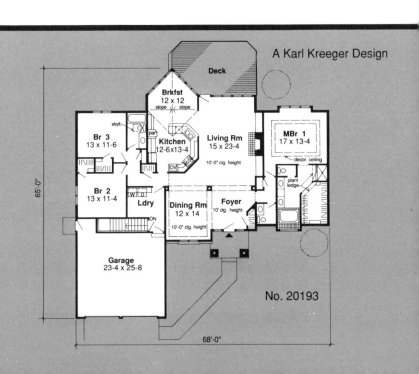

A Karl Kreeger Design

No. 20193

No. 20066
Cathedral Window Graced by Massive Arch

■ This plan features:
— Three bedrooms
— Two full baths

■ A tiled threshold providing a distinctive entrance

■ A comfortable Living Room with a wood-burning fireplace and tiled hearth

■ A Dining Room with vaulted ceiling

■ A Kitchen with central work island, pantry, planning desk, and Breakfast area

■ A Master Suite with decorative ceilings, Master Bath and bow window

FIRST FLOOR — 1,850 SQ. FT.
BASEMENT — 1,850 SQ. FT.
GARAGE — 503 SQ. FT.

TOTAL LIVING AREA:
1,850 SQ. FT.

63'-8"

DECK

BRKFST.
9'-0" X 10'-0"

LIVING ROOM
16'-10" X 19'-6"

MASTER BEDROOM
16'-0 X 13'-4"

B. 1

KITCHEN
13'-0"X 11'-0"

DW

PANT. DESK

DOWN 13 R.

RAIL

CLO.

HALL

52'-0"

DINING ROOM
11'-8" X 11'-10"

FOYER

COURT

S.

LAUN.

W. D.

S.

B. 2

BEDROOM 2
11'-4" X 13'-10"

BEDROOM 3
11'-4" X 13'-10"

2-CAR GARAGE
21'-4" X 21'-8"

W.

No. 20066

FLOOR PLAN

DRIVE

A Karl Kreeger Design

No. 20400
Rustic Contemporary

■ This plan features:
— Three bedrooms:
— Two and a half baths
■ A Master Suite in its own wing, complete with his and her walk-in closets, a luxury bath and private rear deck
■ A two-way fireplace separating the Living Room and Dining Room combination
■ A Kitchen, Breakfast Room and Family Room flowing easily into each other

FIRST FLOOR— 2,279 SQ. FT.
LOFT — 338 SQ. FT.
BASEMENT — 2,317 SQ. FT.
GARAGE — 478 SQ. FT.

TOTAL LIVING AREA:
2,617 SQ. FT.

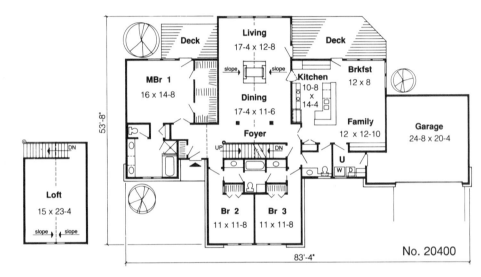

No. 10550
Enjoy the Backyard Views

Karl Kreeger Design

■ This plan features:
— Four bedrooms
— Three full and two half baths
■ Recessed ceilings in the Dining Room and Master Bedroom
■ A sun porch off the Breakfast Nook
■ Two full baths and two convenient baths located on the second floor
■ A full Basement foundation

FIRST FLOOR — 2,069 SQ. FT.
SECOND FLOOR — 821 SQ. FT.
BASEMENT — 2,045 SQ. FT.
GARAGE — 562 SQ. FT.

TOTAL LIVING AREA:
2,890 SQ. FT.

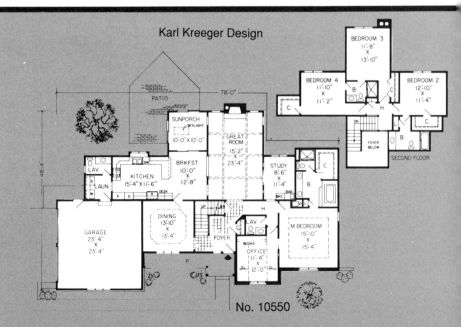

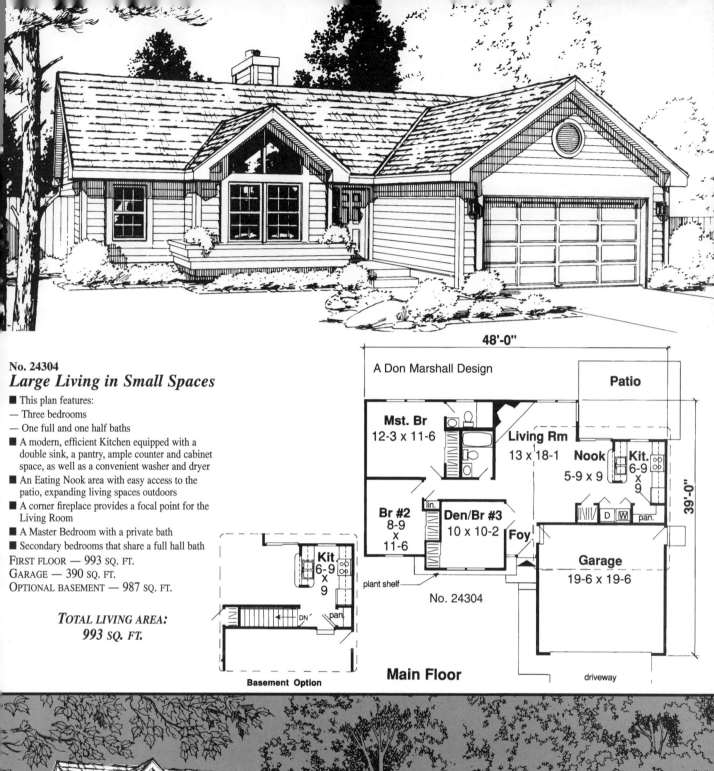

No. 24304
Large Living in Small Spaces

■ This plan features:
— Three bedrooms
— One full and one half baths

■ A modern, efficient Kitchen equipped with a double sink, a pantry, ample counter and cabinet space, as well as a convenient washer and dryer

■ An Eating Nook area with easy access to the patio, expanding living spaces outdoors

■ A corner fireplace provides a focal point for the Living Room

■ A Master Bedroom with a private bath

■ Secondary bedrooms that share a full hall bath

FIRST FLOOR — 993 SQ. FT.
GARAGE — 390 SQ. FT.
OPTIONAL BASEMENT — 987 SQ. FT.

TOTAL LIVING AREA:
993 SQ. FT.

A Don Marshall Design

48'-0"

39'-0"

Patio

Mst. Br
12-3 x 11-6

Living Rm
13 x 18-1

Nook
5-9 x 9

Kit.
6-9 x 9

Br #2
8-9 x 11-6

lin.

Den/Br #3
10 x 10-2

Foy

D W pan.

Garage
19-6 x 19-6

Kit.
6-9 x 9

DN pan.

plant shelf

No. 24304

Basement Option

Main Floor

driveway

No. 10776
Traditional Trend Setter

■ This plan features:
— Three bedrooms
— Two full baths
■ A Living Room with a floor-to-ceiling bay window
■ Active areas sharing the entry level with the fire-placed Living Room
■ A well equipped Kitchen including a built-in pantry and planning desk
■ Front facing bedrooms located over the attached two-car Garage sharing a hall bath
■ A private Master Suite including a private bath

FIRST FLOOR — 1,200 SQ. FT.
BASEMENT — 482 SQ. FT. (FINISHED)
BASEMENT — 548 SQ. FT. (UNFINISHED)
GARAGE — 575 SQ. FT.

TOTAL LIVING AREA:
1,682 SQ. FT.

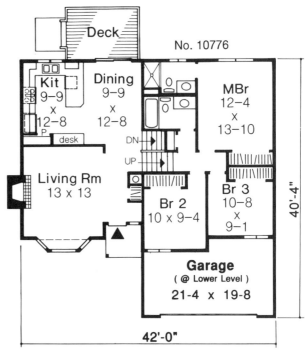

No. 10595
Perfect for a Hillside

■ This plan features:
— Three bedrooms
— Two and one half baths
■ An island Kitchen with a breakfast area leading onto one of two screened porches
■ A huge Recreation Room with a Kitchenette and fireplace
■ A sloping ceiling and fireplace in the spacious Living Room
■ A central staircase directing traffic to all areas of the house

FIRST FLOOR — 1,643 SQ. FT.
SECOND FLOOR — 1,297 SQ. FT.
GARAGE — 528 SQ. FT.

TOTAL LIVING AREA:
2,940 SQ. FT.

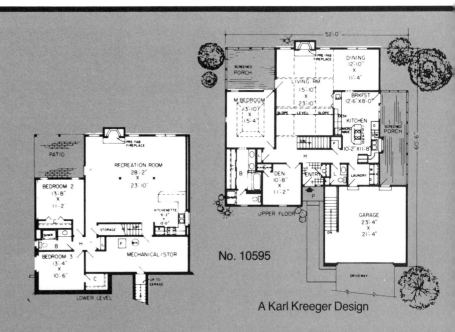

A Karl Kreeger Design

No. 10645
Facade Features Vertical Siding

■ This plan features:
— Four bedrooms
— Three full baths

■ A sheltered entrance leading to a tiled Foyer, an elegant Dining Room with a decorative ceiling and a Great Room with a sloping ceiling and a massive fireplace

■ A U-shaped Kitchen equipped with a snack bar and a planning desk adjacent to the Laundry Room, with a pantry and a Breakfast area with a sliding glass door to the Patio

■ A Master Bedroom with a Dressing area, a private bath and a walk-in closet

■ An additional first floor bedroom offers a boxed window and a large closet

■ Two second floor bedrooms with ample closet space share a full hall bath

First floor — 1,628 sq. ft.
Second floor — 609 sq. ft.
Basement — 1,616 sq. ft.
Garage — 450 sq. ft.

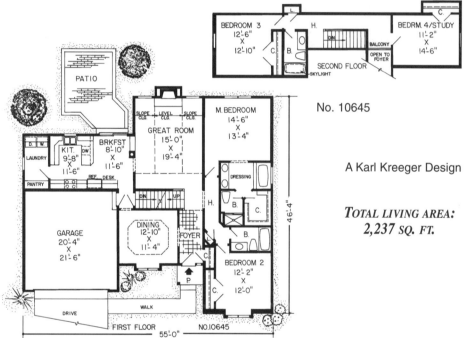

No. 10645

A Karl Kreeger Design

Total living area:
2,237 sq. ft.

No. 20051
Three Bedroom Features Cathedral Ceilings

■ This plan features:
— Three bedrooms
— Two and a half baths
■ A Kitchen with central island, built-in desk, pantry and adjacent Breakfast Nook
■ A fireplaced Living Room with built-in book case that combines with the Dining Room
■ A Master Suite with private full bath

FIRST FLOOR — 1,285 SQ. FT.
SECOND FLOOR — 490 SQ. FT.
BASEMENT — 1,285 SQ. FT.
GARAGE — 495 SQ. FT.

TOTAL LIVING AREA:
1,775 SQ. FT.

A Karl Kreeger Design

No. 20051

No. 10524
Split-level Made for Growing Family

■ This plan features:
— Four bedrooms
— Two and three quarters baths
■ A fireplaced Living Room, stepping up to a Dining Room with adjoining Kitchen
■ An efficient Kitchen featuring an eat-in space and sliding door access to the deck

FIRST FLOOR — 1,470 SQ. FT.
SECOND FLOOR — 711 SQ. FT.
BASEMENT — 392 SQ. FT.
GARAGE — 563 SQ. FT.

TOTAL LIVING AREA:
2,181 SQ. FT.

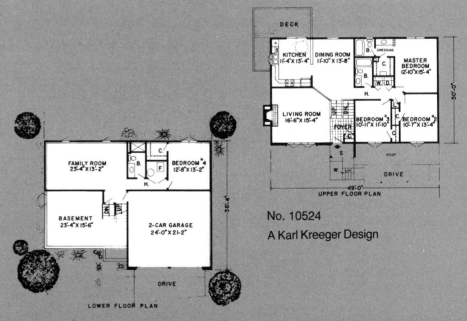

No. 10524
A Karl Kreeger Design

No. 20310

Custom Windows Light Up Contemporary

■ This plan features:

— Three bedrooms

— Two and a half baths

■ A Master Bedroom with a volume ceiling, walk-in closet and private Master Bath

■ A fireplaced Great Room flowing into an elegant Dining Room with floor to ceiling windows

■ An island Kitchen with an eating Nook and easy access to Dining Room

FIRST FLOOR — 1,263 SQ. FT.

SECOND FLOOR — 483 SQ. FT.

GARAGE — 528 SQ. FT.

BASEMENT — 1,263 SQ. FT.

**TOTAL LIVING AREA:
1,746 SQ. FT.**

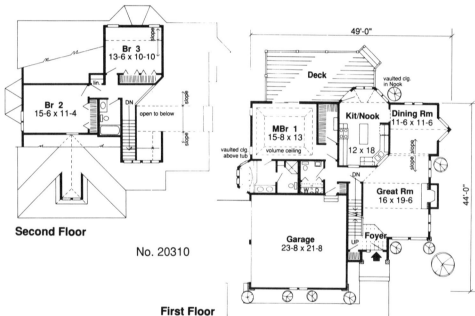

Second Floor

No. 20310

First Floor

No. 34878
Classic Warmth

■ This plan features:
— Three bedrooms
— Two full baths
■ Clapboard and brick exterior
■ Cathedral ceilings gracing the Living and Dining Rooms lending an airy quality
■ A Master Bedroom with private Master Bath and walk-in closet
■ A spacious fireplaced Family Room
■ Sliders leading from both Dining and Family Rooms to the rear patio adding to living space

FIRST FLOOR — 940 SQ. FT.
SECOND FLOOR — 720 SQ. FT.
BASEMENT — 554 SQ. FT.
GARAGE — 418 SQ. FT.
CRAWL SPACE — 312 SQ. FT.

TOTAL LIVING AREA:
1,660 SQ. FT.

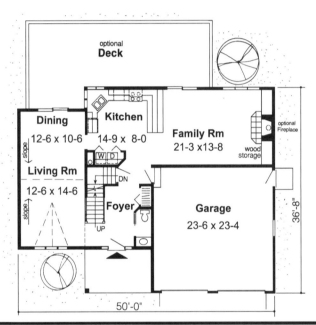

optional
Deck

Dining
12-6 x 10-6

Kitchen
14-9 x 8-0

Family Rm
21-3 x13-8

optional
Fireplace

wood
storage

Living Rm
12-6 x 14-6

W D

DN

Foyer

Garage
23-6 x 23-4

UP

36'-8"

50'-0"

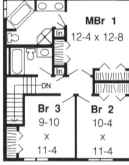

MBr 1
12-4 x 12-8

lin.

lin.

DN

Br 3
9-10
X
11-4

Br 2
10-4
X
11-4

D W

Slab/Crawlspace
Option

No. 34878

No. 10579
Attractive Rock Fireplace in Split Level

■ This plan features:
— Three bedrooms
— Two full baths
■ A covered Porch leads into a tiled Foyer and easy access to the lower level Garage
■ An expansive formal Dining/Great Room accented by an open beamed, sloping ceiling, a bay window and a bold rock fireplace
■ An L-shaped eat-in Kitchen opens to the Patio and the Dining area
■ A spacious Master Suite offering a walk-in closet and a full bath
■ Two bedrooms with oversized closets share a full hall bath
■ A Loft area

FIRST FLOOR — 1,400 SQ. FT.
LOFT — 152 SQ. FT.
BASEMENT — 663 SQ. FT.
GARAGE — 680 SQ. FT.

TOTAL LIVING AREA:
1,542 SQ. FT.

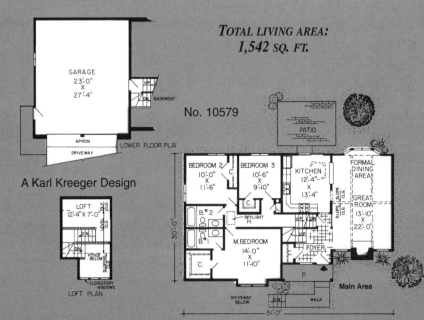

GARAGE
23'-0"
X
27'-4"

UP
DN BASEMENT

APRON

DRIVEWAY

LOWER FLOOR PLAN

No. 10579

A Karl Kreeger Design

LOFT
12'-4" X 7'-0"

DN

FOYER
BELOW

CLERESTORY
WINDOWS
LOFT PLAN

PATIO

BEDROOM 2
10'-0"
X
11'-6"

BEDROOM 3
10'-6"
X
9'-10"

KITCHEN
12'-4"
X
13'-4"

FORMAL
DINING
AREA

GREAT
ROOM
13'-10"
X
22'-0"

B. 2

SKYLIGHT

UP DN

30'-0"

M. BEDROOM
14'-0"
X
11'-10"

C.

FOYER

P.

DRIVEWAY
BELOW

DN

WALK

Main Area

51'-0"

158

No. 10501
Foyer Welcomes Guests

■ This plan features:
— Four bedrooms
— Two full and two half baths
■ A massive welcoming foyer which steps right into the Great Room
■ A Great Room enlarged by a wrap-around deck and highlighted by a fireplace, built-in bookcases, and a wetbar
■ A Kitchen with a built-in desk, an octagonal morning room, and a central island

FIRST FLOOR — 2,419 SQ. FT.
SECOND FLOOR — 926 SQ. FT.
BASEMENT — 2,419 SQ. FT.
GARAGE — 615 SQ. FT.

TOTAL LIVING AREA:
3,345 SQ. FT.

No. 10501

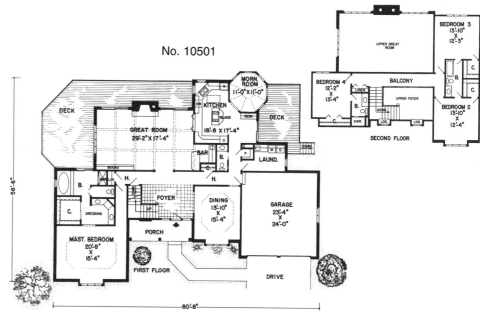

A Karl Kreeger Design

No. 10380
Passive Solar Design with Unique Great Room

■ This plan features:
— Three bedrooms
— Two and one half baths
■ Exposed beams and large expanses of glass
■ A six-sided living area
■ Spiral stairs rising to a loft which overlooks the Great Room
■ Rooms with sloping ceilings containing R-38 insulation
■ Side walls containing R-24 insulation
■ A full Basement foundation

FIRST FLOOR — 2,199 SQ. FT.
LOFT — 336 SQ. FT.
GARAGE — 611 SQ. FT.
BASEMENT — 2,199 SQ. FT.

**TOTAL LIVING AREA:
2,535 SQ. FT.**

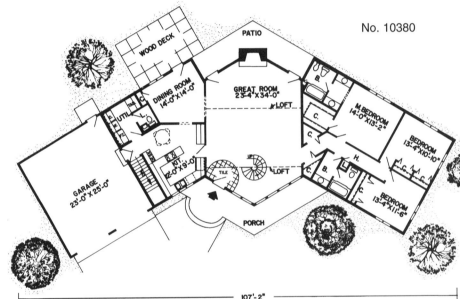

No. 10500
Contemporary Features

A Karl Kreeger Design

No. 10500

■ This plan features:
— Four bedrooms
— Three full and two half baths
■ A Great Room with a fireplace, and a beamed, cathedral ceiling
■ A Kitchen including an angled cooking/snack bar, a center work island and a Breakfast area
■ A Master Suite with a tile tub, an over-sized shower and two vanities
■ Three bedrooms and a Loft, which opens onto the Foyer and Great Room, on the second floor

FIRST FLOOR — 2,188 SQ. FT.
SECOND FLOOR — 1,083 SQ. FT.
BASEMENT — 2,188 SQ. FT.
GARAGE — 576 SQ. FT.

**TOTAL LIVING AREA:
3,271 SQ. FT.**

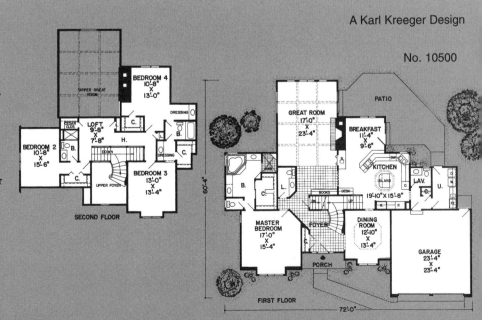

160

No. 10643
Low Maintenance, Southwestern Style

■ This plan features:
— Three bedrooms
— Two full baths
■ A cheerful Kitchen with a Breakfast bar and entry onto the patio
■ A sky-lit bath and huge bay window illuminating the Master Suite
■ A spacious Living Room, convenient Dining Room, and a handy utility room

FIRST FLOOR — 1,285 SQ. FT.
GARAGE — 473 SQ. FT.

TOTAL LIVING AREA:
1,285 SQ. FT.

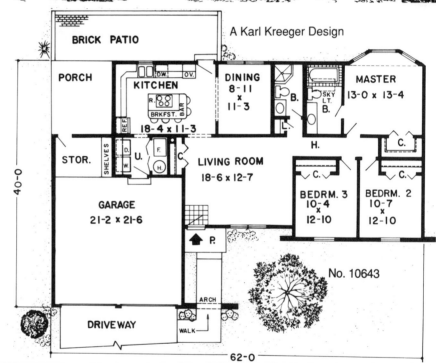

A Karl Kreeger Design

BRICK PATIO

PORCH

KITCHEN
DW. OV.
R.
BRKFST. BAR
18-4 x 11-3

DINING
8-11
x
11-3

B.
SKY
LT.
B.

MASTER
13-0 x 13-4

STOR.

SHELVES
D. F.
U.
W. H.
C.

LIVING ROOM
18-6 x 12-7

H.

C.

C.

40-0

GARAGE
21-2 x 21-6

P.

C.

BEDRM. 3
10-4
x
12-10

BEDRM. 2
10-7
x
12-10

No. 10643

DRIVEWAY

ARCH
WALK

62-0

No. 10292
Airy Design With Decks

■ This plan features:
— Two or three bedrooms
— Two and a half baths

■ Contemporary styling with cathedral ceilings and gable end windows

■ A formal Living Room leading to the formal Dining Room for a smooth transition when entertaining

■ An efficient U-shaped Kitchen with a double sink, ample counter and cabinet space and a built-in broom closet

■ A sunken Family Room equipped with two closets and sliding doors to the patio

■ A Master Bedroom with a full Bath, a walk-in closet and a private deck

■ A bright second bedroom with access, through sliding glass doors, to a large sun deck and conveniently near the full hall bath

■ A sunny Sitting Room with sliding glass doors to the sun deck, could also be the perfect guest room or study

FIRST FLOOR — 1,145 SQ. FT.
SECOND FLOOR — 864 SQ. FT.
BASEMENT — 1,145 SQ. FT.
GARAGE — 568 SQ. FT.

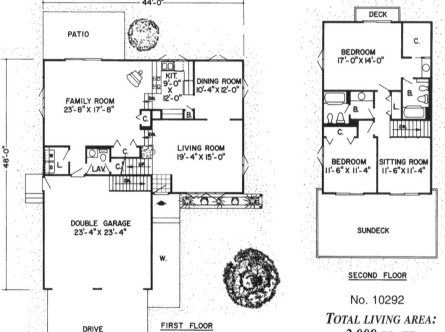

No. 10292
TOTAL LIVING AREA:
2,009 SQ. FT.

No. 10421
Numerous Options Abound

■ This plan features:
— Three bedrooms
— Two full and one half baths

■ A sheltered entrance leading into an Entry which opens into an expansive Living Room featuring a hearth fireplace, built-in shelves and a wall of windows

■ A sunken Dining Room accented by large picture windows and adjacent to Kitchen

■ A well-planned Kitchen includes an eating bar and a Nook with easy access to the Laundry area, the Garage and the covered patio

■ A Master Suite includes a plush bath and double walk-in closets

■ Second floor features two additional bedrooms and a Game Room which share a full hall bath

FIRST FLOOR — 1,605 SQ. FT.
SECOND FLOOR — 732 SQ. FT.
GARAGE — 525 SQ. FT.
PATIO — 395 SQ. FT.

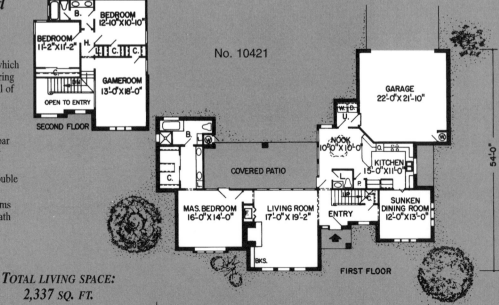

TOTAL LIVING SPACE:
2,337 SQ. FT.

146

No. 24319
Home With Many Views

■ This plan features:
— Three bedrooms
— Two full baths
■ Large Decks and windows taking full advantage of the view
■ A fireplace that divides the Living Room from the Dining Room
■ A Kitchen flowing into the Dining Room
■ A Master Bedroom with full Master Bath
■ A Recreation Room sporting a whirlpool tub and a bar

MAIN FLOOR — 728 SQ. FT.
UPPER FLOOR — 573 SQ. FT.
LOWER FLOOR — 379 SQ. FT.
GARAGE — 240 SQ. FT.

TOTAL LIVING AREA:
1,680 SQ. FT.

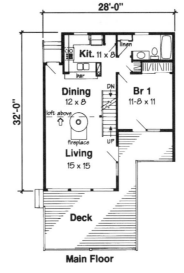

Main Floor

28'-0"
32'-0"

Kit. 11 x 8
linen
Dining 12 x 8
bar
Br 1 11-8 x 11
DN
loft above
fireplace
Living 15 x 15
UP
Deck

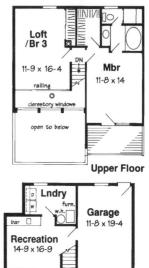

Upper Floor

Loft /Br 3 11-9 x 16-4
railing
clerestory windows
open to below
DN
Mbr 11-8 x 14

Lower Floor

Lndry
D W
furn.
w.h.
Garage 11-8 x 19-4
bar
Recreation 14-9 x 16-9
whirlpool tub
UP

No. 24319

A Don Marshall Design

No. 20171
Family Home with Flair

■ This plan features:
— Three bedrooms
— Two full baths

■ A classic brick and clapboard exterior

■ A central foyer to an island Kitchen with adjoining formal Dining Room made elegant by floor-to ceiling window

■ A spacious Living Room with soaring ceilings and sizzling fireplace with sliders to an outdoor deck

FIRST FLOOR — 1,349 SQ. FT.
SECOND FLOOR — 590 SQ. FT.
BASEMENT — 1,342 SQ. FT.
GARAGE — 480 SQ. FT.

TOTAL LIVING AREA:
1,939 SQ. FT.

No. 20171
First Floor

A Karl Kreeger Design

Second Floor

No. 20193
Interesting Angles

■ This plan features:
— Three bedrooms
— Two full and one half baths

■ A wrap-around shaped Kitchen with built-in pantry, snack bar counter and double sinks

■ A diamond-shaped Breakfast area that overlooks the deck

■ A spacious Living Room with a wonderful fireplace to add warmth and atmosphere

■ A Master Suite with decorative ceiling and luxury bath with walk-in closet

■ Two additional bedrooms that share a sky-lit full hall bath

FIRST FLOOR — 2,250 SQ. FT.
GARAGE — 573 SQ. FT.
BASEMENT — 2,291 SQ. FT.

TOTAL LIVING AREA:
2,250 SQ. FT.

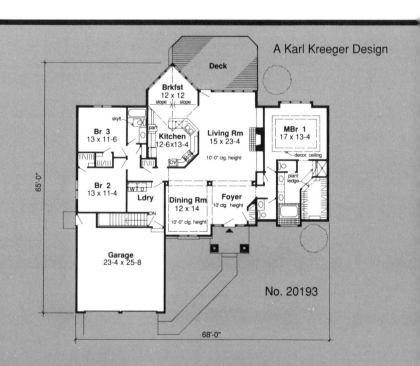

A Karl Kreeger Design

No. 20193

No. 20066

Cathedral Window Graced by Massive Arch

■ This plan features:
— Three bedrooms
— Two full baths
■ A tiled threshold providing a distinctive entrance
■ A comfortable Living Room with a wood-burning fireplace and tiled hearth
■ A Dining Room with vaulted ceiling
■ A Kitchen with central work island, pantry, planning desk, and Breakfast area
■ A Master Suite with decorative ceilings, Master Bath and bow window

FIRST FLOOR — 1,850 SQ. FT.
BASEMENT — 1,850 SQ. FT.
GARAGE — 503 SQ. FT.

TOTAL LIVING AREA:
1,850 SQ. FT.

No. 20066

FLOOR PLAN

A Karl Kreeger Design

No. 20400
Rustic Contemporary

■ This plan features:
— Three bedrooms:
— Two and a half baths

■ A Master Suite in its own wing, complete with his and her walk-in closets, a luxury bath and private rear deck

■ A two-way fireplace separating the Living Room and Dining Room combination

■ A Kitchen, Breakfast Room and Family Room flowing easily into each other

FIRST FLOOR— 2,279 SQ. FT.
LOFT — 338 SQ. FT.
BASEMENT — 2,317 SQ. FT.
GARAGE — 478 SQ. FT.

TOTAL LIVING AREA:
2,617 SQ. FT.

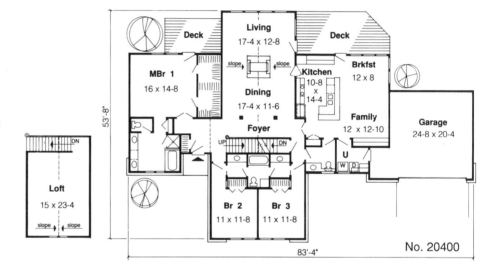

No. 10550
Enjoy the Backyard Views

Karl Kreeger Design

■ This plan features:
— Four bedrooms
— Three full and two half baths

■ Recessed ceilings in the Dining Room and Master Bedroom

■ A sun porch off the Breakfast Nook

■ Two full baths and two convenient baths located on the second floor

■ A full Basement foundation

FIRST FLOOR — 2,069 SQ. FT.
SECOND FLOOR — 821 SQ. FT.
BASEMENT — 2,045 SQ. FT.
GARAGE — 562 SQ. FT.

TOTAL LIVING AREA:
2,890 SQ. FT.

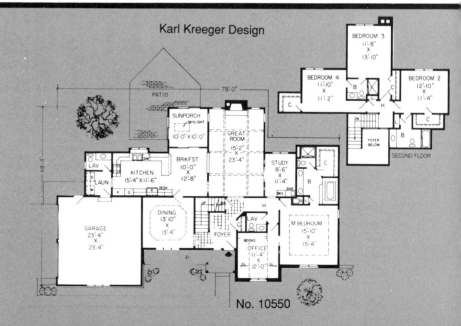

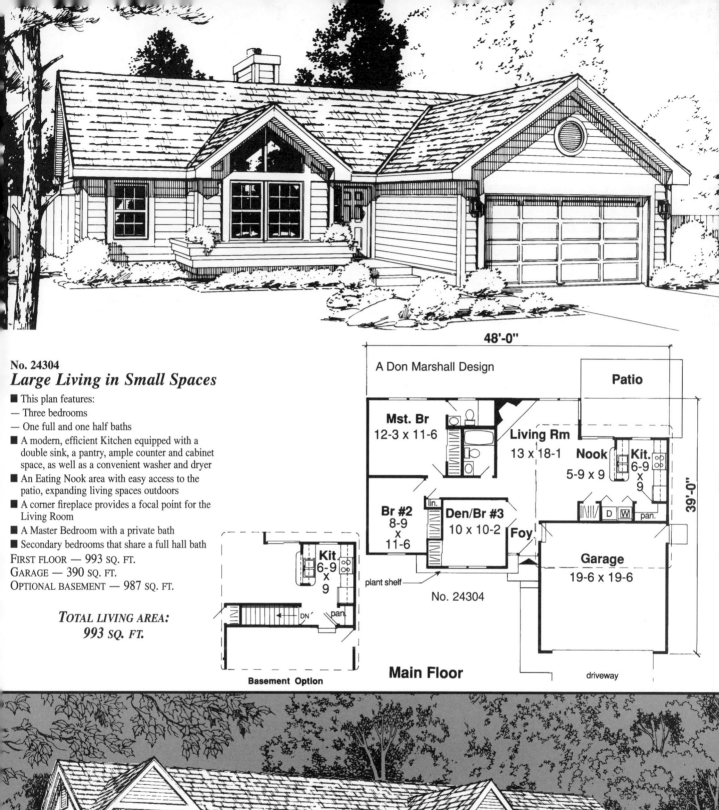

No. 24304
Large Living in Small Spaces

■ This plan features:
— Three bedrooms
— One full and one half baths

■ A modern, efficient Kitchen equipped with a double sink, a pantry, ample counter and cabinet space, as well as a convenient washer and dryer

■ An Eating Nook area with easy access to the patio, expanding living spaces outdoors

■ A corner fireplace provides a focal point for the Living Room

■ A Master Bedroom with a private bath

■ Secondary bedrooms that share a full hall bath

FIRST FLOOR — 993 SQ. FT.
GARAGE — 390 SQ. FT.
OPTIONAL BASEMENT — 987 SQ. FT.

TOTAL LIVING AREA: 993 SQ. FT.

Kit. 6-9 x 9

DN

pan.

Basement Option

A Don Marshall Design

Patio

48'-0"

Mst. Br 12-3 x 11-6

Living Rm 13 x 18-1

Nook 5-9 x 9

Kit. 6-9 x 9

39'-0"

Br #2 8-9 x 11-6

lin.

Den/Br #3 10 x 10-2

Foy

D W pan.

plant shelf

No. 24304

Garage 19-6 x 19-6

Main Floor

driveway

No. 10776
Traditional Trend Setter

■ This plan features:
— Three bedrooms
— Two full baths

■ A Living Room with a floor-to-ceiling bay window

■ Active areas sharing the entry level with the fireplaced Living Room

■ A well equipped Kitchen including a built-in pantry and planning desk

■ Front facing bedrooms located over the attached two-car Garage sharing a hall bath

■ A private Master Suite including a private bath

FIRST FLOOR — 1,200 SQ. FT.
BASEMENT — 482 SQ. FT. (FINISHED)
BASEMENT — 548 SQ. FT. (UNFINISHED)
GARAGE — 575 SQ. FT.

TOTAL LIVING AREA:
1,682 SQ. FT.

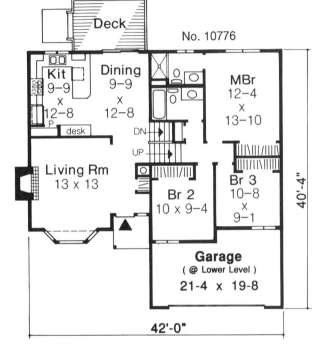

No. 10595
Perfect for a Hillside

■ This plan features:
— Three bedrooms
— Two and one half baths

■ An island Kitchen with a breakfast area leading onto one of two screened porches

■ A huge Recreation Room with a Kitchenette and fireplace

■ A sloping ceiling and fireplace in the spacious Living Room

■ A central staircase directing traffic to all areas of the house

FIRST FLOOR — 1,643 SQ. FT.
SECOND FLOOR — 1,297 SQ. FT.
GARAGE — 528 SQ. FT.

TOTAL LIVING AREA:
2,940 SQ. FT.

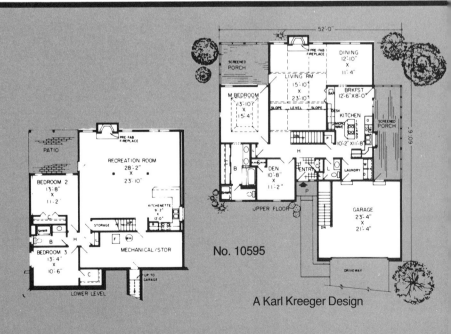

A Karl Kreeger Design

No. 10645
Facade Features Vertical Siding

■ This plan features:
— Four bedrooms
— Three full baths

■ A sheltered entrance leading to a tiled Foyer, an elegant Dining Room with a decorative ceiling and a Great Room with a sloping ceiling and a massive fireplace

■ A U-shaped Kitchen equipped with a snack bar and a planning desk adjacent to the Laundry Room, with a pantry and a Breakfast area with a sliding glass door to the Patio

■ A Master Bedroom with a Dressing area, a private bath and a walk-in closet

■ An additional first floor bedroom offers a boxed window and a large closet

■ Two second floor bedrooms with ample closet space share a full hall bath

FIRST FLOOR — 1,628 SQ. FT.
SECOND FLOOR — 609 SQ. FT.
BASEMENT — 1,616 SQ. FT.
GARAGE — 450 SQ. FT.

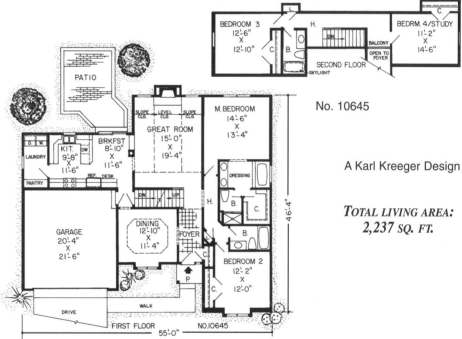

No. 10645

A Karl Kreeger Design

TOTAL LIVING AREA:
2,237 SQ. FT.

No. 20051
Three Bedroom Features Cathedral Ceilings

■ This plan features:

— Three bedrooms

— Two and a half baths

■ A Kitchen with central island, built-in desk, pantry and adjacent Breakfast Nook

■ A fireplaced Living Room with built-in book case that combines with the Dining Room

■ A Master Suite with private full bath

FIRST FLOOR — 1,285 SQ. FT.

SECOND FLOOR — 490 SQ. FT.

BASEMENT — 1,285 SQ. FT.

GARAGE — 495 SQ. FT.

TOTAL LIVING AREA:
1,775 SQ. FT.

A Karl Kreeger Design

No. 20051

No. 10524
Split-level Made for Growing Family

■ This plan features:

— Four bedrooms

— Two and three quarters baths

■ A fireplaced Living Room, stepping up to a Dining Room with adjoining Kitchen

■ An efficient Kitchen featuring an eat-in space and sliding door access to the deck

FIRST FLOOR — 1,470 SQ. FT.

SECOND FLOOR — 711 SQ. FT.

BASEMENT — 392 SQ. FT.

GARAGE — 563 SQ. FT.

TOTAL LIVING AREA:
2,181 SQ. FT.

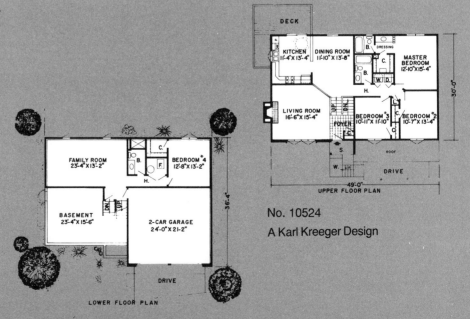

No. 10524

A Karl Kreeger Design

No. 20310
Custom Windows Light Up Contemporary

■ This plan features:

— Three bedrooms

— Two and a half baths

■ A Master Bedroom with a volume ceiling, walk-in closet and private Master Bath

■ A fireplaced Great Room flowing into an elegant Dining Room with floor to ceiling windows

■ An island Kitchen with an eating Nook and easy access to Dining Room

FIRST FLOOR — 1,263 SQ. FT.

SECOND FLOOR — 483 SQ. FT.

GARAGE — 528 SQ. FT.

BASEMENT — 1,263 SQ. FT.

TOTAL LIVING AREA:
1,746 SQ. FT.

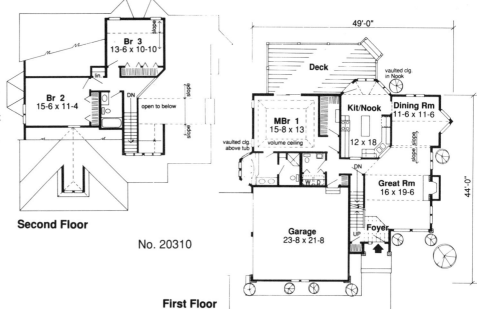

Second Floor

Br 3
13-6 x 10-10

Br 2
15-6 x 11-4

lin.

DN

open to below

slope

No. 20310

First Floor

49'-0"

Deck

vaulted clg. in Nook

MBr 1
15-8 x 13
volume ceiling

Kit/Nook
12 x 18

Dining Rm
11-6 x 11-6

vaulted clg. above tub

W D

DN

Great Rm
16 x 19-6

Garage
23-8 x 21-8

UP

Foyer

44'-0"

No. 34878
Classic Warmth

■ This plan features:
— Three bedrooms
— Two full baths
■ Clapboard and brick exterior
■ Cathedral ceilings gracing the Living and Dining Rooms lending an airy quality
■ A Master Bedroom with private Master Bath and walk-in closet
■ A spacious fireplaced Family Room
■ Sliders leading from both Dining and Family Rooms to the rear patio adding to living space

FIRST FLOOR — 940 SQ. FT.
SECOND FLOOR — 720 SQ. FT.
BASEMENT — 554 SQ. FT.
GARAGE — 418 SQ. FT.
CRAWL SPACE — 312 SQ. FT.

TOTAL LIVING AREA:
1,660 SQ. FT.

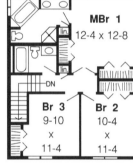

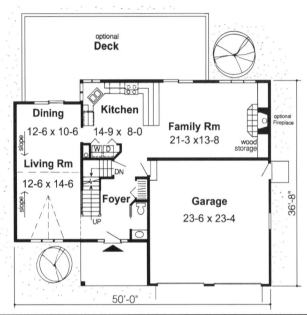

Slab/Crawlspace Option

No. 34878

No. 10579
Attractive Rock Fireplace in Split Level

■ This plan features:
— Three bedrooms
— Two full baths
■ A covered Porch leads into a tiled Foyer and easy access to the lower level Garage
■ An expansive formal Dining/Great Room accented by an open beamed, sloping ceiling, a bay window and a bold rock fireplace
■ An L-shaped eat-in Kitchen opens to the Patio and the Dining area
■ A spacious Master Suite offering a walk-in closet and a full bath
■ Two bedrooms with oversized closets share a full hall bath
■ A Loft area

FIRST FLOOR — 1,400 SQ. FT.
LOFT — 152 SQ. FT.
BASEMENT — 663 SQ. FT.
GARAGE — 680 SQ. FT.

TOTAL LIVING AREA:
1,542 SQ. FT.

No. 10579

A Karl Kreeger Design

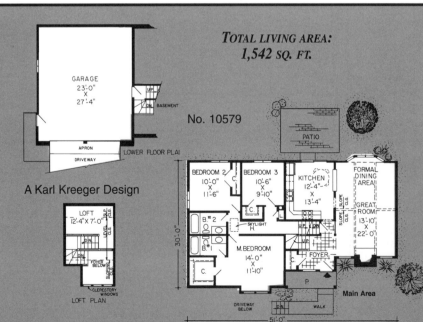

No. 10501
Foyer Welcomes Guests

- This plan features:
  — Four bedrooms
  — Two full and two half baths
- A massive welcoming foyer which steps right into the Great Room
- A Great Room enlarged by a wrap-around deck and highlighted by a fireplace, built-in bookcases, and a wetbar
- A Kitchen with a built-in desk, an octagonal morning room, and a central island

FIRST FLOOR — 2,419 SQ. FT.
SECOND FLOOR — 926 SQ. FT.
BASEMENT — 2,419 SQ. FT.
GARAGE — 615 SQ. FT.

TOTAL LIVING AREA: 3,345 SQ. FT.

No. 10501

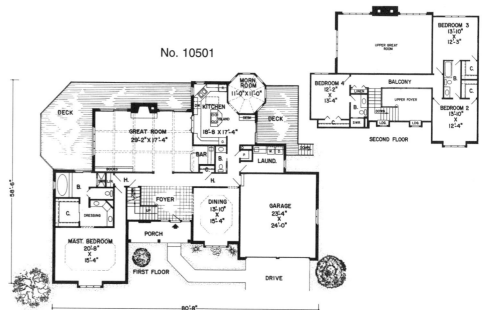

A Karl Kreeger Design

No. 10380
Passive Solar Design with Unique Great Room

■ This plan features:
— Three bedrooms
— Two and one half baths

■ Exposed beams and large expanses of glass

■ A six-sided living area

■ Spiral stairs rising to a loft which overlooks the Great Room

■ Rooms with sloping ceilings containing R-38 insulation

■ Side walls containing R-24 insulation

■ A full Basement foundation

FIRST FLOOR — 2,199 SQ. FT.
LOFT — 336 SQ. FT.
GARAGE — 611 SQ. FT.
BASEMENT — 2,199 SQ. FT.

**TOTAL LIVING AREA:
2,535 SQ. FT.**

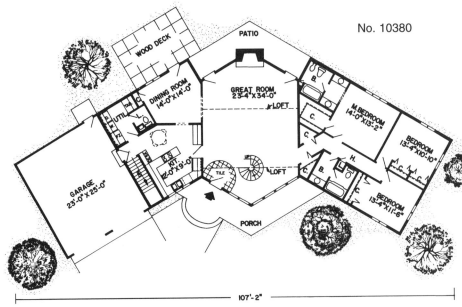

No. 10380

No. 10500
Contemporary Features

A Karl Kreeger Design

No. 10500

■ This plan features:
— Four bedrooms
— Three full and two half baths

■ A Great Room with a fireplace, and a beamed, cathedral ceiling

■ A Kitchen including an angled cooking/snack bar, a center work island and a Breakfast area

■ A Master Suite with a tile tub, an over-sized shower and two vanities

■ Three bedrooms and a Loft, which opens onto the Foyer and Great Room, on the second floor

FIRST FLOOR — 2,188 SQ. FT.
SECOND FLOOR — 1,083 SQ. FT.
BASEMENT — 2,188 SQ. FT.
GARAGE — 576 SQ. FT.

**TOTAL LIVING AREA:
3,271 SQ. FT.**

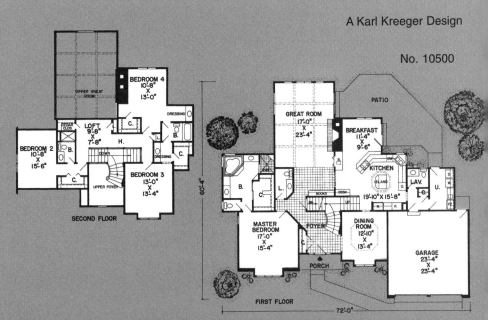

No. 20069
Stylish and Practical Plan

■ This plan features:
— Three bedrooms
— Two and one half baths

■ A Kitchen with a Breakfast Area large enough for most informal meals

■ A spacious Living Room with a fireplace

■ A formal Dining Room with a decorative ceiling for comfortable entertaining

■ A first floor Master Bedroom providing a private retreat and a lavish Master Bath

FIRST FLOOR — 1,340 SQ. FT.
SECOND FLOOR — 651 SQ. FT.
BASEMENT — 1,322 SQ. FT.

TOTAL LIVING AREA: 1,991 SQ. FT.

A Karl Kreeger Design

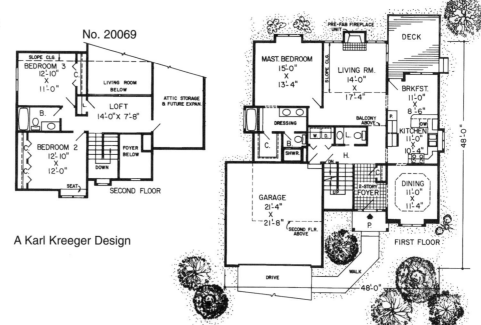

No. 10778
Balcony Offers Sweeping Views

■ This plan features:
— Three bedrooms
— Three and one half baths

■ A Living Room and a formal Dining Room located off the foyer

■ A convenient island Kitchen steps away from both the Dining Room and the Three Season Porch

■ A cozy Master Suite including a fireplace and a large bath area

FIRST FLOOR — 1,978 SQ. FT
SECOND FLOOR — 1,768 SQ. FT.
BASEMENT — 1,978 SQ. FT.

TOTAL LIVING AREA:
3,746 SQ. FT.

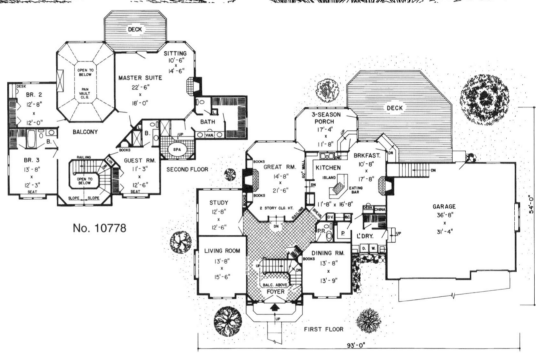

No. 10778

No. 24303
Affordable Living

■ This plan features:
— Three bedrooms
— Two full baths

■ A simple, yet gracefully designed exterior

■ A sheltered entrance into a roomy Living Room graced with a large front window

■ A formal Dining Room flowing from the Living Room, allowing for ease in entertaining

■ A well-appointed U-shaped Kitchen with double sinks and adequate storage

■ A Master Bedroom equipped with a full Bath

■ Two additional bedrooms that share a full hall bath complete with a convenient laundry center

■ A covered Patio, tucked behind the garage, perfect for a cook out or picnic

MAIN AREA — 936 SQ. FT.
BASEMENT — 948 SQ. FT.
GARAGE — 280 SQ. FT.
OPT. 2-CAR GARAGE — 384 SQ. FT.

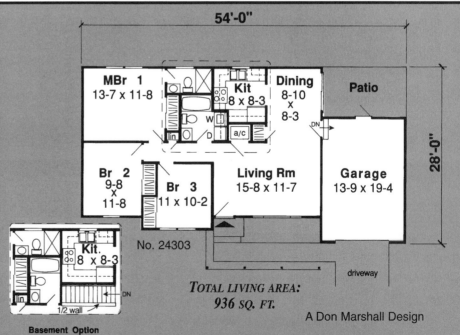

Basement Option

No. 24303

TOTAL LIVING AREA:
936 SQ. FT.

A Don Marshall Design

No. 20404
Spacious Saltbox

■ This plan features:
— Five bedrooms
— Three full baths

■ Flower boxes and a friendly front porch introducing an updated saltbox

■ A formal Dining Room and Parlor adjoining the open Foyer offers a classic arrangement with a contemporary approach

■ A wonderful gathering place, where the Kitchen, Breakfast area, and Family Room join together, enhanced by a cozy fireplace and a wall of windows overlooking the Deck

■ A Guest Suite including a full Bath with handicap access

■ A private Deck and luxurious Bath highlighting the Master Suite

■ A Balcony that links two, optional three, bedrooms and a full bath together on the second floor

FIRST FLOOR — 2,285 SQ. FT.
SECOND FLOOR — 660 SQ. FT.
GARAGE — 565 SQ. FT.

No. 20404

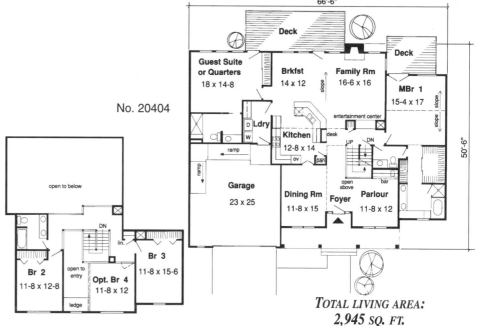

TOTAL LIVING AREA:
2,945 SQ. FT.

No. 10583
Loft Overlooks Foyer

■ This plan features:
— Four bedrooms
— Three full baths
■ Enormous rooms and two Garages
■ An island Kitchen with an eating peninsula for informal dining
■ A sun-filled Great Room with a massive fireplace and open-beamed ceiling
■ A large wrap-around deck to expand the outdoor living area
■ A Master Bedroom suite with a private deck, two large walk-in closets, and a lavish sky-lit tub
■ A large Recreation Room on the lower floor with access to the rear patio

FIRST FLOOR — 2,367 SQ. FT.
LOWER FLOOR — 1,241 SQ. FT.
BASEMENT (UNFINISHED) — 372 SQ. FT.
LOFT — 295 SQ. FT.
GARAGE (UPPER) — 660 SQ. FT.
GARAGE (LOWER) — 636 SQ. FT.

TOTAL LIVING AREA:
3,903 SQ. FT.

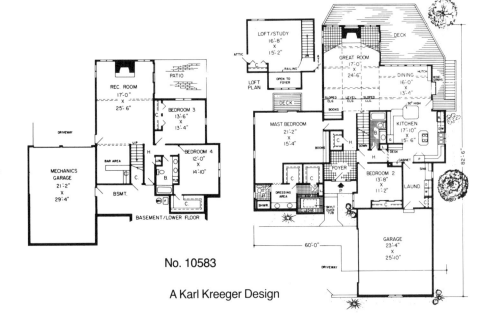

No. 10583

A Karl Kreeger Design

No. 20061
Options Abound

■ This plan features:
— Three bedrooms
— Two full baths
■ A striking exterior featuring vertical siding, shake shingles, and stone
■ A Kitchen with built-in pantry and appliances
■ An open beamed Master Bedroom

FIRST FLOOR — 1,674 SQ. FT.
BASEMENT — 1,656 SQ. FT.
GARAGE — 472 SQ. FT.

TOTAL LIVING AREA:
1,674 SQ. FT.

No. 20061

A Karl Kreeger Design

No. 20097
Balcony Affords Splendid View

■ This plan features:

— Three bedrooms

— Two and one half baths

■ A Living Room with a two-story ceiling pierced by a skylight

■ Living and Dining Rooms flowing together in one spacious unit

■ A handy Kitchen with a breakfast bar peninsula

■ A large Master Bedroom with an abundance of closet space and a private bath with a separate shower and tub

FIRST FLOOR — 1,752 SQ. FT.

SECOND FLOOR — 897 SQ. FT.

BASEMENT — 1,752 SQ. FT.

GARAGE — 531 SQ. FT.

TOTAL LIVING AREA:
2,649 SQ. FT.

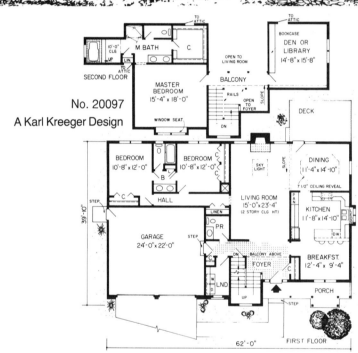

No. 20097
A Karl Kreeger Design

No. 10780
Veranda Mirrors Two-Story Bay

■ This plan features:

— Four bedrooms

— Two and one half baths

■ A huge foyer flanked by the formal Parlor and Dining Room

■ An island Kitchen with an adjoining pantry

■ A Breakfast bay and sunken Gathering Room located at the rear of the home

■ Double doors opening to the Master Suite and the book-lined Master Retreat

■ An elegant Master Bath including a raised tub and adjoining cedar closet

First floor — 2,108 sq. ft.
Second floor — 2,109 sq. ft.
Basement — 1,946 sq. ft.
Garage — 764 sq. ft.

Total living area: 4,217 sq. ft.

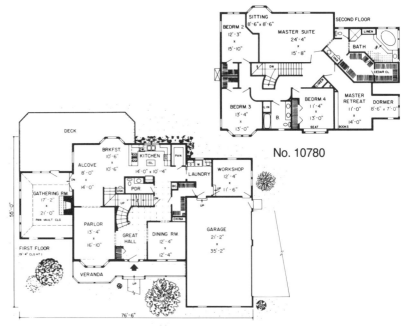

No. 10780

No. 10678
Entry Hints At Appealing Interior

■ This plan features:

— Three bedrooms

— Two and one half baths

■ A Family Room with a fireplace opening to a convenient Kitchen with built-in desk, pantry and near-by Laundry area

■ A Dining Room surrounded by a deck and open to the Living Room with vaulted ceilings.

■ A Den and deck upstairs and a Study downstairs

First floor — 1,375 sq. ft.
Second floor — 1,206 sq. ft.
Basement — 1,375 sq. ft.

Total living area: 2,581 sq. ft.

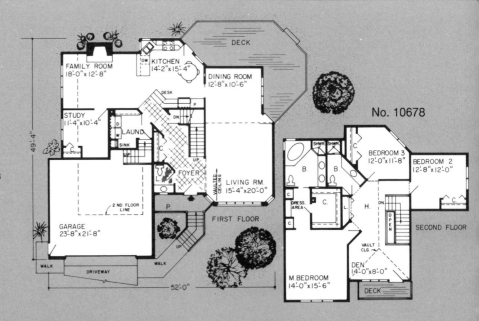

No. 10678

No. 20351
Elegant Master Suite Crowns Victorian

■ This plan features:

— Three bedrooms

— Two and one half baths

■ A formal Living Room with a charming fireplace

■ A formal Dining Room flowing off of the Living Room for ease in entertaining

■ A convenient Kitchen that has an open layout between the Breakfast area and the Family Room

■ A second fireplace in the Family Room and a romantic window seat

■ A Master Suite with his and her walk-in closets and whirlpool tub, step-in shower and double vanities

■ Two additional bedrooms that share a full hall bath

FIRST FLOOR — 1,304 SQ. FT.

SECOND FLOOR — 1,009 SQ. FT.

BASEMENT — 1,304 SQ. FT.

GARAGE — 688 SQ. FT.

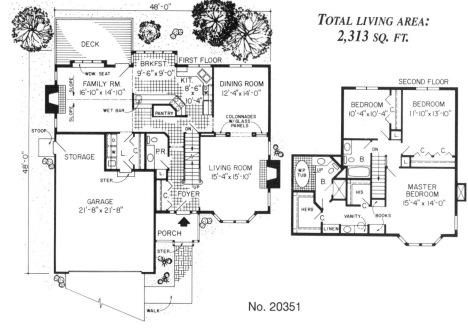

TOTAL LIVING AREA: 2,313 SQ. FT.

No. 20351

No. 10734
Sunny and Warm

■ This plan features:
— Four bedrooms
— Three full baths and two half baths

■ The children's rooms upstairs, sharing a full bath with a double vanity and just steps away from a loft ideal for a playroom

■ An island cook top, loads of counter space and a Breakfast nook in the Kitchen

■ A Deck, Sun Room, and Utility room

■ A Master Bedroom with a fireplace, a walk-in closet and a Study

FIRST FLOOR — 2,887 SQ. FT.
SECOND FLOOR — 1,488 SQ. FT.
BASEMENT — 2,888 SQ. FT.
GARAGE — 843 SQ. FT.

**TOTAL LIVING AREA:
4,375 SQ. FT.**

A Karl Kreeger Design

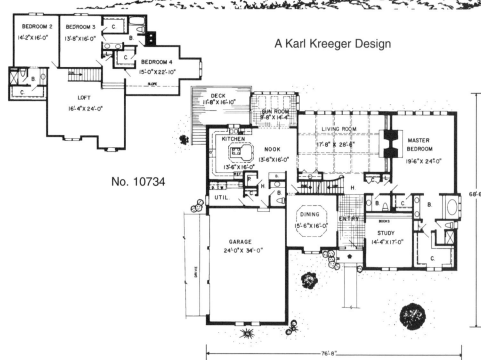

No. 10734

No. 24251
Skylight Brightens Breakfast Nook

■ This plan features:
— Three bedrooms
— Two full and one half bath

■ A covered porch entry welcomes guests

■ A vaulted ceiling and bay window in the Dining Room adjoining the formal Living Room for an easy transition in entertaining

■ A center island Kitchen, with a double basin sink and numerous amenities

■ A skylight naturally illuminating the Breakfast Nook gives a cheerful start to the day

■ Built-in bookshelves or entertainment center around the fireplace in the Family Room

■ A wetbar convenient to the entertainment areas

■ A Master Suite with a cathedral ceiling, a walk-in closet, a double vanity, a separate shower and a tub in the bath

■ Two additional bedrooms share full hall bath

No. 24251

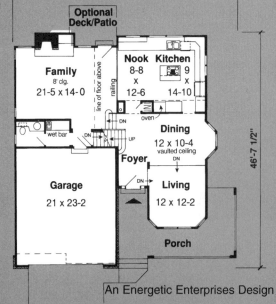

FIRST FLOOR — 1,157 SQ. FT.
SECOND FLOOR — 907 SQ. FT.

**TOTAL LIVING AREA:
2,064 SQ. FT.**

An Energetic Enterprises Design

No. 10761
Tudor for Today & Tomorrow

- This plan features:
— Four bedrooms
— Three and one half baths
- Double doors opening to a huge entry foyer flanked by a formal Dining Room and a sunken Living Room
- The cozy elegance of a book-lined Library
- A Kitchen with a rangetop island and a sunny Breakfast room
- A Master Suite with a fireplace, sitting area, and his-n-her closets

FIRST FLOOR — 1,926 SQ. FT.
SECOND FLOOR — 1,606 SQ. FT.
BASEMENT — 1,926 SQ. FT.
GARAGE — 840 SQ. FT.

**TOTAL LIVING AREA:
3,532 SQ. FT.**

No. 10761

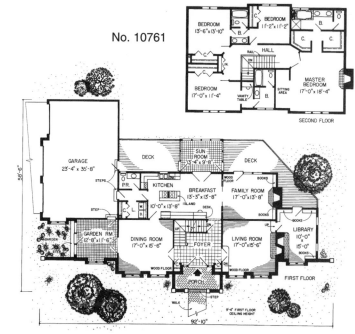

No. 34353
Classic Ranch Has Contemporary Flavor

■ This plan features:
— Three bedrooms
— Two full baths
■ A Galley-styled Kitchen easily serving Dining Room
■ A Living Room with bump out window and fireplace
■ Ample closet space
■ An optional slab or crawl space foundation available — please specify when ordering
■ A Master Bedroom with private bath with shower

FIRST FLOOR — 1,268 SQ. FT.
BASEMENT — 1,248 SQ. FT.

TOTAL LIVING AREA:
1,268 SQ. FT.

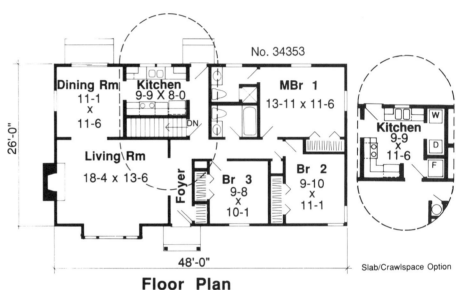

No. 34353

Dining Rm 11-1 x 11-6

Kitchen 9-9 X 8-0

MBr 1 13-11 x 11-6

Living Rm 18-4 x 13-6

Foyer

Br 3 9-8 x 10-1

Br 2 9-10 x 11-1

26'-0"

48'-0"

Kitchen 9-9 x 11-6

Slab/Crawlspace Option

Floor Plan

No. 10594
Lots of Room in Ranch Design

■ This plan features:
— Two bedrooms (with optional third bedroom)
— Two full baths
■ A sloping, open-beamed ceiling and a wood-burning fireplace in the Great Room
■ A Dining Room with sliding glass doors leading onto a large wooden deck
■ A laundry room nearby the Kitchen and Dining Room

FIRST FLOOR — 1,565 SQ. FT.
BASEMENT — 1,576 SQ. FT.
GARAGE — 430 SQ. FT.

TOTAL LIVING AREA:
1,565 SQ. FT.

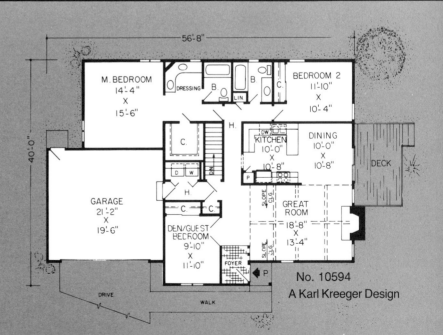

56'-8"

40'-0"

M. BEDROOM 14'-4" x 15'-6"

BEDROOM 2 11'-10" x 10'-4"

DRESSING

KITCHEN 10'-0" x 10'-8"

DINING 10'-0" x 10'-8"

DECK

GARAGE 21'-2" x 19'-6"

GREAT ROOM 18'-8" x 13'-4"

DEN/GUEST BEDROOM 9'-10" x 11'-10"

FOYER

DRIVE

WALK

No. 10594
A Karl Kreeger Design

No. 20063
First-Time Owner's Delight

■ This plan features:
— Three bedrooms
— Two and one half baths

■ A distinctive exterior of wood veneer siding with a large, multi-paned picture window

■ A foyer leading directly into the Living Room which has a wood burning fireplace and opens to the Dining Room

■ A laundry room conveniently placed between the Kitchen and the Garage

■ A Master Bedroom on the first floor with a full bath and a walk-in closet

A loft area open to the Living Room below

FIRST FLOOR — 1,161 SQ. FT.
SECOND FLOOR — 631 SQ. FT.

TOTAL LIVING AREA: 1,792 SQ. FT.

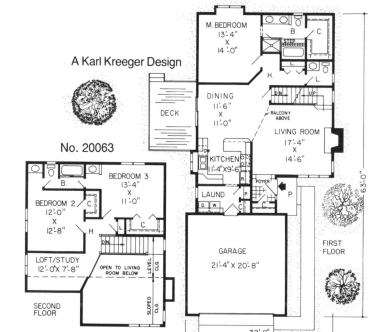

A Karl Kreeger Design

No. 20063

M. BEDROOM
13'-4" X 14'-0"

DINING
11'-6" X 11'-0"

DECK

LIVING ROOM
17'-4" X 14'-6"

KITCHEN
11'-4" X 9'-6"

LAUND.

FOYER

GARAGE
21'-4" X 20'-8"

FIRST FLOOR

63'-0"

32'-0"

BEDROOM 3
13'-4" X 11'-0"

BEDROOM 2
12'-0" X 12'-8"

LOFT/STUDY
12'-0" X 7'-8"

OPEN TO LIVING ROOM BELOW

SECOND FLOOR

No. 10514
Circular Kitchen is Center of Family Activities

■ This plan features:
— Three bedrooms
— Two baths
■ A Kitchen enhanced by tiled hallways
■ A Dining Room opening onto the patio with large glass doors
■ A large Family Room with a fireplace and a wood storage area
■ A Master Suite with a private patio, bay window, five piece bath and large walk-in closet

MAIN AREA — 1,870 SQ. FT.
SUN ROOM — 110 SQ. FT.
GARAGE — 434 SQ. FT.

TOTAL LIVING AREA: 1,980 SQ. FT.

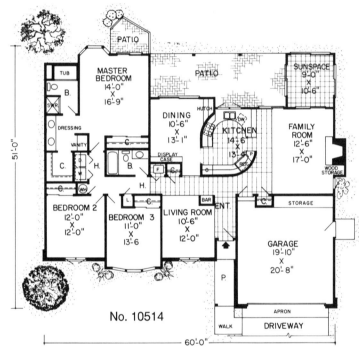

No. 10514

No. 10020
Colonial Detailing Enlivens Exterior

■ This plan features:
— Four bedrooms
— Two and one half baths
■ Fireplaces gracing both Living Room and Family Room.
■ An expansive terrace
■ A highly functional Kitchen with a nearby laundry room

FIRST FLOOR — 2,512 SQ. FT.
BASEMENT — 2,512 SQ. FT.
GARAGE — 648 SQ. FT.

TOTAL LIVING AREA: 2,512 SQ. FT.

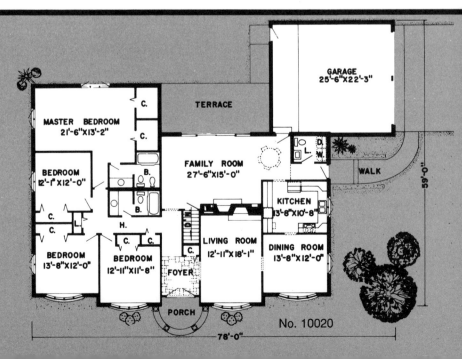

No. 10020

No. 10768
Upper Deck Affords Roadside View

■ This plan features:
— Five bedrooms
— Two and one half baths

■ A wetbar in the Family Room, built-in seating in the Breakfast Room, and an island Kitchen with a planning desk and room sized pantry

■ A magnificent Master Suite including a fireplace, access to a private deck, an abundance of closet space and a tub in a bow window setting

FIRST FLOOR — 2,573 SQ. FT.
SECOND FLOOR — 2,390 SQ. FT.
BASEMENT — 1,844 SQ. FT.
CRAWL SPACE — 793 SQ. FT.
GARAGE — 1,080 SQ. FT.

TOTAL LIVING AREA: 4,963 SQ. FT.

No. 10686
A Library in Every Room

■ This plan features:
— Four bedrooms
— Two and one half baths

■ An open staircase leading to the bedrooms and dividing the space between the vaulted Living and Dining Rooms

■ A wide family area including the Kitchen, Dinette and Family Room complete with built-in bar, bookcases, and fireplace

■ A Master Bedroom with a vaulted ceiling, spacious closets and Jacuzzi

FIRST FLOOR — 1,786 SQ. FT.
SECOND FLOOR — 1,490 SQ. FT.
BASEMENT — 1,773 SQ. FT.
GARAGE — 579 SQ. FT.

TOTAL LIVING AREA:
3,276 SQ. FT.

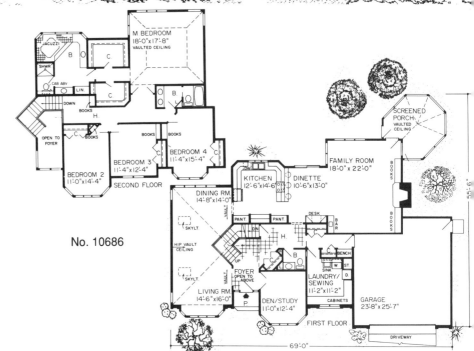

No. 10686

No. 10527
Hearth Room Highlights
Four Bedroom Plan

■ This plan features:
— Four bedrooms
— Three full and one half baths

■ A cozy Hearth Room off the efficient Kitchen

■ A large, sunken Family Room highlighted by a built-in bar and a fireplace flanked by bookcases

■ A Master Bedroom including two walk-in closets and a five piece bath

FIRST FLOOR — 1,697 SQ. FT.
SECOND FLOOR — 1,624 SQ. FT.
BASEMENT — 1,697 SQ. FT.
GARAGE — 586 SQ. FT.

TOTAL LIVING AREA:
3,321 SQ. FT.

WIDTH 64'-0"
DEPTH 52'-0"

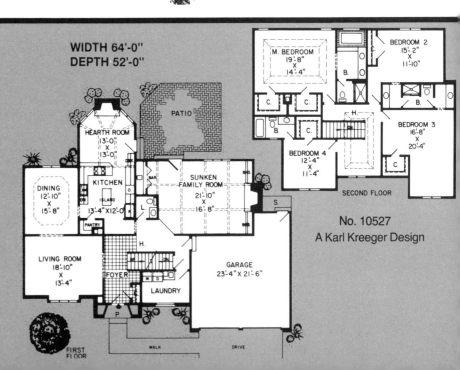

No. 10527
A Karl Kreeger Design

No. 20205
Small But Room To Grow

■ This plan features:
— Three Bedrooms
— Two full Baths
■ A Master Suite with a vaulted ceiling and its own skylit Bath
■ A fireplaced Living Room with a sloped ceiling
■ An efficient Kitchen with a Breakfast Nook
■ Options for growth on the lower level

MAIN AREA — 1,321 SQ. FT.
LOWER LEVEL — 286 SQ. FT.
GARAGE — 655 SQ. FT.

TOTAL LIVING AREA:
1,607 SQ. FT.

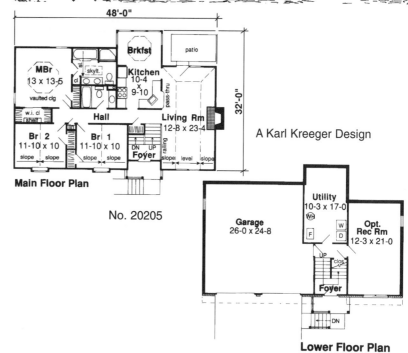

A Karl Kreeger Design

No. 20205

Main Floor Plan

Lower Floor Plan

No. 20368
Spacious Stucco

■ This plan features:
— Three bedrooms
— Two and one half baths
■ A vaulted foyer flanked by a soaring Living Room with huge palladium windows
■ A Family Room with a massive two-way fireplace
■ A Master Suite with garden spa, private deck access, and a walk in closet

FIRST FLOOR — 1,752 SQ. FT.
SECOND FLOOR — 620 SQ. FT.
BASEMENT — 1,726 SQ. FT.
GARAGE — 714 SQ. FT.

TOTAL LIVING AREA:
2,372 SQ. FT.

Second Floor

Br 2
13-2 x 13-10
shelves

Loft

linen
DN

Br 3
12-6 x 10-8

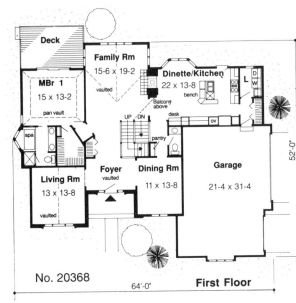

Deck

Family Rm
15-6 x 19-2

MBr 1
15 x 13-2
pan vault

vaulted

Dinette/Kitchen
22 x 13-8
bench

Balcony above

UP DN
desk

pantry

spa

Living Rm
13 x 13-8

Foyer
vaulted

Dining Rm
11 x 13-8

Garage
21-4 x 31-4

vaulted

No. 20368   64'-0"   **First Floor**

52'-0"

No. 20125
Angular Fireplace Adds Interest

■ This plan features:
— Three bedrooms
— Two and a half baths
■ A cozy fireplaced Living Room and an elegant formal Dining Room
■ A Master Suite with walk-in closet and private Master Bath
■ Two additional bedrooms sharing full hall bath

FIRST FLOOR — 1,340 SQ. FT.
SECOND FLOOR — 455 SQ. FT.
BASEMENT — 347 SQ. FT.
GARAGE — 979 SQ. FT.

TOTAL LIVING AREA:
1,795 SQ. FT.

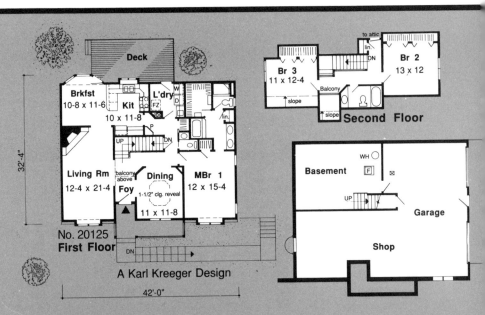

Deck

Brkfst
10-8 x 11-6

Kit
10 x 11-8

L'dry

Living Rm
12-4 x 21-4

balcony above

Dining
1-1/2" clg. reveal
11 x 11-8

Foy

MBr 1
12 x 15-4

UP   DN

No. 20125
First Floor

DN

32'-4"

42'-0"

to attic

Br 3
11 x 12-4

Br 2
13 x 12

Balcony

slope

slope   **Second Floor**

WH

Basement   F

UP

Garage

Shop

A Karl Kreeger Design

No. 20355

Sturdy Stucco Boasts Sunny Atmosphere

■ This plan features:
— Three bedrooms
— Three full baths

■ A sunken Dining Room with a bay window

■ A sunken Parlor with an elegant bay window

■ A book-lined, Family Room made cozy warm by a fireplace

■ A Master Suite with spacious Master Bath and a large walk-in closet

■ Two additional bedrooms that share a full hall bath

FIRST FLOOR — 2,424 SQ. FT.
SECOND FLOOR — 638 SQ. FT.
BASEMENT — 2,207 SQ. FT.
GARAGE — 768 SQ. FT.

TOTAL LIVING AREA:
3,062 SQ. FT.

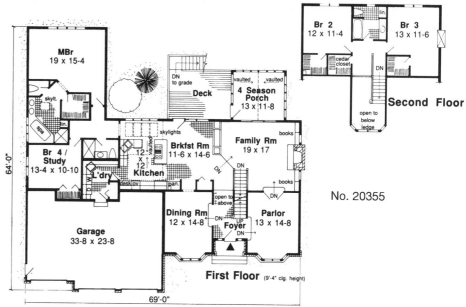

No. 20355

No. 10574
Easy-Living Plan

- This plan features:
  — Three bedrooms
  — Two and one half baths
- A design grouping together the Kitchen, Breakfast and Laundry area
- Expansive windows and fireplaces in both the Family Room and Living Room
- A Master Suite with double vanities and a room-sized closet

FIRST FLOOR — 2,215 SQ. FT.
SECOND FLOOR — 1,025 SQ. FT.
BASEMENT — 1,634 SQ. FT.
GARAGE AND STORAGE — 618 SQ. FT.
CRAWL SPACE — 581 SQ. FT.

TOTAL LIVING AREA:
3,240 SQ. FT.

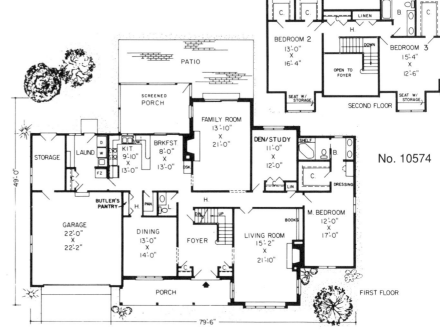

No. 10574

No. 21124
Old-Fashioned Charm

- This plan features:
  — Two bedrooms
  — Two full baths
- An old-fashioned, homespun flavor created by the use of lattice work, horizontal and vertical placement of wood siding, and full-length porches
- An open Living Room, Dining Room and Kitchen
- A Master Suite finishing the first level
- Wood floors throughout adding a touch of country

FIRST FLOOR — 835 SQ. FT.
SECOND FLOOR — 817 SQ. FT.

TOTAL LIVING AREA:
1,652 SQ. FT.

No. 21124

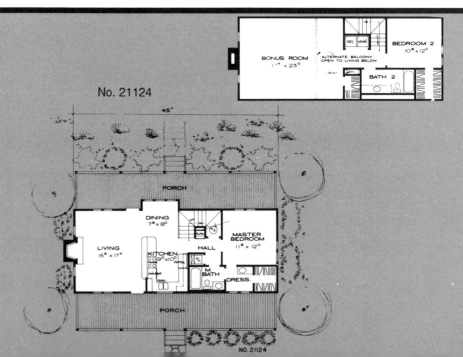

No. 24301
From Times Gone By

■ This plan features:
— Four bedrooms
— Two and one half baths
■ A Family Room opening to a large deck in rear
■ A Master Bedroom with a private bath and ample closet space
■ A large Living Room with a bay window
■ A modern Kitchen with many amenities

FIRST FLOOR — 987 SQ. FT.
SECOND FLOOR — 970 SQ. FT.
BASEMENT — 985 SQ. FT.

**TOTAL LIVING AREA:
1,957 SQ. FT.**

Donald L. Marshall Architect

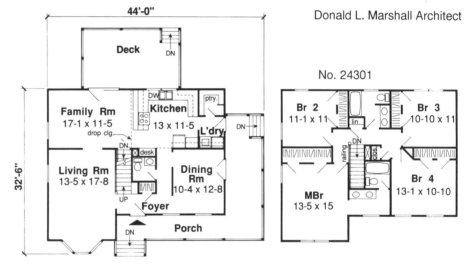

No. 24301

First Floor

Second Floor

No. 9870
Master Bedroom Suite Accentuates Luxury

■ This plan features:
— Three bedrooms
— Two and one half baths
■ A French Provincial design adorned with pillars and a bow window
■ The Kitchen centered between a laundry room and Kitchen Nook for added convenience
■ A spacious Family Room which opens to the terrace
■ A Master Bedroom complete with a full bath and sitting room placed to allow full privacy

FIRST FLOOR — 2,015 SQ. FT.
BASEMENT — 2,015 SQ. FT.
GARAGE — 545 SQ. FT.

TOTAL LIVING AREA:
2,015 SQ. FT.

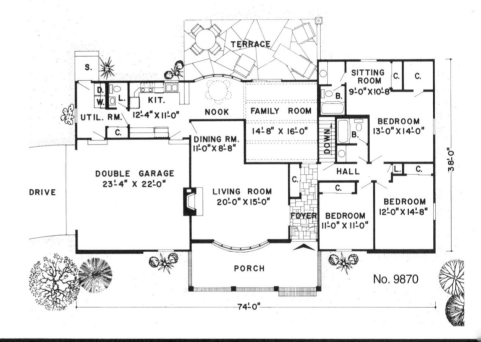

No. 25002
You'll Enjoy the Peace and Quiet

■ This plan features:
— Four bedrooms
— Two and one half baths
■ The bedrooms clustered together, yet none sharing a wall with another
■ A family Playroom downstairs, along with the fourth bedroom, a bath, laundry area, and storage
■ A large fireplace in the Living Room and Dining Room
■ A Master Bedroom with a private bath

FIRST FLOOR — 2,263 SQ. FT.
LOWER FLOOR — 1,290 SQ. FT.
GARAGE — 528 SQ. FT.

TOTAL LIVING AREA:
3,553 SQ. FT.

No. 6687
Simplicity In Design

■ This plan features:
— Two bedrooms
— One full bath

■ An open Living Room with a wood-burning fire-place

■ A Formal Dining Room easily accessible from Kitchen

■ Bedrooms naturally lit by four windows and having large closets

FIRST FLOOR — 1,380 SQ. FT.

TOTAL LIVING AREA: 1,380 SQ. FT.

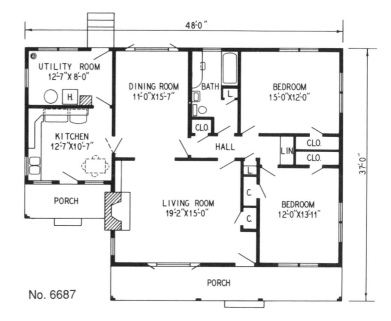

No. 6687

No. 20068
Wonderful Views

■ This plan features:
— Three bedrooms
— Two and one half full baths
■ A fireplaced Living Room with sloped ceiling
■ A second floor balcony
■ A huge Master Bedroom featuring a lavish bath
■ Walk-in closets for all bedrooms

FIRST FLOOR — 1,266 SQ. FT.
SECOND FLOOR — 489 SQ. FT.
BASEMENT — 1,266 SQ. FT.
GARAGE — 484 SQ. FT.

TOTAL LIVING AREA:
1,755 SQ. FT.

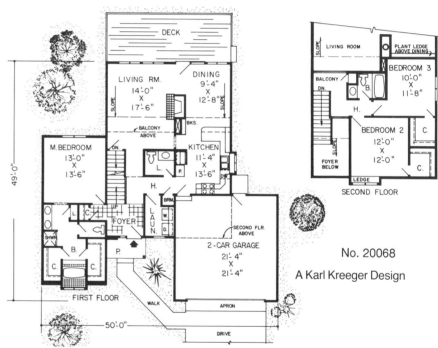

No. 20068

A Karl Kreeger Design

No. 20155
Built-in Beauty

■ This plan features:
— Four bedrooms
— Four and one half bath
■ An L-shaped Living and Dining Room arrangement with a fireplace flanked by bookcases and a decorative ceiling in the Dining area
■ A gourmet Kitchen with range-top island/snack bar, built-in pantry and double sinks
■ A massive fireplace with wood storage that separates the Hearth/Breakfast Room from the skylit Sun Room
■ A Master Suite with a decorative ceiling, walk-in closet, elegant bath and private access to the screened porch
■ Three additional bedrooms that share use of a full hall bath

FIRST FLOOR — 2,800 SQ. FT.
SECOND FLOOR — 1,113 SQ. FT.
BASEMENT — 2,800 SQ. FT.
SCREEN PORCH — 216 SQ. FT.
GARAGE — 598 SQ. FT.

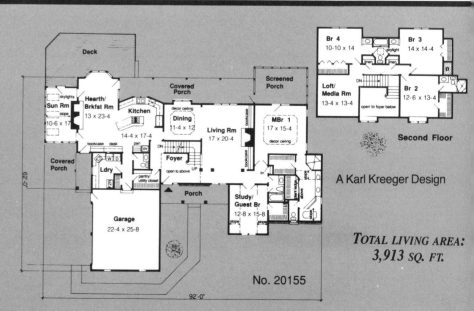

A Karl Kreeger Design

TOTAL LIVING AREA:
3,913 SQ. FT.

No. 20155

No. 20367
Clapboard Contemporary

- This plan features:
  - Three bedrooms
  - Two and one half baths
- An exciting window wall gracing the dramatic two-story Living Room
- A Kitchen with double sink, built-in desk and easy access to Dining Room
- A step down to sunken Family Room with fireplace
- A Master Bedroom with luxurious Master Bath and unique balcony

FIRST FLOOR — 1,108 SQ. FT.
SECOND FLOOR — 786 SQ. FT.
BASEMENT — 972 SQ. FT.
GARAGE — 567 SQ. FT.

TOTAL LIVING AREA:
1,894 SQ. FT.

No. 20367

Second Floor

- Br 2 12-2 x 10
- MBr 1 12 x 15-8
- Br 3 11 x 11-2
- lin.
- lin.
- DN
- open to below

First Floor

- Deck
- Kitchen 11-4 x 12-8
- Family Rm 17 x 12-6
- bar
- desk
- DN
- Dining Rm 12 x 11-6
- DN
- W D
- Garage 23-8 x 23-8
- line of floor above
- Living Rm 15-6 x 12-6
- UP
- Foyer
- slope
- slope
- 39'-6"
- 52'-0"

No. 20407
Sunny Charm

- This plan features:
- — Three bedrooms
- — Two and one half baths
- Wide-open spaces characterizing the active areas
- A sky-lit, columned foyer that divides the Dining Room from the Study
- A rear-facing Master Suite with soaring elegance
- A Living Room with a large fireplace, a handy wetbar, shelf-lined walls, and access to the large rear deck
- A sunny Breakfast area and Family Room surrounding the well-appointed Kitchen

FIRST FLOOR — 2,753 SQ. FT.
GARAGE — 440 SQ. FT.

TOTAL LIVING AREA:
2,753 SQ. FT.

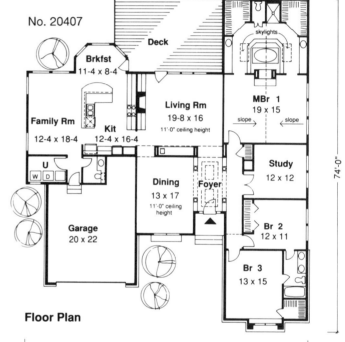

No. 20407

Deck

Brkfst
11-4 x 8-4

skylights

Living Rm
19-8 x 16
11'-0" ceiling height

MBr 1
19 x 15
slope → ← slope

Family Rm
12-4 x 18-4

Kit
12-4 x 16-4

Study
12 x 12

U
W D

Dining
13 x 17
11'-0" ceiling height

Foyer

Br 2
12 x 11

Garage
20 x 22

Br 3
13 x 15

74'-0"

65'-2"

Floor Plan

No. 10657
Designed for Privacy

- This plan features:
- — Three bedrooms
- — Two and one half baths
- A Kitchen with island cooking that opens to a Morning Room accessing the deck and sunroom with a hot tub
- A Master Suite including a room- sized closet, double vanity and sky-lit tub with separate shower
- Ample room throughout, including the Living Room with a fireplace and the formal Dining Room with recessed ceilings

FIRST FLOOR — 1,838 SQ. FT.
SECOND FLOOR — 798 SQ. FT.
BASEMENT — 1,831 SQ. FT.
GARAGE — 800 SQ. FT.

TOTAL LIVING AREA:
2,636 SQ. FT.

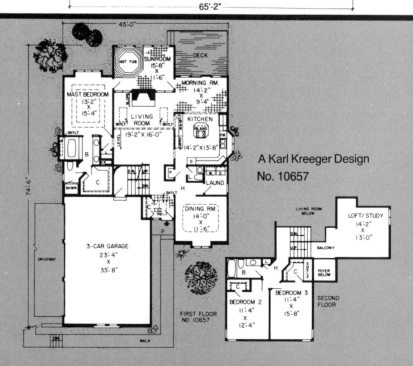

45'-0"

HOT TUB

SUNROOM
15'-8" X 11'-6"

DECK

MAST BEDROOM
13'-2" X 15'-4"

MORNING RM.
14'-2" X 9'-4"

LIVING ROOM
19'-2" X 16'-0"

KITCHEN
14'-2"X13'-8"
ISLAND

SHWR
C

LAUND

74'-6"

DINING RM.
14'-0" X 11'-6"

A Karl Kreeger Design
No. 10657

LIVING ROOM BELOW

LOFT/ STUDY
14'-2" X 13'-0"

BALCONY

FOYER BELOW

3-CAR GARAGE
23'-4" X 33'-8"

DRIVEWAY

DECK

BEDROOM 2
11'-4" X 12'-4"

BEDROOM 3
11'-4" X 15'-8"

SECOND FLOOR

FIRST FLOOR
NO 10657

WALK

No. 10683

Enjoy a Crackling Fire on a Chilly Day

■ This plan features:
— Three bedrooms
— Two and one half baths
■ A dramatic two-story entry
■ Cathedral ceilings in both the Dining Room and the sunken Living Room
■ An efficient corner Kitchen
■ A sunken Great Room with a fireplace
■ An angular staircase leading to the Master Bedroom

FIRST FLOOR — 990 SQ. FT.
SECOND FLOOR — 721 SQ. FT.
BASEMENT — 934 SQ. FT.
GARAGE — 429 SQ. FT.

TOTAL LIVING AREA: 1,711 SQ. FT.

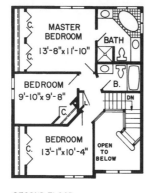

MASTER BEDROOM
13'-8"x11'-10"

BATH

BEDROOM
9'-10"x 9'-8"

B.

DN

BEDROOM
13'-1"x10'-4"

OPEN TO BELOW

SECOND FLOOR

No. 10683

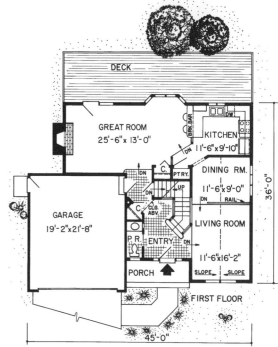

DECK

GREAT ROOM
25'-6"x 13'-0"

BRK. BAR

KITCHEN
11'-6"x9'-0"

DN

DINING RM.
11'-6"x9'-0"

GARAGE
19'-2"x21'-8"

PT RY.

C.

DN

UP

DN

RAIL

C.

CLG. ABV.

LIVING ROOM
11'-6"x16'-2"

P.R.

ENTRY

DN

PORCH

SLOPE   SLOPE

36'-0"

45'-0"

FIRST FLOOR

No. 10666
Arches Dominate Facade

■ This plan features:
— Five bedrooms
— Three and one half baths
■ A window wall and French doors linking the in-ground pool
■ A wetbar with wine storage and built-in book-cases in the Living Room
■ A Library on the second floor with room for the largest book collection
■ Dressing rooms and adjoining baths in all the bedrooms

FIRST FLOOR — 3,625 SQ. FT.
SECOND FLOOR — 937 SQ. FT.
GARAGE — 636 SQ. FT.

TOTAL LIVING AREA:
4,562 SQ. FT.

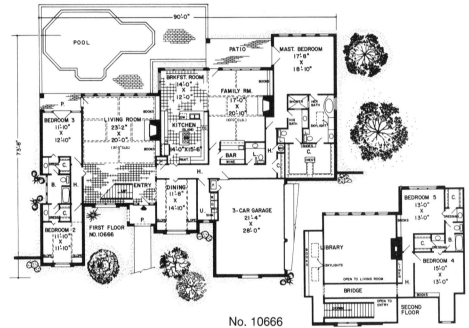

No. 10666

No. 20405
Past Luxuries Revisited

■ This plan features:
— Four bedrooms (with optional fifth bedroom)
— Four and one half baths
■ An arched entry to the formal Living and Dining Rooms, divided by columns for an open feeling
■ A short hall leading past the sunny Library to the private Master Suite with a luxury garden spa and private access to the veranda
■ An open arrangement of the Kitchen, Breakfast area, and Family Room creating a spacious atmosphere
■ A lofty Game Room on the second floor, perfect for recreation or just relaxing

FIRST FLOOR — 2,423 SQ. FT.
SECOND FLOOR — 1,235 SQ. FT.
GARAGE — 507 SQ. FT.

TOTAL LIVING AREA:
3,658 SQ. FT.

204

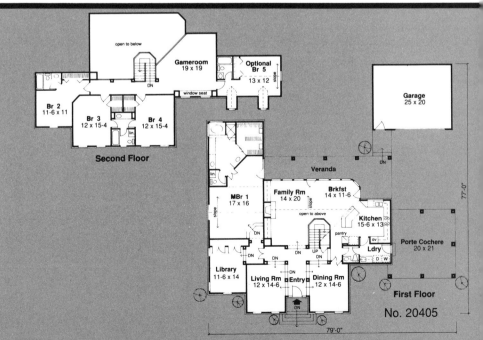

No. 20405

No. 10615
Surround Yourself with Luxury

■ This plan features:
— Five bedrooms
— Five full baths

■ Luxury and stately surroundings in all bedrooms

■ A tiled foyer and a grand staircase with a landing that leads to both wings

■ A vast Living Room for formal entertaining and a Kitchen designed to serve the eating areas and Family Room

■ A patio, pool, second floor deck and court yard

FIRST FLOOR — 4,075 SQ. FT.
SECOND FLOOR — 1,179 SQ. FT.
GARAGE — 633 SQ. FT.

**TOTAL LIVING AREA:
5,254 SQ. FT.**

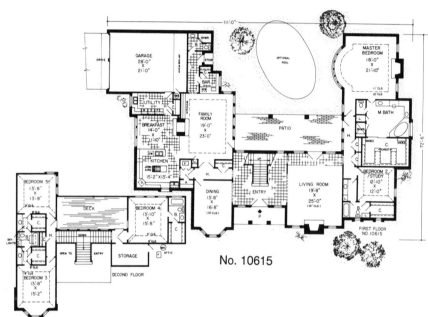

No. 10615

No. 84056
Convenient Single Level

■ This plan features:
— Three bedrooms
— Two full baths

■ A well-appointed U-shaped Kitchen that includes a view of the front yard and a built-in pantry

■ An expansive Great Room with direct access to the rear yard, expanding the living space

■ A Master Bedroom equipped with two closets—one is a walk-in, and a private bath

■ Two additional bedrooms that share a full hall bath

■ A step-saving, centrally located laundry center

FIRST FLOOR — 1,644 SQ. FT.
GARAGE — 576 SQ. FT.

TOTAL LIVING AREA:
1,644 SQ. FT.

No materials list available

Alternate Plan
w/ Crawlspace

No. 84056

52'-0"

Breakfast 10-4 x 12-6
Kit 10 x 15-2
Dining/Living 25-8 x 15
Br 1 12 x 15-10
Optional Garage 24 x 24
DN pan.
Breakfast 10 x 12-6
Kit 10 x 12-6
Entry
Br 2 10-8 x 11-8
Br 3 12 x 11-8

32'-0"

No. 10483
Intelligent Use of Space

■ This plan features:
— Three bedrooms
— Two full baths

■ Lots of living packed into this well-designed home

■ A combined Kitchen and Dining Room

■ A highly functional Kitchen, including a corner sink under double windows

■ A Living Room accentuated by a large fireplace and well-placed skylight

■ A sleeping area containing three bedrooms and two full baths

MAIN AREA — 1,025 SQ. FT.
GARAGE — 403 SQ. FT.

TOTAL LIVING AREA:
1,025 SQ. FT.

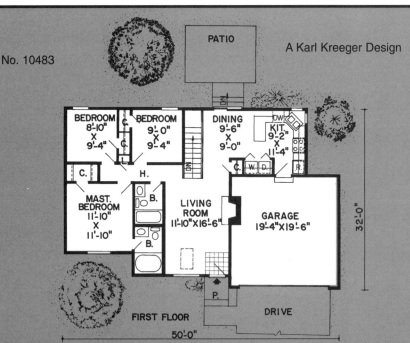

No. 10483

A Karl Kreeger Design

PATIO

BEDROOM 8'-10" X 9'-4"
BEDROOM 9'-0" X 9'-4"
DINING 9'-6" X 9'-0"
KIT. 9'-2" X 11'-4"
MAST. BEDROOM 11'-10" X 11'-10"
LIVING ROOM 11'-10" X 16'-6"
GARAGE 19'-4" X 19'-6"

32'-0"

FIRST FLOOR
DRIVE
50'-0"

No. 34827
Comfortable Family Home Leaves Room to Grow

■ This plan features:

— Three bedrooms

— Two and one half baths

■ Formal Living and Dining Rooms off the central foyer for ease in entertaining

■ A Family Room with a large fireplace adjoining the Breakfast area with a bay window

■ A short hall leading past the powder room, linking the formal Dining Room with the Kitchen

■ Each bedroom containing a walk-in closet

■ A Master Suite including both a raised tub and a step-in shower

FIRST FLOOR — 1,212 SQ. FT.

SECOND FLOOR — 1,030 SQ. FT.

BASEMENT — 1,212 SQ. FT.

GARAGE — 521 SQ. FT.

TOTAL LIVING AREA: 2,242 SQ. FT.

No. 34827

No. 20008
Contemporary Convenience

■ This plan features:
— Three bedrooms
— Two full baths
■ A Living Room with vaulted ceilings and a fireplace
■ A Master Suite with vaulted ceilings, walk-in closet and the privacy of a Master Bath
■ An open Kitchen with a Breakfast Bay arrangement

FIRST FLOOR — 1,545 SQ. FT.
BASEMENT — 1,545 SQ. FT.
GARAGE — 396 SQ. FT.

TOTAL LIVING AREA:
1,545 SQ. FT.

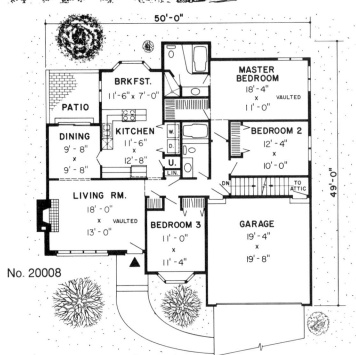

No. 20008

No. 10748
Outdoor-Lovers' Delight

■ This plan features:
— Three bedrooms
— Two full baths
■ A roomy Kitchen and Dining Room
■ A massive Living Room with fireplace and access to the wrap-around porch via double French doors
■ An elegant Master Suite amid spacious bedrooms and close to the laundry area

FIRST FLOOR — 1,540 SQ. FT.
PORCHES — 530 SQ. FT.

TOTAL LIVING AREA:
1,540 SQ. FT.

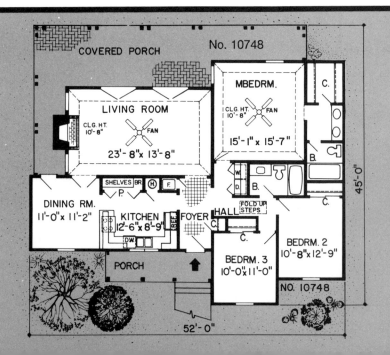

No. 20364
Lofty Views

- ■ This plan features:
- — Three bedrooms
- — Two and one half baths
- ■ A two-story foyer with lofty views
- ■ A spacious Living and Dining Room arrangement with vaulted ceilings
- ■ An efficient island Kitchen opening to a sunny Breakfast room with sliders to the rear patio
- ■ A Family Room with a large fireplace and views of the backyard
- ■ A Master Suite complete with a private bath

FIRST FLOOR — 1,060 SQ. FT.
SECOND FLOOR — 990 SQ. FT.
BASEMENT — 1,060 SQ. FT.
GARAGE — 462 SQ. FT.

TOTAL LIVING AREA:
2,050 SQ. FT.

MBr
14-10 x 14-2

Loft

Br 3
10 x 13

Br 2
10 x 10-6

DN

open to below

lin.

Second Floor

No. 20364

Patio   46'-0"

Family Rm
15 x 14

Brkfst
9 x 15-6

Kitchen
9 x 15-6

Dining Rm
11-6 x 12-6

desk   pan.

lin.

vaulted

Garage
20-8 x 20-8

DN   UP   **Foyer**

Living Rm
11-6 x 12-6

Porch

38'-6"

First Floor

No. 24317
Natural Light Creates Bright Living Spaces

■ This plan features:
— Three bedrooms
— Two full baths

■ A generous use of windows throughout the home, creating a bright living space

■ A center work island and a built-in pantry in the Kitchen

■ A sunny Eating Nook for informal eating and a formal Dining Room for entertaining

■ A large Living Room with a cozy fireplace to add atmosphere to the room as well as warmth

■ A Master Bedroom with a private bath and double closets

■ Two additional bedrooms that share a full, compartmented hall bath

MAIN AREA — 1,620 SQ. FT.

TOTAL LIVING AREA:
1,620 *SQ.* FT.

No. 24317

Main Floor

A Don Marshall Design

No. 34376
Charming Exterior Hints at Inviting Interior

■ This plan features:
— Three bedrooms
— Two full baths

■ An arched window and a covered porch entry

■ An open Living Room and Dining Room arrangement spanning the full depth of the home

■ A Kitchen, including a corner sink with a window overlooking the backyard

■ Twin bay windows adding light and space to the informal Dining area and Master Suite

■ An attached street-side Garage adding a sound buffer for the three bedrooms

FIRST FLOOR — 1,748 SQ. FT.
BASEMENT — 1,693 SQ. FT.
GARAGE — 541 SQ. FT.

TOTAL LIVING AREA:
1,748 *SQ.* FT.

No. 34376

Crawlspace Option

No. 24318
Master Suite Offers Privacy

■ This plan features:
— Four bedrooms
— Two full baths

■ A large covered porch and dormer windows, creating a friendly invitation to enter

■ A Living Room with a beamed ceiling access to the Patio through an atrium door

■ A Dining Room adjoining the Living Room and Kitchen making entertaining easy

■ A efficient, U-shaped Kitchen with a curved counter that serves as a pass-through and a snack bar

■ A exclusive Master Suite on second floor, offering a quiet place with a double vanity Bath

■ Three bedrooms on the first floor sharing a full hall bath

FIRST FLOOR — 1,044 SQ. FT.
SECOND FLOOR — 354 SQ. FT.

TOTAL LIVING AREA:
1,398 SQ. FT

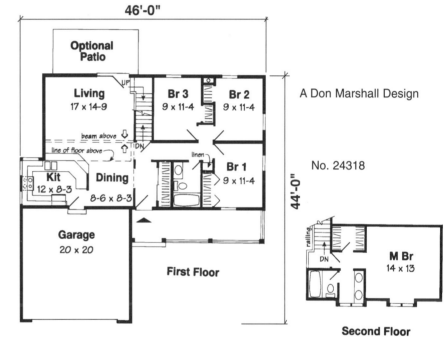

46'-0"

A Don Marshall Design

No. 24318

Optional Patio

Living 17 x 14-9

UP

Br 3 9 x 11-4

Br 2 9 x 11-4

beam above
line of floor above

DN

Kit 12 x 8-3

Dining 8-6 x 8-3

linen

Br 1 9 x 11-4

Garage 20 x 20

First Floor

44'-0"

railing

DN

M Br 14 x 13

Second Floor

No. 10417
Kitchen is Gourmet's Heaven

■ This plan features:

— Four bedrooms

— Five full baths

■ Cedar shake roofing which contrasts nicely with the brick exterior

■ Double entry doors ushering you into a two-story entrance with a curving staircase

■ Ten foot ceilings throughout the lower level, nine foot ceilings in the second level

■ A spacious Kitchen which will appeal to the gourmet cook in everyone

FIRST FLOOR — 3,307 SQ. FT.

SECOND FLOOR — 837 SQ. FT.

GARAGE — 646 SQ. FT.

PORCH AND PATIOS — 382 SQ. FT.

**TOTAL LIVING AREA:
4,144 SQ. FT.**

No. 9850
Home Recalls the South

■ This plan features:

— Three bedrooms

— Two and one half baths

■ A Master Bedroom suite with a private Study

■ Fireplaces enhancing the formal Living Room and spacious Family Room

■ A lovely screened porch/patio skirting the Family Room and Kitchen

■ A utility room with access into the storage and garage area

FIRST FLOOR — 2,466 SQ. FT.

BASEMENT — 1,477 SQ. FT.

GARAGE — 664 SQ. FT.

**TOTAL LIVING AREA:
2,466 SQ. FT.**

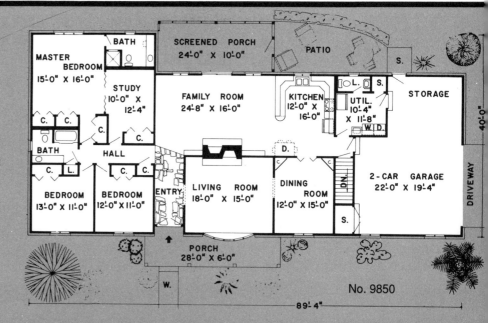

No. 10698
Vaulted Ceilings Make Every Room Special

■ This plan features:
— Five bedrooms
— Five full baths
■ An enjoyable view from the island Kitchen which is separated from the Morning Room by only a counter
■ Access to the pool from the covered patio or from the Living and Family Rooms
■ The Living and Family Rooms with beamed ten-foot ceilings and massive fireplaces
■ A Master Suite with a raised tub, built-in dressing tables and a fireplaced Sitting room with vaulted ceiling

FIRST FLOOR — 4,014 SQ. FT.
SECOND FLOOR — 727 SQ. FT.
GARAGE — 657 SQ. FT.

**TOTAL LIVING AREA:
4,741 SQ. FT.**

No. 10698

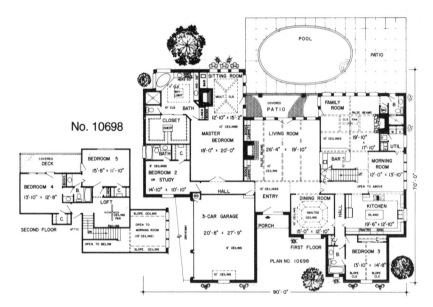

No. 20096
Traditional Sun Catcher

■ This plan features:
— Three bedrooms
— Three and one half baths

■ Windows and skylights in all shapes and sizes, giving this home an airy feeling

■ A sky-lit Breakfast nook off the Kitchen

■ A large rear deck accessible from the Living Room and the Breakfast nook

■ Three bedrooms opening to a balcony overlooking the floor below

■ A Master Suite with a walk-in closet, double vanities, and a raised sky-lit tub

FIRST FLOOR — 1,286 SQ. FT.
SECOND FLOOR — 957 SQ. FT.
BASEMENT — 1,286 SQ. FT.
GARAGE — 491 SQ. FT.

No. 20096

TOTAL LIVING AREA:
2,243 SQ. FT.

A Karl Kreeger Design

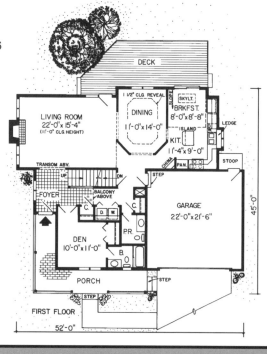

No. 10016
Studio Enhances Dutch Colonial

■ This plan features:
— Three bedrooms
— Two full and one half baths

■ A convenient Foyer area leads to a large Living Room with a fireplace and sliding doors to a terrace

■ The U-shaped Kitchen offers efficiency and easy access to the Family Room and a half bath with laundry center

■ The informal, airy Family Room opens onto the front porch and a second terrace and leads to an upstairs multi-purpose Studio

■ Three bedrooms with two full baths, one private, complete the upstairs level

FIRST FLOOR — 1,256 SQ. FT.
SECOND FLOOR — 815 SQ. FT.
GAME ROOM — 384 SQ. FT.
GARAGE — 576 SQ. FT.
BASEMENT — 936 SQ. FT.

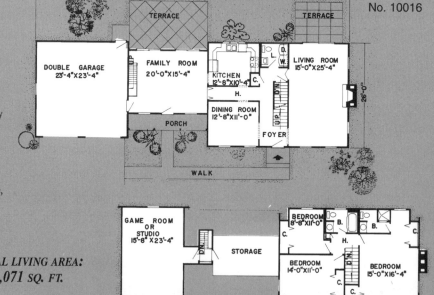

No. 10016

TOTAL LIVING AREA:
2,071 SQ. FT.

No. 10696
Lunch by the Pool

■ This plan features:
— Four bedrooms
— Four full baths

■ A Master wing with a sky-lit bath, room-sized closets and a book-lined Study

■ A foyer leading into the formal Living Room or Family Room with an adjoining bar and patio

■ An island Kitchen with a huge pantry and a Breakfast nook overlooking the pool

FIRST FLOOR — 3,252 SQ. FT.
SECOND FLOOR — 873 SQ. FT.
GARAGE — 746 SQ. FT.

TOTAL LIVING AREA:
4,125 SQ. FT.

No. 10696

No. 24308
Leisure Time Getaway

- This plan features:
— One bedroom
— One full bath
- The simplicity of an A-frame with a spacious feeling achieved by the large, two-story Living Room
- An entrance deck leads into the open Living Room accented by a spiral staircase to the Loft
- A small, but efficient Kitchen serves the Living area easily, and provides access to the full bath with a shower and a storage area
- A first floor bedroom and a Loft area provide the sleeping quarters

FIRST FLOOR — 660 SQ. FT.
LOFT — 163 SQ. FT.

TOTAL LIVING AREA:
823 SQ. FT.

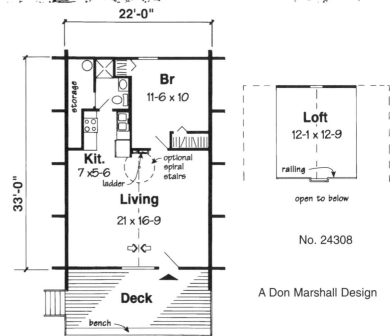

No. 24308

A Don Marshall Design

Main Floor

No. 9850
Home Recalls the South

- This plan features:
— Three bedrooms
— Two full and one half baths
- A Master Bedroom Suite with a private Study
- Fireplaces enhancing the formal Living Room and spacious Family Room
- A lovely, screened porch/patio skirting the Family Room and the Kitchen
- A Utility Room with access into the storage and garage areas

FIRST FLOOR — 2,466 SQ. FT.
BASEMENT — 1,477 SQ. FT.
GARAGE — 664 SQ. FT.

TOTAL LIVING AREA:
2,466 SQ. FT.

No. 9850

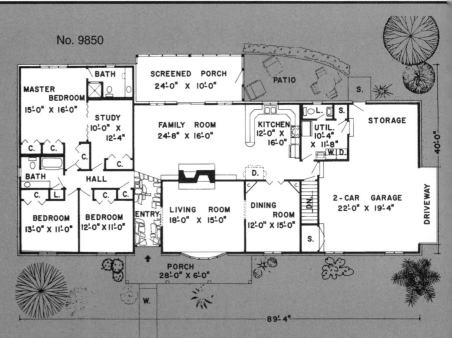

216

No. 20093
Porch Adorns Elegant Bay

■ This plan features:

— Three bedrooms

— Two and one half baths

■ A Master Suite with romantic bay window and full Bath

■ Bedrooms with huge closets and use of the hall full bath

■ A roomy island Kitchen with modern, efficient layout

■ A Formal Dining Room with recessed decorative ceiling

■ Sloping sky lit ceilings illuminating the fireplaced Living Room

■ A rear Deck accessible from both the Kitchen and the Living Room

FIRST FLOOR — 1,027 SQ. FT.

SECOND FLOOR — 974 SQ. FT.

GARAGE — 476 SQ. FT.

TOTAL LIVING AREA:
2,001 SQ. FT.

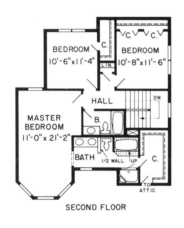

SECOND FLOOR

No. 20093

A Karl Kreeger Design

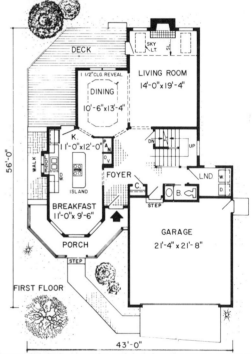

FIRST FLOOR

You've Picked Your Dream Home!

You can already see it standing on your lot... you can see yourselves in your new home... enjoying family, entertaining guests, celebrating holidays. All that remains ahead are the details. That's where we can help. Whether you plan to build-it-yourself, be your own contractor, or hand your plans over to an outside contractor, your Garlinghouse blueprints provide the perfect beginning for putting yourself in your dream home right away.

We even make it simple for you to make professional design modifications. We can also provide a materials list for greater economy.

My grandfather, L.F. Garlinghouse, started a tradition of quality when he founded this company in 1907. For over 85 years, homeowners and builders have relied on us for accurate, complete, professional blueprints. Our plans help you get results fast... and save money, too! These pages will give you all the information you need to order. So get started now... I know you'll love your new Garlinghouse home!

Sincerely,

TYPICAL WALL SECTIONS

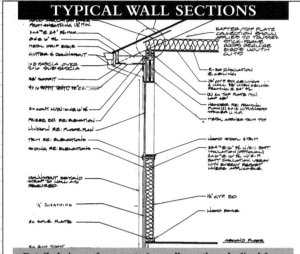

Detailed views of your exterior walls, as though sliced from top to bottom. These drawings clarify exterior wall construction insulation, flooring, and roofing details. Depending on your specific geography and climate, your home will be built with either 2x4 or 2x6 exterior walls. Most professional contractors can easily adapt plans for either requirement.

KITCHEN & BATH CABINET DETAILS

These plans or, in some cases, elevations show the specific details and placement of the cabinets in your kitchen and bathrooms as applicable. Customizing these areas is simpler beginning with these details. Kitchen and bath cabinet details are available for most plans featured in our collection.

EXTERIOR ELEVATIONS

Exact scale views of the front, rear and both sides of your home, showing exterior materials, details, and all necessary measurements.

DETAILED FLOOR PLANS

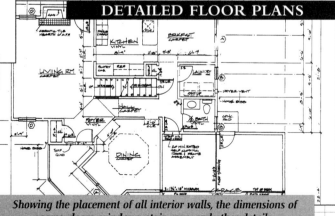

Showing the placement of all interior walls, the dimensions of rooms, doors, windows, stairways, and other details.

ake Your Dream Come True!
for home designs by respected professionals.

FIREPLACE DETAILS

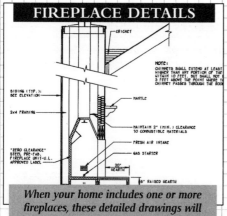

When your home includes one or more fireplaces, these detailed drawings will help your mason with their construction and appearance. It is easy to review details with professionals when you have the plans for reference.

TYPICAL CROSS SECTION

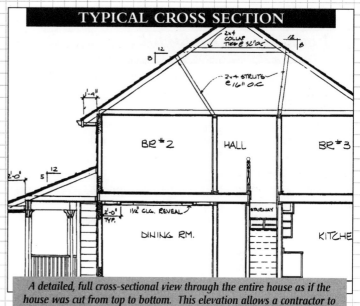

A detailed, full cross-sectional view through the entire house as if the house was cut from top to bottom. This elevation allows a contractor to better understand the interconnections of the construction components.

FOUNDATION PLAN

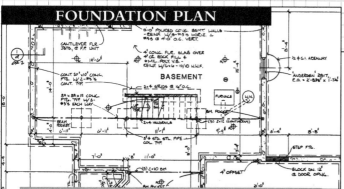

With footings and all load-bearing points applicable to your home, including all necessary notation and dimensions. The type of foundation supplied varies from home to home. Local conditions and practices will determine whether a basement, crawlspace or a slab is best for you. Your professional contractor can easily make the necessary adaption.

SCHEMATIC ELECTRICAL LAYOUTS

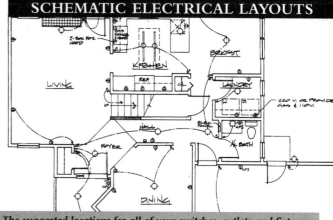

The suggested locations for all of your switches, outlets and fixtures are indicated on these drawings. They are practical as they are, but they are also a solid taking-off point for any personal adaptions.

ROOF PLAN

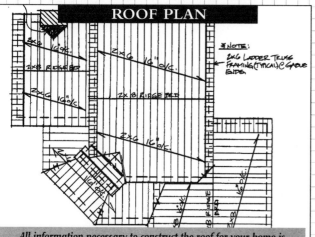

All information necessary to construct the roof for your home is included. Many blueprints contain framing plans showing all of the roof elements, so you'll know how these details look and fit together.

STAIR DETAILS

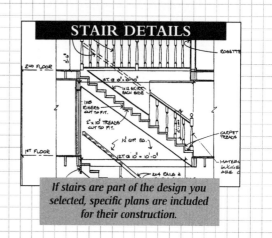

If stairs are part of the design you selected, specific plans are included for their construction.

GARLINGHOUSE OPTIONS & EXTRAS MAKE THE DREAM TRULY YOURS.

Reversed Plans Can Make Your Dream Home Just Right!

"That's our dream home... if only the garage were on the other side!"

You could have exactly the home you want by flipping it end-for-end. Check it out by holding your dream home page of this book up to a mirror. Then simply order your plans "reversed". We'll send you one full set of mirror-image plans (with the writing backwards) as a master guide for you and your builder.

The remaining sets of your order will come as shown in this book so the dimensions and specifications are easily read on the job site... but they will be specially stamped "REVERSED" so there is no construction confusion.

We can only send reversed plans with multiple-set orders. But, there is no extra charge for this service.

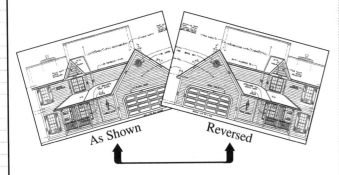

As Shown   Reversed

Modifying Your Garlinghouse Home Plan

Easy modifications to your dream home such as minor non-structural changes and simple material substitutions, can be made between you and your builder and marked directly on your blueprints. However, if you are considering making major changes to your design, we strongly recommend that you purchase our reproducible vellums and use the services of a professional designer or architect. Modifications are not available for plan numbers 90,000 and above. For additional information call us at 1-203-343-5977.

Our Reproducible Vellums Make Modifications Easier

With a vellum copy of our plans, a design professional can alter the drawings just the way you want, then you can print as many copies of the modified plans as you need. And, since you have already started with our complete detailed plans, the cost of those expensive professional services will be significantly less. Refer to the price schedule for vellum costs. Call for vellum availability for plan numbers 90,000 and above.

Reproducible vellum copies of our home plans are only sold under the terms of a license agreement that you will receive with your order. Should you not agree to the terms, then the vellums may be returned unopened for a full refund.

Yours FREE With Your Order

FREE

SPECIFICATIONS AND CONTRACT FORM

provides the perfect way for you and your builder to agree on the exact materials to use in building and finishing your home before you start construction. A must for homeowner's peace of mind.

Remember To Order Your Materials List

It'll help you save money. Available at a modest additional charge, the Materials List gives the quantity, dimensions, and specifications for the major materials needed to build your home. You will get faster, more accurate bids from your contractors and building suppliers — and avoid paying for unused materials and waste. Materials Lists are available for all home plans except as otherwise indicated, but can only be ordered with a set of home plans. Due to differences in regional requirements and homeowner or builder preferences... electrical, plumbing and heating/air conditioning equipment specifications are not designed specifically for each plan. However, detailed typical prints of residential electrical, plumbing and construction guidelines can be provided. Please see next page for additional information.

Questions?

Call our customer service number at 1-203-343-5977.

222